The Gender Balanced Scorecard

Forum Personalmanagement
Human Resource Management

Herausgegeben von Michel E. Domsch/Désirée H. Ladwig

Band 8

PETER LANG

Frankfurt am Main · Berlin · Bern · Bruxelles · New York · Oxford · Wien

Sonja W. Floeter-van Wijk

The Gender Balanced Scorecard

A Management Tool to Achieve Gender Mainstreaming
in Organisational Culture

PETER LANG
Internationaler Verlag der Wissenschaften

Bibliographic Information published by the Deutsche Nationalbibliothek
The Deutsche Nationalbibliothek lists this publication in the Deutsche Nationalbibliografie; detailed bibliographic data is available in the internet at <http://www.d-nb.de>.

Zugl.: Hamburg, Helmut-Schmidt-Universität / Univ. der Bundeswehr, Diss., 2007

D 705
ISSN 1438-6971
ISBN 978-3-631-56711-1

© Peter Lang GmbH
Internationaler Verlag der Wissenschaften
Frankfurt am Main 2007

Printed in Germany 1 2 3 4 5   7

www.peterlang.de

Foreword

A wide variety of economic, partly interdisciplinary, studies on equality and WorkLifeBalance repeatedly show: highly qualified and career-oriented women are mostly interested in – besides secure employment with a challenging job profile – gender equality and compatibility of work and private-life.

However, this is definitely not just a 'women's subject' because more and more men, in all occupations and age groups, set the same priorities in their professional lives. But, in reality there is a significant 'gender gap' here. For this reason both science and practice focus on ways to reduce this gap using gender-mainstreaming activities. The necessity for increased efforts in this area is accepted nationally and internationally (it is one of the aims of the European Union), and by politicians, unions, universities, non-governmental organisations and others alike. Also, the number of gender-aware companies is growing. On the other hand, the demand for action rather than words has been ongoing for over twenty years, mainly owing to the fact that little or only very slow progress has been made in the business world. Particularly, the fact that women are reaching higher levels of education and the shortage on the labour market make it more interesting, i.e. inevitable for companies to consider women as a target group.

In this publication Ms Floeter-van Wijk discusses this subject with a scientific and at the same time practical approach. She develops an instrument for leadership ('the gender balanced scorecard') that will be, when applied as strategic management tool, of great value for achieving gender mainstreaming targets and as a consequence results in economic success for the organisation.

Prof. Dr. Michel E. Domsch   Hamburg, May 2007

Acknowledgement

I would like to use this opportunity to name all persons who have contributed to the realisation of this ambitious project. First of all, I would like to thank *Professor Dr. Michel E. Domsch* for his supervision of this dissertation and for giving me the unique opportunity to research this specific subject. Throughout the process of research and writing he has provided me with all the feedback and support needed to keep motivated and challenged. I also enjoyed it very much to discuss the actual changes that are nowadays taking place in Germany and Europe in this area of work-life/private-life balance with him, as his opinions have proven to be very valuable to me personally and for this project.

Secondly, I would like to thank *Professor Dr. Peter Nieder* for accepting the responsibility of reviewing this dissertation and for his expert opinions about this work.

I also return my thanks to the organisations, managers and experts participating in the empirical part of this research. It is their support and precious time that made it possible to successfully complete the in-depth research interviews.

Without hesitation I can say that this process has felt like climbing a very high mountain. Enthusiasm, determination and lots of discipline were important ingredients to reach the top. However, the critical success factor was the support of my family. It is for this reason that I would like to thank my husband. *Knut*, thank you for our endless discussions about work-life/family-life balance and I am sure that more discussions about this subject will follow. I am happy that we were able to arrange our 'balance' successfully through this project and I am sure that we will be able to continue this also in the future as a dual-career couple. Then, I would like to give a big hug to our amazing and beautiful children *Lars* and *Julia*, who also have supported and inspired me in their own special ways with the completion of this dissertation.

Following this, I would like to thank my sister *Janny van Wijk*, who has done the proofreading of this dissertation. Then, I would like to thank my family and friends for all the support I received throughout the process which has helped me in a myriad of ways.

It is also here that I would like to thank my parents, *Ties and Jeltje van Wijk*, who have supported and motivated me to continue and widen my educational/professional career in all phases of my life. It is to you both that I dedicate this work.

Sonja Floeter-van Wijk

Preface

The writing of this dissertation has been a great challenge for me but also has proved to be a great opportunity. In my personal life I have reached the phase were finding the balance between work-life and family-life receives high priority. Everywhere around me I noticed how this became a real issue, especially, for women who attempt to combine their professional career with motherhood. It is this dilemma that many women face at a certain time in life. It is therefore, out of personal interest, that I selected this topic for my research. I wanted to try to find solutions which could assist organisations when they attempted to improve their level of maturity towards gender mainstreaming and gender equality.

Gender mainstreaming has increased its importance for organisations. The economic, legal and demographic changing situation demands adaptations from organisations. To get the best possible workforce means that all high potentials need to be reviewed without excluding a large part of the population, i.e. the female half. When organisations have selected the high qualified employees they need from the total labour pool the next challenge arises. To keep the workforce motivated and satisfied because this will lead to better business results and higher competitiveness. How to keep the complete workforce motivated is a challenge which has been researched often. But, the specific challenge of keeping female employees satisfied and motivated is an even more difficult challenge. Reason for this is that a majority of the high qualified female employees still face a dilemma with balancing their work-life with their family-life. For this reason, it is important that organisations develop gender specific initiatives which assist female employees with finding a better balance, which will enable them to stay on the labour market and use their skills and education without giving them the feeling that they are lacking in their family life. It has to be said that these balance issues also start to become more important for male employees, however, the traditional ways still mostly prevail and the amount of men for which this applies is still small in comparison to the number of women who are directly facing this challenge.

The official political answer to this dilemma is gender mainstreaming. This term should take care that a gender perspective becomes an integral part of all strategies of a company (or a government) instead of being separately analysed and handled, i.e. gender perspectives and initiatives should become 'mainstream'. Theoretical this is a good idea but the practical implementation is very difficult and research in this area is still very limited. If gender perspectives should be 'mainstream' in organisations it is essential that the organisational culture/climate, that is the way people think, is changed.

However, according to half of the respondents that participated in the primary research the organisational culture is an obstacle to gender mainstreaming. For this reason this project researches whether an adapted balanced scorecard, i.e. a gender balanced scorecard, could be an instrument that could assist organisations with achieving gender mainstreaming in organisational culture. It is important to develop an instrument that is widely recognised and accepted because this instrument has to convince the top management and leaders of the organisations that it is worth to invest in.

The design of the gender balanced scorecard would include the four traditional balanced scorecard perspectives, financial, customer, internal business processes and learning and growth and would be expanded with the organisational culture perspective and three additional (optional) perspectives: community, leadership commitment and workforce profile. These optional perspectives depend on the situation of the organisation as each gender balanced scorecard would be unique and especially designed for each organisation. From the primary research it was found that first of all general awareness and the levels of acceptance should be raised towards the issue of gender equality and gender mainstreaming before a gender balanced scorecard could be developed.

A gender balanced scorecard could be designed, developed and implemented successfully, even though this would be a complex issue, when it would be supported by all four promoters, including the power promotor (CEO/Top management), of the promoter model. This is also the main problem with the instrument as *resistance* is the biggest obstacle to its development in the first place. If the level of maturity towards- and awareness about gender issues increases the gender balanced scorecard could be an instrument that could assist organisations with changing their organisational culture into a culture that facilitates and incorporates gender mainstreaming.

I hope that the outcome of this work will assist organisations with their efforts to become organisations where gender equality is the norm, more specifically, organisations where gender mainstreaming is an ingrained part of the organisational culture. Because, it is these organisations where all employees, including the female employees, will be able to find a good balance between work-life and family-life, and as a consequence, the organisations will be better equipped, with highly motivated employees, who create a competitive advantage for the organisation that will help them deal successfully with the challenges the future will bring.

11

Table of contents

13

15

List of tables

16

List of figures

18

Part I: Introduction

1 Introduction

"The world we have created is a product of our way of thinking.
It cannot be changed without changing the way that we think."
-Albert Einstein-

The above opening quote is very relevant to the central focus of this work, namely, to enable more organisations to benefit from the opportunity gender mainstreaming can offer them. The discussion around gender equality on all levels in society and in organisations has been an ongoing discussion for many years. A central issue why gender equality is still 'under discussion' is that it is very difficult to change the way people think. This is the main reason why gender inequality has continued to exist and is still part of our way of life today. However, recent developments and changes in society and in economic situations in the world have led to a new focus in dealing with this issue.

Organisations in the 21st century have to take into account the wants and needs of all their stakeholders for a number of reasons. First of all, because the stakeholders otherwise could rebel and refuse to cooperate with the organisation if it does not satisfy their wants and needs. Secondly, because organisations have legal, moral, and ethical responsibilities towards their stakeholders. Thirdly, in this age of ever-present media and special interest groups, they also have hard-won reputations to protect (Neely, Adams & Kennerley, 2002). How should companies deal with this challenge and particularly in terms of measurement what should be included and how can companies best design their measurement system and their strategy to keep all stakeholders satisfied? This challenge to keep stakeholders happy and to motivate employees shows organisations that they need a good performance measurement system but also demands that companies focus more on their company image. Organisations can attract the best employees when they are able to offer them the best working conditions and environment. Therefore, it has become more important for organisations to invest in programmes that focus on a diverse workforce and with this also to become an employer who deals with gender inequality.

The addition of female employees to the workforce can provide organisations with an important competitive advantage. It offers human resource advantages as well as marketing advantages and furthermore, cost savings can be considerable. However, to attract and retain the best female employees requires that the organisation is woman-friendly. Nowadays, it is very often the case that women think that they are confronted with the following paradox: work commitment is defined as family neglect and family involvement is defined as a lack of work commitment (Jacobs and Gerson, 2004, 202). Work life needs to be in balance with private life for women to be able to perform to their best ability. This dilemma has become such an important issue for higher educated women in many countries nowadays that they increasingly decide to choose for a career instead of for a family life with children. This will lead to a considerable change in demographics of the developed countries, especially since the population of many western European countries is already facing the challenge of an ageing population. Organisations will be faced with a limited pool of highly qualified personnel to select their workforce from and therefore it becomes even more important that also highly qualified female employees are given the opportunity to work in balance with their private family life.

The measures organisations can take to enable more women to enter and reach management level vary. The common measures asked for by female employees include flexible working hours, flexible workplace (e.g. home office), equal pay and promotional and training opportunities. Organisations can also change the recruitment of personnel in order to attract female potential, assist with child care to improve work-life/private-life balance or have women representatives or a diversity council in the organisation. Many measures focus on immediate action, however, it is also important that the long-term point of view of organisations is changed and this can be done by focussing on changing the organisational culture. This requires a change of strategy by the organisation and for this reason the use of a management tool could be helpful.

The balanced scorecard has proven itself to be such a successful management tool that can assist organisations with implementing a new strategy and achieving change initiatives. It is very difficult to measure intangible assets and intellectual capital and therefore it is also very difficult to demonstrate that gender initiatives contribute to the organisation's 'bottom line', i.e. that it brings positive financial results. The aim to achieve gender equality will need to be aligned with the other strategic goals and objectives of the organisation and the balanced scorecard is a management tool that offers the possibility to achieve this. It is the aim of this research to examine the balanced scorecard as a management tool to achieve gender mainstreaming in the organisational culture.

1.1 Relevance of research; gender mainstreaming between theory and practice

The growing legal focus on the issue of gender mainstreaming, for example, by the European Union (as defined in the Treaty of Amsterdam), has also been the basis for an increase in interest in dealing with the gender issue more intensely on different levels, namely, on the governmental-, the political-, the educational- and also on the organisational level. But, this is only one reason for the increase in importance that gender mainstreaming should be given.

Another important reason can be found by reviewing the economic and demographic situation that many European countries are faced with. In short, companies (and countries) are faced with the challenge that a smaller population (low birth rates) will have to support a larger ageing population. This will create the situation, as agreed by many politicians and experts, that everybody who can work should work full-time, and they should work longer hours (to put the pension age back is being discussed in several European countries), to be able to meet the demand and carry the future costs. This would mean that also the large female labour force should be totally included (there are many women who are currently working only part-time or not at all).

A third reason is that the markets have changed from homogeneous towards more heterogeneous markets which also demand a more diverse approach from organisations. Diversity in work teams and in all levels of organisations can give the organisation the competitive advantage to deal with a diverse customer base and to identify all different opportunities of diverse markets. Therefore, a diverse employee base seems to be a requirement for a successful organisation.

Further reasons for an increasing interest in gender mainstreaming are that the nature of work has changed. These changes include changes in the workplace (e.g. restructuring, flatter organisational structures, etc.), a flexible workforce (changing notion in career planning), virtual organisations (home office workers), job insecurity (in times of recession) and long working hours (organisational culture changes). Some of these changes are positive for achieving gender equality but some are also additional challenges. This shall be explained in further detail in chapter 3.4 (page 44).

These reasons explain why, in theory, the gender mainstreaming opportunity should be dealt with by governments and organisations. However, an easy way to implement gender mainstreaming in practise is still relatively unknown. There are no practical manuals or guidelines that can help organisations to implement gender mainstreaming. Research in this field often focuses on short-term individual measures to promote equality for woman in the workplace. Research on how to change organisations long term, in order that they embrace gender mainstreaming in their culture, is still limited. In this research the balanced scorecard will be analysed to determine whether this could be the 'right' management tool to use in order to achieve this long-term change in organisational culture to include gender mainstreaming. Furthermore, the balanced scorecard is also a controlling tool that can be used to reveal whether the organisation has really embraced gender mainstreaming in their culture.

1.2 Research objectives

The main objective of this research will be: *to contribute to the discussion around gender mainstreaming and, in particular, to offer both short-term and long-term practical solutions for the use of the balanced scorecard as a management tool to implement gender mainstreaming within the organisational culture.*

The following sub-objectives can be identified:
- Analyse whether the balanced scorecard is an appropriate tool to change organisational culture in such a way that gender mainstreaming becomes part of it
- Conduct a primary research of a sample of German and Dutch organisations and their organisational cultures with respect to gender mainstreaming issues and solutions
- Offer practical recommendations for organisations in general which can assist them with implementing gender mainstreaming in their organisational culture by using the balanced scorecard

1.3 Plan of action

There are a number of elements involved in creating the organisation that embraces gender equality and a balance between work-life and private-life as common ingredients. In figure 1 below the project plan including all four theoretical elements that are part of this project can be found.

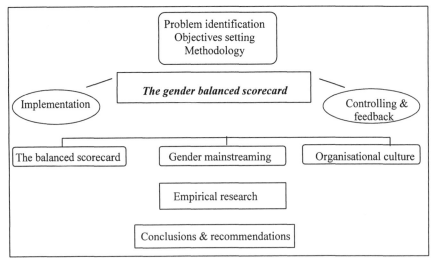

Figure 1: Project plan

As can be seen in figure 1 the project is built on three theoretical foundations which are: the balanced scorecard, the gender mainstreaming foundation and the organisational culture foundation. The last section is the primary research which is done in organisations in the Netherlands and Germany.

There are four parts to the project:
Part I: The first part of the project includes the introduction, the identification of the problem and setting the objectives for the work.
Part II: In part two the three theoretical foundations will be described in detail.
Part III: In the third part the methodology will be the subject and the empirical research will be introduced and analysed.
Part IV: The fourth part will include the conclusions and recommendations.

Part II: Theoretical Foundations

2 The balanced scorecard

2.1 Introduction
In this chapter the balanced scorecard, will be introduced. First of all, the balanced scorecard will be defined and explained. Then the structure, the scope and the strategic importance of the balanced scorecard as a management tool will be researched. Following this, the actual implementation process will be reviewed.

2.2 Literature review on the balanced scorecard
The traditional performance measurement systems that companies use have always been based on financial results and analysis. The need to produce performance measurement systems that would support performance initiatives within the organisation became a major point of concern for managers since the 1990s. The need to bring non-financial measures into the performance measurement arena has been mentioned by many authors in the past, for example, as far back as Parker in 1979, Kaplan in 1984 and Brignall in 1991. Parker emphasised that too much stress was placed by organisations on corporate financial objectives, which ignores the fact that organisations have multiple objectives (Parker, 1979). Other objectives may relate to sales growth, market share, employee relations, quality or social responsibility. The early ideas of Parker, who argued that the organisation should use a balanced assessment of divisional performance which is measured by a composite mix of quantitative and qualitative indices, provided the basis for the development of the balanced view by Kaplan and Norton, who elaborated on this idea in 1992.

Robert Kaplan, a professor at Harvard University, and David Norton, a consultant from the Boston area, developed the balanced scorecard. They summarised the idea behind it in three Harvard Business Review articles. The central theme in the first Kaplan & Norton article, "The Balanced Scorecard: Measures that Drive Performance", is the connection between the traditional performance measures which are financial in nature and the non-financial performance measures (Kaplan & Norton, 1992, 71-92). The balanced scorecard was successfully implemented by a number of companies in the four years following the first publication and in 1996 Kaplan and Norton published a book ("The Balanced Scorecard") that describes these positive results and the learning that followed from these companies. Since this time the balanced scorecard has become a huge success around the world, not only for the fortune 1000 companies, but it was also adapted and implemented by public sector- and not-for-profit organisations. The scorecard has been so widely accepted and effective that the Harvard Business Review recently hailed it as one of the 75 most influential ideas of the twentieth century (Hubbard, 2004).

2.2.1 The balanced scorecard defined

In their first article about the balanced scorecard Kaplan and Norton describe it as follows: *"a set of measures that gives top managers a fast but comprehensive view of the business. The balanced scorecard includes financial measures that tell the results of actions already taken. And it complements the financial measures on customer satisfaction, internal processes, and the organization's innovation and improvement activities – operational measures that are the drivers of future financial performance"* (Kaplan & Norton, 1992, 72).

2.2.2 The four original balanced scorecard perspectives explained

After further development by Kaplan and Norton, the idea and the balanced scorecard can be explained as a conceptual framework for translating an organisation's vision into a set of performance indicators distributed over the following four perspectives (Kaplan and Norton, 2001):
1. Financial
2. Customer
3. Internal business processes
4. Learning and growth

1. The financial perspective

The financial perspective is the strategy for growth, profitability, and risk viewed from the perspective of the shareholder. Most companies traditionally relied solely on the financial data to review a company's performance. This overall and exclusive use of financial measures has been criticised by some who say that it (Hubbard, 2004, 122):

- *is not consistent with today's business realities.* Value creating activities are not captured by tangible fixed assets but value rests in the ideas of the people (intellectual capital) scattered throughout the organisation
- *is like driving by rear-view mirror.* Financial measures review past performance but have no predictive power for the future.
- *tends to reinforce functional silos.* Financial statements are usually prepared by functional area and they ignore the cross-functional work taking place in many organisations today.
- *sacrifices long-term thinking.* Many change programmes feature cost-cutting measures that may have positive impact on the firm's short-term financial statements but they have a negative impact on long-term change plans.
- *is not relevant to many levels of the organisation.* Financial statements are very abstract and difficult to use by most managers and employees. Employees at all levels in the organisation need performance and environment data they can act on.

Given these limitations of financial measures why should they actually be part of a balanced scorecard? The answer is, that like the name already mentions, it needs to be a *balanced* overview of company performance (Hubbard, 2004). As Hubbard states: "financial statements will remain an important tool for organisations because they ultimately determine whether improvements in diverse customer satisfaction, quality, on-time delivery, workplace culture, leadership competencies for a diverse workforce, and innovation are leading to improved financial performance and wealth creation for shareholders (Hubbard, 2004, 124)."

2. The customer perspective
The customer perspective focuses on the strategy for creating value and differentiation from the perspective of the customer. "This perspective typically includes several core or generic measures of the successful outcomes of a well formulated and implemented strategy (Kaplan & Norton, 1996, 26)." Kaplan and Norton state that some of the core outcome measures should include customer satisfaction, customer retention, new customer acquisition, customer profitability, and market and account share in targeted segments (Kaplan & Norton, 1996). "The customer perspective will enable business unit managers to articulate the customer and market-based strategy that will deliver superior future financial returns (Kaplan & Norton, 1996, 26)."

3. Internal business processes.
"In the internal-business-process perspective, executives identify the critical internal processes in which the organisation must excel (Kaplan & Norton, 1996, 26)." These processes enable the business unit to deliver the value that will attract and retain customers in targeted market segments and it will satisfy shareholder expectations of excellent financial returns (Kaplan & Norton, 1996). According to Kaplan and Norton: "the scorecard approach does not only measure existing business processes but it also can identify entirely new and innovative processes that the organisation must excel at to meet customer and financial objectives. Secondly, the balanced scorecard can focus on and improve existing operations that represent the short wave of value creation (short wave being the complete process from receipt of order from customer to delivery of product to customer). But, in addition the balanced scorecard also can focus on the long wave of value creation, i.e. the innovation process, which is for many companies a more powerful driver of future financial performance than the short-term operating cycle (Kaplan & Norton, 1996, 28)."

4. The learning and growth perspective.
The learning and growth perspective aims to create a climate that supports organisational change, innovation, and growth. "This perspective identifies the

infrastructure that the organisation must build to create long-term growth and improvement (Kaplan & Norton, 1996, 28)." Organisational learning and growth come from three principal sources: people, systems and organisational procedures (Kaplan & Norton, 1996, 28). As in the customer perspective, employee based measures include a mixture of generic outcome measures – employee satisfaction, retention, training and skills – along with specific drivers of these generic measures, such as detailed, business-specific indexes of the particular skills required for the new competitive environment (Kaplan & Norton, 1996, 29).

According to Kaplan and Norton balanced scorecard indicators are maintained to measure an organisation's progress towards achieving its vision. Through the balanced scorecard, an organisation monitors both its current performance (finances, customer satisfaction, and business process results) and its efforts to improve processes, motivate and educate employees, and enhance information systems i.e. its ability to learn and improve. "While retaining an interest in financial performance, the balanced scorecard clearly revealed the drivers of superior, long-term value and competitive performance (Kaplan & Norton, 2001, 23)." The financial measures can be called *lag indicators* as they are outcomes of actions previously taken (Hubbard, 2004). The balanced scorecard complements these lag indicators with the drivers of future economic performance, or *lead indicators* (Hubbard, 2004). All performance measures, i.e. both lead and lag indicators are derived from the organisation's strategy.

2.2.3 A fifth perspective?
"Some organisations have added other perspectives, such as quality, environment, safety, health or community (Cokins, 2004, 51)." For example, a chemical manufacturer may choose a fifth perspective because of its huge responsibility for the surroundings of its facilities (Cokins, 2004). Additional perspectives, if desired, facilitate construction of the organisation's strategy map and elevate the importance of strategic objectives related to these topics (Cokins, 2004). Also several organisations have looked at the possibility to develop scorecards for different purposes like Human Resource Management or for promoting diversity initiatives. These options will be discussed in further detail later (see chapter 5.3 page 75).

2.3 Main reasons for using the balanced scorecard
The business environment has changed rapidly during the last years and companies have to deal with many new challenges and technologies. Competition is fierce and companies have answered by changing organisational structures in order to be more flexible to deal with the fast changing environment. As organisations flatten their structures and tilt 90 degrees from

being hierarchical to more process-based and customer-focused, core processes replace the artificial boundaries of functional silos (Cokins, 2004). Things get more complicated and many employees multi-task in two or more processes which increases the need for matrixed management (Cokins, 2004). Organisational charts divide the organisation into work units and although these lines are drawn and constantly redrawn, the hierarchy will never disappear because individuals continue to need mentoring, coaching, career development counselling and direction (Cokins, 2004). Performance measurement is all about converting formulated strategies into execution, outcomes and results and because of the increase in complexity in organisations and their structures the need for the discipline of performance measurement is only become more important. Cokins mentions: "the rising specialisation, complexity, and value-adding services cause the need for more, not less, performance measurement (Cokins, 2004, 17)."

As organisations have attempted to transform themselves to compete successfully in the future, they are turning to a variety of improvement initiatives (Kaplan & Norton, 1996, 6):
- Total Quality Management
- Just-in-time (JIT) production and distribution systems
- Time-based competition
- Lean production, lean enterprise
- Building customer focused organisations
- Activity-based cost management
- Employee empowerment
- Reengineering

And, even though, each of these improvement programmes has had demonstrated success stories there have also been disappointing results. The programmes are often fragmented and they may not be linked to the organisations strategy (Kaplan & Norton, 1996). Furthermore, they may not be designed to achieve specific financial and economic outcomes (Kaplan & Norton, 1996). However, after reviewing the traditional balanced scorecard perspectives it can be said that Kaplan and Norton have used the ideas of some other well known and widely used management tools (see table 1).

Balanced scorecard perspectives:	Comparison to other management tools:
Financial perspective	Shareholder value
Customer perspective	Target costing
Internal business processes	Total Quality Management (TQM) Lean management
Learning and growth perspective	The learning organisation

Table 1: The balanced scorecard perspectives compared to other management tools

Breakthroughs in performance require major change and that includes changes in the measurement and management systems used by an organisation. "Navigating to a more competitive, technological, and capability-driven future cannot be accomplished merely by monitoring and controlling financial measures of past performance (Kaplan & Norton, 1996, 6)." The balanced scorecard offers this connection of past results and future direction and it is a translation of the organisation's strategy.

One of the other reasons that led to an increasing interest in scorecards is the major frustration of executives regarding their inability to get their employees to carry out the executive's strategies they have so carefully formulated (Cokins, 2004). Especially, in cases where strategies are changing and being adapted the employees often continue to work as usual. This does not happen with the key performance indicator measures which are put in the scorecard as these figures become reality.

2.4 The balanced scorecard; how do organisations actually use it?
The balanced scorecard is now widespread used by companies around the world in many different industries and sectors. Each balanced scorecard is unique to the organisation that developed it as it is a translation of their specific strategy and vision. Different market situations, product strategies, and competitive environments require different scorecards. Business units devise customised scorecards to fit their mission, strategy, technology and culture (Kaplan and Norton, 1993).

In many organisations, and research into best practices of scorecard use, the balanced scorecard serves at least three functions for organisations (Hubbard, 2004, 126):
1. A measurement system
2. A strategic management system
3. A communication tool

2.4.1 The balanced scorecard as measurement system
The balanced scorecard as measurement system can be seen in figure 2. As Kaplan and Norton described, it actually is the translation of the organisation's vision and strategy into the four perspectives of the balanced scorecard.

The balanced scorecard allows an organisation to translate its vision and strategies by providing a new framework for the organisation's strategy (Hubbard, 2004). "Scorecards communicate strategic objectives to the workforce in terms that are meaningful to them, scorecards allow organisations to coordinate the efforts and behaviour of large numbers of employees, and,

35

scorecards can assure that the vision and mission created in the boardroom are achieved by the organisation (Cokins, 2004, 51)."

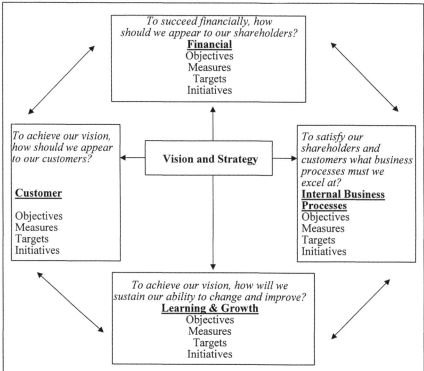

Figure 2: The balanced scorecard / translating vision and strategy: four perspectives (adapted from: Kaplan and Norton, January/February 1996, 76)

2.4.2 The balanced scorecard as strategic management system

After the initial use of the balanced scorecard as a measurement system there were also a number of companies identified by Kaplan and Norton that have gone further and discovered the scorecard's value as the cornerstone of a new strategic management system (Kaplan and Norton, 1996). Traditional management systems rely on financial measures with little relation to progress in achieving long-term strategic objectives, but, the scorecard introduces four new processes that help companies connect long-term objectives with short-term actions (Kaplan and Norton, 1996). In figure 3 "managing strategy: four processes" these four processes and the connection to the balanced scorecard can be seen.

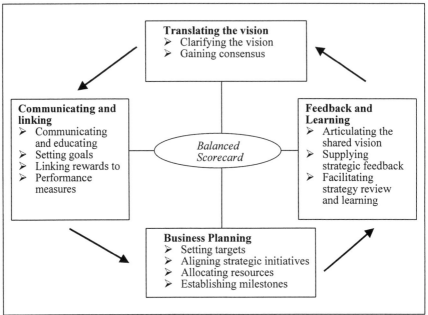

Figure 3: The balanced scorecard / Managing strategy: four processes (source: Kaplan
and Norton, January/February 1996, 77)

The four processes are the following (Kaplan and Norton, 1996, 77):
1) Translating the vision – helps managers build a consensus around the
company's strategy and express it in terms that can guide action at the local
level.
2) Communicating and linking – lets managers communicate their strategy up
and down the organisation and link it to unit and individual goals.
3) Business planning – enables companies to integrate their business and
financial plans.
4) Feedback and learning – gives companies the capacity for strategic learning,
which consists of gathering feedback, testing the hypotheses on which strategy
was based, and making the necessary adjustments.

Kaplan and Norton found that most organisations did not intend to develop a
new strategic management system when they implemented the balanced
scorecard. However, when the senior executives started to build the scorecard
they started a process of change that usually went well beyond the original idea
of simply broadening the company's performance measures (Kaplan and
Norton, 1996).

2.4.3 The balanced scorecard as communication tool

The initial use of the balanced scorecard was as a pure balanced measurement system. By implementing it and using it as measurement system a number of companies found out that it could also be helpful for developing a strategic management system. However, the most basic and most valuable part of the entire balanced scorecard system is its ability to communicate the translation of the organisation's strategy and telling its story to all employees (Hubbard, 2004). Hubbard mentions that a well-constructed scorecard describes the organisation's strategy and makes the vague and imprecise world of visions and strategies come alive through the clear and objective performance measures chosen (Hubbard, 2004). Or as Cokins writes, the overriding goal of a strategy map and scorecard system is to make strategy everyone's job (Cokins, 2004).

2.4.4 Strategy maps

There are authors who have expressed criticism regarding the balanced scorecard. For example Neely, Adams and Kennerley (2002) mention that with the focus on only the four perspectives the balanced scorecard downplays the importance of other stakeholders, such as employees, suppliers, regulators and communities. An organisation's key stakeholders are likely to be a combination of the following: investors, customers and intermediaries, employees and labour unions, suppliers and alliance partners, regulators, pressure groups and communities (Neely, Adams and Kennerley, 2002).

This might be one of the reasons why Kaplan & Norton (2001, 2004) further developed the balanced scorecard in their latest books in such a way that they add a next layer to it which is described as a strategy map. Here also other stakeholders are included. Strategy maps are like geographical maps that visually aid in understanding how one gets from point A (the present capability, organisation, and focus of the enterprise) to destination B (the future desired state of capabilities, organisation, and focus, as laid out in the enterprise vision, mission and strategy plan). "Scorecards are like a cockpit enabling managers and employee teams to navigate and steer. Scorecards without strategy maps may lead to failure especially because when scorecards are built and reported in isolation, there is no direct linkage to strategy (Cokins, 2004, 42)." As Cokins continues: "strategy maps and scorecards go hand in hand, once created, they embody the strategic intent of the organisation and communicate to all both the strategic objectives the organisation intends to meet as well as the critical measures of success for attaining those objectives – be they strategic, tactical, or operational measures (Cokins, 2004, 43)."

Kaplan and Norton define a strategy map as: "a visual representation of the cause-and-effect relationships among the components of an organisation's strategy (Kaplan and Norton, 2004, 9)." The general strategy map evolved from the simple, four-perspective model of the balanced scorecard. The strategy map adds a second layer of detail that illustrates the time-based dynamics of a strategy. Kaplan and Norton developed the strategy map to be the missing link between strategy formulation and strategy execution. The strategy map is based on several principles:

1) Strategy balances contradictory forces
2) Strategy is based on a differentiated customer value proposition
3) Value is created through internal business processes

The internal business processes are then classified into four clusters:
- Operations management
- Customer management
- Innovation
- Regulatory and social

Here Kaplan and Norton deal with the stakeholders that, according to some critics, were neglected by the balanced scorecard, namely the regulatory and social element. In this way they focus on the issue that organisations should enhance their reputation in the community. Some people have criticised the balanced scorecard, believing that people cannot focus on twenty-five different measures and indeed if the scorecard is viewed as twenty-five independent measures, it will be to complicated, but, this is also the wrong way to think about the balanced scorecard. "The strategy map shows how the multiple measures on a properly constructed balanced scorecard provide the instrument for a single strategy (Kaplan and Norton, 2004, 54)." "Strategy maps and scorecards provide a framework for literally keeping score of the functions and processes that are the most important to the success of an organisation (Cokins, 2004, 43)."

2.5 Implementation of the balanced scorecard

As was already mentioned before, each balanced scorecard is unique and therefore also the development of the scorecard is unique and specifically designed for the company requirements. However, it is possible to make a typical project profile as Kaplan & Norton did in their 1993 article. A comprehensive view of the process of developing a balanced scorecard in an organisation can be seen in figure 4.

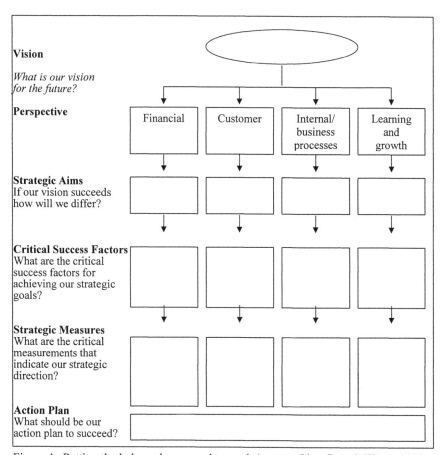

Figure 4: Putting the balanced scorecard to work (source: Olve, Roy & Wetter 2000, 42 / Original source: Kaplan & Norton, September / October 1993, 139)

There are three principles that enable an organisation's balanced scorecard to be linked to its strategy (i.e. they assist in developing the measures on the scorecard) and these are (Kaplan and Norton, 1996, 149):
1) Cause-and-effect relationships
2) Performance drivers
3) Linkage to financials

A strategy is a set of hypotheses about cause and effect which can be expressed by a sequence of *if–then* statements (e.g. *if* we can achieve this, *then* this will happen) (Kaplan and Norton, 1996, 149). All balanced scorecards use certain generic measures which tend to be the lag indicators. However, the performance drivers, the lead indicators are the ones that tend to be unique for a particular business unit and they reflect the uniqueness of the business unit's strategy. A good balanced scorecard should have a mix of outcome measures (lagging indicators) and performance drivers (leading indicators). And, finally, causal paths from all the measures on a scorecard should be linked to financial objectives (Kaplan and Norton, 1996, 150). Kaplan and Norton (2001, 63) have identified five principles of a strategy-focussed organisation to achieve breakthrough performance, which are:

1. Translate the strategy to operational terms
2. Align the organisation to the strategy
3. Make strategy everyone's everyday job
4. Make strategy a continual process
5. Mobilise leadership for change

However, there are also problems with implementing the balanced scorecard and not all organisations become a strategy-focussed organisation. The most common implementation failures include the following (Kaplan and Norton, 2001, 361):

- Lack of senior management commitment
- Too few individuals involved
- Keeping the scorecard at the top
- Too long a development process; the balanced scorecard as a one-time measurement project
- Treating the balanced scorecard as a systems project
- Hiring inexperienced consultants
- Introducing the balanced scorecard only for compensation

When the implementation has taken place and the scorecard is being used also the aspects of feedback and learning become important. The capacity for organisational learning at the executive level, i.e. the strategic learning, is perhaps the most innovative aspect of the balanced scorecard (Kaplan and Norton, 1996, 269). The balanced scorecard also facilitates team learning as the scorecard should be developed and used by the management team for performance monitoring which can take the form of hypothesis testing and double-loop learning (Kaplan and Norton, 1996, 270). The scorecard needs to be reviewed and adapted regularly to keep up with competitive pressures and market changes. "A learning organisation improves a company's ability to react to, adapt to, and capitalise on changes in its internal and external situation. While individual learning is important as a foundation for collective learning, in the long run it is of limited value to the company. What is learned should also be accessible to others at the company and preferably tied to it in a more lasting manner (i.e. structural capital) (Olve, Roy and Wetter, 2000, 256)." The balanced scorecard can assist organisations with continuous learning as continuous changes are a requirement for successful scorecard performance.

2.6 Acceptance of the balanced scorecard

One issue with the implementation and the use of the balanced scorecard is that many organisations state that they already use both financial and non-financial measures, so, in a way they have a balanced scorecard. However, very often their non-financial measures only exist of lagging measures and they are generic measures. This means that the organisation is lacking leading measures that can be communicated to the employees to show them what they must improve on in order to stay competitive in the future.

Other issues with wrongful implementation or use of the balanced scorecard can occur when the development of the scorecard is not done by the top management team but is delegated to middle management. "For the balanced scorecard to be effective, it must reflect the strategic vision of the senior executive group (Kaplan and Norton, 1996, 285)." Another point here is that the top management team must also use the balanced scorecard for their reviews and feedback about the results of the organisation. If they do not do so the chances are high that the focus of the top management is still short-term instead of long-term.

Finally, it is important that organisations realise that their balanced scorecard is unique to them and should not be a reflection of a benchmarking study, i.e. based on the best practices in the industry. Balanced scorecards are unique and should be dynamic and continually reviewed, assessed and updated to reflect new competitive, market and technological conditions.

To finalise this review about the issues with- and the acceptance of the balanced scorecard two final questions should be reviewed.

Who do scorecards help more – senior management or the workers?
The answer is that there should be a win-win result for both groups. Management and employees equally benefit from scorecards. However, it is important to note that the scorecard should not become a report card (Cokins, 2004). Scorecards are not about who was right or wrong but it is a tool that assists the overall organisation to achieve its strategy and vision. If scorecards are used for punishing employees for individual behaviour the purpose of the scorecard is lost and the employees will resist against using the scorecard. Also Kaplan and Norton agreed that: "the organisation may first wish to get some experience in managing with the balanced scorecard before explicitly tying compensation to it (Kaplan and Norton, 1996, 283)." However, they also state that incentive compensation motivates employees and that reward and punishment must eventually be tied to the balanced set of objectives if the organisation wants to use the balanced scorecard as the central organising

framework for its management systems (Kaplan and Norton, 1996). According to Meyer (2003) by the mid 1990s between a third and two-thirds of US companies had adopted the balanced scorecard or some variant of it for purposes of appraising and compensating their managers (Meyer, 2003, 82). "Using the balanced scorecard to appraise and compensate performance is more difficult than using the scorecard for strategic measurement, especially, to find the right scorecard measures (particularly those non-financial measures that look ahead) is essential for appraising and compensating performance (Meyer, 2003, 82)."

Are strategy maps and scorecards going to be a management fad?
According to the following authors scorecards definitely are a very good management tool:
• Strategy maps and scorecards do make sense, address a true need, and will likely be a keeper for organisations that are willing to try new ideas (Cokins, 2004, 81).
• So widely accepted and effective has the scorecard been that the Harvard Business Review recently hailed it as one of the 75 most influential ideas of the twentieth century (Hubbard, 2004).
• Also Olve, Roy and Wetter agree that the balanced scorecard has its place and an important role to play as the concept is an aid in the essential process of arriving at a shared view of the business environment and of the company and because it provides a new foundation for strategic control (Olve, Roy and Wetter, 2000, 11).

And, Kaplan and Norton state:
• Information age companies will succeed by investing in and managing their intellectual assets (Kaplan and Norton, 1996, 19).
• Management processes built around the scorecard enable the organisation to become aligned and focused on implementing the long-term strategy (Kaplan and Norton, 1996, 19).

One of the main deficits of the balanced scorecard is that it is still difficult to use for performance appraisal and compensation as this may lead to uncertainty and less effective working behaviour among the employees. This maybe an area where more research and further development of the balanced scorecard should take place especially since many companies already have made their learning experiences with this issue. If this can be improved and made easier, then the balanced scorecard is a very good management tool to communicate the strategy and vision of the organisation to the employees at all levels. Secondly, it assists the organisation as measurement system to review performance. And thirdly, it has been used successfully on many occasions as a strategic management tool.

The balanced scorecard is already so widely used and integrated not only as performance measurement system but also as strategic management system in many companies around the world that it will be a tool that will probably still be used for many years to come and probably by many generations to come, as Max Planck once wrote:

"A new scientific truth does not triumph by convincing its opponents and making them see the light, but rather because its opponents eventually die out, and a new generation grows up that is familiar with it."

Max Planck, physicist and originator of the Quantum Theory,
in the Philosophy of Physics (1936)

2.7 Conclusion

In this chapter the balanced scorecard as management tool was the central focus. The balanced scorecard was defined and explained and the main reasons why organisations should use it were reviewed. Then, the actual ways in which organisations have used it were analysed followed by the implementation process. Finally practical issues with the balanced scorecard and the actual acceptance level of the balanced scorecard were mentioned. The overall conclusion of the chapter is that the balanced scorecard is not just a management fad but that it is a management tool that is here to stay. In the next chapter gender mainstreaming will be discussed and explained. What is gender mainstreaming and why is it important to organisations. The gender mainstreaming chapter is the second theoretical foundation.

3 Gender Mainstreaming

3.1 Introduction

Now that the balanced scorecard is introduced it is important to look at the gender mainstreaming theoretical foundation. In this chapter the meaning of the terms gender, gender equality/equity and gender mainstreaming need to be determined. Furthermore, a short historical overview of the changes in gender perspectives will be a good basis for explaining what gender mainstreaming is and why gender mainstreaming offers an important opportunity for organisations to achieve competitive advantage nowadays.

3.2 Gender perspectives; a brief historical overview

The ideas about achieving equality for women have changed significantly over the years. In the 1960s and 1970s the Women in Development (WID) approach was based on the rationale that, women constituted a large untapped resource which should be recognised as being potentially valuable in economic development (Commonwealth Secretariat, 1999).

An alternative approach that followed in the 1980s was called the Gender and Development approach (GAD approach). This approach questioned the previous tendency to view women's problems in terms of their sex, i.e. their biological differences from men, rather than in terms of their gender, i.e. the social relationship between women and men in which women have been subordinated and oppressed (Commonwealth Secretariat, 1999). The GAD approach supports the WID view that women should be given the opportunity to participate on equal terms in all aspects of life, but its primary focus is to examine gender relations of power at all levels in society, so that interventions can bring about equality and equity between women and men in all spheres of life (Commonwealth Secretariat, 1999). The state is expected to assist in this process and legislation plays a big role in the GAD approach.

Under the GAD approach women are seen as agents of change rather than as passive recipients of development assistance and from the GAD perspective the intervention strategies seek to bring about a structural change and shifts in power relationships and in doing so eliminate gender biases at all levels (Commonwealth Secretariat, 1999). This can be seen as the basis for the gender mainstreaming development which will be described in more detail later on.

3.3 Definition of terms

It is important to review several definitions in order to understand gender and this can then serve as the basis for constructing the definition of gender mainstreaming which will be used for the purpose of this research.

What is gender? In a guide to gender impact assessment by the European Commission **gender** is defined as: "the social differences between women and men that are learned, changeable over time and have wide variations both within and between cultures (www.europa.eu.int)." The Commonwealth Secretariat (1999, 8) uses the following definition for **gender**: "Gender refers to the socially constructed, rather than the biologically defined, sex roles and attributes of females and males." The 1995 Commonwealth plan of action defines gender as: "the socially defined/constructed differences between women and men that result in women's subordination and inequality in opportunity to a better life."

So gender refers to historical and social relationships between women and men. And if it is the aim to increase the life quality and standards of everybody it is the specific gender focus that adds an extra factor of control towards reviewing the impact of this improvement especially for women. If gender is being analysed – as this research aims to do – the differences in the status and experiences between women and men can be made visible. In many cases specific measures need to be taken to ensure that women can enjoy the same rights, levels of achievements and standard of living that men do.

What is gender equality and gender equity? Gender equality and gender equity are used very often as if they are interchangeable. However, the Commonwealth Secretariat (1999, 9) identifies the difference between these two terms as follows:
"Gender equality refers to sameness or uniformity in quantity, amount, value and intensity of provisions made and measures implemented for women and men. Equality can usually be legislated.
Gender equity refers to doing whatever is necessary to ensure equality of outcomes in the life experiences of women and men. Equity is difficult to legislate: identical treatment may satisfy the equality, but not the equity criterion."

What is diversity and inclusion? It is also relevant to define the terms diversity and inclusion as these are often used in literature to refer to managing, among others, gender equality. According to Krell (2004) the concept of gender mainstreaming should actually be changed into the concept of managing diversity which would be a more modern concept and which might be a management concept that could reach more people. She also argues that top managers in private organisations often link gender mainstreaming to bureaucracy and paperwork, whereas they have accepted managing diversity as a modern management concept (translated from Krell, 2004).

Rajan, Martin and Latham (2003, 1) define these two terms as follows:
"Diversity covers personal identity defined by gender, ethnicity, age, disability and religion. It also covers personal styles and approaches with respect to learning, working and managing.
Inclusion is about engaging people to do their best. It is influenced by the way they are managed and by the environment in which they work: for example being respected as an individual, being treated fairly, having opportunities to influence and be heard, and receiving recognition for doing a good job."

3.3.1 Gender mainstreaming
Gender mainstreaming is a relatively new concept which was developed during the third World Conference on Women in Nairobi in 1985. A global platform for action was adopted at the fourth World Conference on Women in Beijing in 1995 which requested governments and other actors: "to mainstream a gender perspective into all policies and programmes, so that, before decisions are taken, an analysis is made of the effects on women and men respectively (www.europa.eu.int)." Also the Treaty of Amsterdam formalises the mainstreaming commitment at the European level as it explicitly mentions: "the elimination of inequalities and the promotion of equality between women and men" among the tasks and objectives of the community (Articles 2 & 3, Treaty of Amsterdam). The Commonwealth Secretariat (1999, 10) explains that gender mainstreaming means "the consistent use of a gender perspective at all stages of the development and implementation of policies, plans, programmes and projects." "Mainstreaming gender differs from previous efforts to integrate women's concerns into government activities in that, rather than 'adding on' a women's component to existing policies, plans, programmes and projects, a gender perspective informs these at all stages, and in every aspect of the decision-making process (the Commonwealth Secretariat, 1999, 10)."

For the purpose of this research **gender mainstreaming** will be defined as: *a fundamental transformation process which changes the underlying paradigms in national cultures, organisational cultures and also on the individual level in persons to embrace gender equality at all levels and in all activities.*

For this research the term gender mainstreaming will be used instead of diversity management or inclusion. Reason for this is that the focus of this project is solely on gender initiatives and, therefore, the other focuses (i.e. ethnicity, age, disability and religion) which are included in the term diversity management are excluded here.

According to the Commonwealth Secretariat (1999, 13) the process of mainstreaming gender for nations involves the following steps:
1) Questioning the underlying paradigm on which national policy, goals and objectives have been based
2) Joint programming with other development entities, including government ministries and departments, intergovernmental and non-governmental organisations
3) Aligning with other entities' priorities, activities and critical issues; placing gender-sensitive women and men in strategic positions in policy-setting and decision-making
4) Making women visible in all data
5) Providing training in gender analysis, methodology and awareness
For the purpose of this research the above steps will be adapted for organisations by reviewing the balanced scorecard as management tool in chapter 5 (page 74).

In the European Union the legal base for gender mainstreaming includes the following (www.europa.eu.int):
Article 2 of the EC Treaty: "The promotion of equality between men and women is a task of the European Community"
Article 3 of the EC Treaty: "In all its activities the community shall aim to eliminate inequalities and to promote equality between men and women"
Article 23 (1) of the Charter of Fundamental Rights of the European Union: "Equality between men and women must be ensured in all areas, including employment, work and pay."

The method the European Commission wants to use to achieve gender main-streaming is a dual approach where gender mainstreaming is combined with specific actions. Also gender impact assessment and gender proofing are methods chosen by the European commission. Furthermore, they decided on training for and awareness raising among key personnel in addition to monitoring, benchmarking and breakdown of data and statistics by sex. These actions are to be implemented by: a group of commissioners in equal oppor-tunities, inter-service groups on gender equality and an advisory committee of equal opportunities for women and men (www.europa.eu.int).

3.4 Advantages of gender mainstreaming for organisations
Now that gender mainstreaming and gender equality are explained and defined it is important to explore the reasons for implementing these concepts in organi-sations. What are the advantages of gender mainstreaming for organisations? The short answer is that the successful implementation of gender main-streaming, i.e. equality can provide the organisation with an important *competitive advantage* (translated from Krell, 2004, 14).

Wellington agrees when she states: "the winners are going to be the organisations that view diversity as truly a mechanism to gain competitive advantage" (Wellington, 1998, 57). Or as Hubbard mentions: "the ability to utilise a diverse mixture of human and other resources to create a unique blend of strategy-focused solutions, by its very nature, creates an innovative competitive process that is difficult to copy – thus making it a competitive advantage (largely invisible to competitors) (Hubbard, 2004, 5)."

Figure 5 shows that organisations have started to align their workplace and workforce to the changing, more global and more diverse marketplace. "This interaction between markets, businesses and workforce is clearly at the heart of national competitiveness (Rajan, Martin and Latham, 2003, 2)." The figure shows why the demand for a more diverse workforce exists and that it can provide organisations with competitive advantages in the more diverse markets.

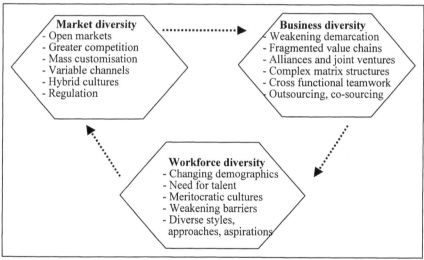

Figure 5: Aligning the workplace with the marketplace (source: Rajan, Martin and Latham, 2003, 2)

To determine the benefits of gender mainstreaming for organisations in further detail a number of important arguments, which can also be seen in figure 5 above, can be reviewed under the following three main advantages of gender mainstreaming that organisations can profit from (translated from Krell 2004):
1) The human resource advantage
2) The marketing advantage
3) The cost element

The advantages gender mainstreaming offers to organisations can be seen in table 2 below and will be outlined individually in more detail next.

Area of advantage:	Advantage for organisation:
Human resource advantages	• Loyal & motivated employees – reduce absenteeism • Positive effect on company image • Suitable organisational structures • More women in management positions • Diverse work teams • Better use of the total workforce available
Marketing advantages	• Do female customers prefer to buy from female employees? • Do female customers prefer to buy from women friendly organisations? • The company image improvement from a marketing point of view
Cost savings advantages	• Avoid fines for discrimination • Loss of motivation of workforce & reduced productivity • High retention costs • Price of rebuilding a corporate image

Table 2: Overview of advantages of gender mainstreaming initiatives for organisations

3.4.1 The human resource advantage

From a human resource point of view there are several reasons why companies would gain competitive advantages when they implement gender mainstreaming in their organisational culture. The following are examples of the advantages:

• *Loyal and motivated employees – reduce absenteeism*
From the human resource perspective an organisation which achieves or promotes gender equality will have advantages on the labour market as the organisation will be able to attract highly qualified employees who will be loyal and very motivated to work for the organisation (translated from Krell, 2004). A highly motivated and loyal labour force can give a company the competitive edge it needs to survive and expand even in times of recession. Secondly, highly motivated and satisfied employees are less likely to be absent, to come in late or to leave early compared to unsatisfied employees. Employees witnessing and/or experiencing hostile work environments and harassment are often away more frequently and are less productive (Hubbard, 2004). Productivity is directly affected by the cost of absenteeism.

• *Positive effect on company image*
Secondly, a gender equality company can utilise this to improve and promote their company image in a very positive way to potential employees but also towards governments and other organisations. Especially, since governments are focussing more on gender mainstreaming and since it is legally defined as a requirement for governments and organisations the company can use this

favourable image to deal with government issues or contracts. The corporate reputation quotient of Harris-Fombrun is a comprehensive measuring method of corporate reputation that was created especially to capture the perceptions of any corporate stakeholder group such as consumers, investors, employees, or key influential persons (Fombrun, van Ciel, 2003). The instrument enables research on the drivers of a company's reputation as well as comparisons of reputation both within and across industries. The model has the following 6 drivers of corporate reputation with subsequent attributes:

➢ Emotional appeal (good feeling about the company, admire and respect the company, trust the company)

➢ Products and services (stands behind products/services, offers high quality, develops innovations, offers high value)

➢ Vision and leadership (has excellent leadership, has a clear vision for the future, recognises/takes advantages of market opportunities)

➢ Workplace environment (is well managed, looks like a good company to work for, looks like it has good employees)

➢ Financial performance (record of profitability, looks like a low risk investment, strong prospects for future growth, tends to outperform its competitors)

➢ Social responsibility (supports good causes, environmentally responsible, treats people well)

The corporate reputation is receiving increased attention and focus nowadays. Gender equality and equal/good treatment of all employees is an important component of the organisation's reputation and will be reviewed by potential, high talented, new employees. Also Leary-Joyce describes how companies can become an employer of choice by creating the sort of great company atmosphere that will attract top people who will deliver excellent results (Leary-Joyce, 2004). Thus, gender mainstreaming can have a huge effect on the company image and can help the organisation to become an employer of choice for high talented employees.

- *Suitable organisational structures*

Also, from a human resource point of view, some recent changes in the workplace show that equality for women in organisations can provide these organisations with competitive advantages. A review of changes in organisational structures makes clear why women fit very well in the structures organisations choose more frequently nowadays. In the 1980s the 'enterprise culture' became popular with mergers & acquisitions, strategic alliances, joint ventures, process reengineering, etc. transforming workplaces into free market hothouse cultures (Cooper & Lewis; in Powell, 1999, 37). The 1990s saw the most profound changes in the workplace. The early years were dominated by the effects of recession and globalisation, as organisations downsized, delayered, flattened or right sized (Cooper & Lewis; in Powell, 1999, 37). The trend toward a short-term contract and freelance culture has led to what employers euphemistically refer to as the 'flexible workforce'. The psychological contract between employers and employees in terms of relatively permanent employment for a job well done is being undermined as more and more workers do not regard their job as secure and growing numbers engage in part-time work (Cooper & Lewis; in Powell, 1999, 38). With employers preferring flexible workers it makes sense for them to hire women because of their historical background and experience with part-time and contract work. Women everywhere are historically more familiar with discontinuous career patterns, flowing in and out of the labour market, working part-time and on short-term contracts (Cooper & Lewis; in Powell, 1999, 39). Even though in the past the opportunities connected to these jobs were minimal, nowadays, there is a clear tendency that also part-time jobs and contract work become more challenging as companies are often downsizing the number of employees on a permanent basis. Also job-sharing has become an option to fill a full-time job position with two persons working both part-time. For men it is much harder to deal with these changes. They prefer a job for life and flexibility is much harder to accept. A cross-national qualitative study of orientations to work and family among young people (under 30) in five European countries by Lewis (in 1998) suggests that especially less highly educated men and working-class men had problems to adapt to shifts in the nature of work and the changing roles in family and relationships (Cooper & Lewis; in Powell, 1999, 40). Most of the women hoped to be financially independent, be in egalitarian relationships and have satisfying careers, mostly defined as a series of jobs fitting around family obligations. Also highly educated professional men in this study expressed similar ideas (Cooper & Lewis; in Powell, 1999, 40).

- *More women in management positions*

Even though it is still very often the case that men are situated in top management teams (and it is unlikely that they will give up this power easily) several changes are taking place which allow more women to reach managerial positions. There are several reasons why this also can lead to a competitive advantage for the organisation. Above it was already stated that many organisations have changed their organisational structure in order to deal with the challenges of globalisation and recessions. Flatter structures are often asked for to handle the challenges and different career paths that come with it. A discontinuous career path is often more suitable for women as they already have experiences with this issue. This does not correspond to the traditional male career notions which were more suited to bureaucratic and hierarchical organisations. With these changes in structure and careers also a new management style based on different management skills might be better. Being a good manager nowadays is less about competitiveness, aggression and task orientation (the characteristics of the traditional macho male managers) but more about good communication, coaching and people skills and being intuitive and flexible, all more typically or at least stereotypically associated with women (Cooper & Lewis; in Powell, 1999, 41). Evidence shows that female leaders tend to be more open, approachable, and encouraging (Gibson, 1995; Rosener, 1990), and are more likely to display transformational leadership (Bass, Avolio & Atwater, 1996) and stimulate an atmosphere of participative safety in teams (Atkins & Dunning, 1998), all essential skills in the rapidly changing workplace (From: Cooper & Lewis; in Powell, 1999, 41). Thus organisations with modern flatter structures and flexible career notions are more likely to have women in management positions which can give the organisation a competitive advantage because it fully exploits and implements the chosen structure and allows the organisation to use the advantages of this structure to deal with the challenges of change. More women in management will also impact the organisational culture which will be discussed in further detail in chapter 4.3 (page 66). For organisations that are not very women-friendly the risk is also very high that high-powered female employees will leave their position. As Solomon mentions: "when women are frustrated by inflexible work environments and stubborn barriers to the top echelons, they are less tolerant of glass ceilings and glass walls and they actually will leave to start their own business, work for smaller firms or go to competitors that offer more of what they want (Solomon, 2001)."

- *Diverse work teams*
Diverse work teams have been found to possess the potential to achieve higher levels of performance than homogeneous teams, especially since diverse groups of people bring a broad range of skills, knowledge, abilities, and perspectives to organisational challenges (Hubbard, 2004, 16). This shows that it could be really valuable to include women in work teams as this will offer different perspectives and can lead to achieving competitive advantage.

- *Better use of the total workforce available*
Looking at the economic and demographic situation in many European countries it becomes clear that many organisations will need to focus on the complete workforce in the future because high quality labour might become scarcer in the near future. Companies (and countries) are faced with the challenge that a smaller population (low birth rates) will have to support a larger ageing population. This will create a situation (as agreed by many politicians and experts) in which everybody who can work must work full-time, and they should work longer hours to meet the demand from organisations for labour and to carry the future costs of the ageing population. Therefore, also the large female labour force should be included (there are many women who are

currently working only part-time or not at all). It is interesting to review that workforce projections put forth by the U.S. Department of Labour have indicated that only 15% of the new entrants to the workforce in the USA will be white males and nearly 85% will be women, minorities and immigrants (Hubbard, 2004, 10). He further writes that workers 55 and older are the fastest growing segment of the workforce in the United States (Hubbard, 2004, 11). Companies who are already preparing for this future challenge and make their organisation accessible to women will have a competitive advantage in the longer run.

3.4.2 The marketing advantage

From a marketing point of view there are also several advantages organisations can achieve when they implement gender mainstreaming:

- *Do female customers prefer to buy from female employees?*

Krell (2004) also looks at the marketing argument to show why gender mainstreaming can offer organisations a competitive advantage. Here it is important to recognise that many organisations have a large female customer base and that it could be beneficial if female employees would approach them. Actually, by one estimate, women in the United States have "more purchasing power than the total economic output of any other country, including Japan" (Katz & Katz, 1997). Hence organisations have to take this large female customer base into account when planning their marketing. However, to some industries (for example technological, information technology or other typically male areas) this does not necessarily apply and their customer base could prefer to be served and assisted by male employees rather than female employees. Clearly, this advantage should be reviewed for each individual organisation. Furthermore, it needs to be noted here that there is not much evidence supporting the statement that women prefer to buy from female employees and therefore, more research should be done in this field to establish whether it can provide companies with a competitive advantage. However, as Hubbard states: "it is clear that globalisation and changing domestic markets reflect a changing buying public and there is little doubt that an organisation that is serious about diversity can gain an improved understanding of diverse customers' needs and therefore foster better customer service to an increasingly diverse (and also large female) market. So, in addition to attracting and retaining the best workforce, successful businesses must also attract and retain clients (Hubbard, 2004, 10)."

- *Do female customers prefer to buy from women friendly organisations?*

Katz & Katz argue that women can put their purchasing power to work in different ways by supporting women-friendly companies (Katz & Katz, 1997). To help women in this endeavour Katz & Katz rate companies, states and countries using a variety of criteria, including the number of women on the board, number of female top officers, the company's benefits programme and pay disparities (Gutek, Cherry and Goth; in Powell, 1999). This could mean that an organisation with a women-friendly image could achieve a competitive advantage. And, now that gender mainstreaming is so high on the agenda of governments and politicians and as a consequence also receives more attention from the general public this could really become an important argument in favour of gender mainstreaming in organisations nowadays.

- *The company image improvement from a marketing point of view*
More awards are being introduced in the different countries which are given to companies for good practices with respect to achieving equality for women in the organisation. Some examples include the Catalyst Company in the USA, which is a non-profit organisation with the mission of furthering women's advancement in corporations and professional firms. The Catalyst award recognises corporate or professional initiatives promoting women's leadership (Wellington, 1998, 233). In Germany a 'total E-Quality' award was introduced which is also awarded to companies who align their personnel policies to achieve equal opportunities in the best way possible (www.total-e-quality.de; Krell, 2004, 2). Another initiative was developed in Germany which is called the genderdax (www.genderdax.de). Here companies are examined according to different criteria with regards to gender equality and then they are rated accordingly. It has become more interesting for organisations to focus on equal opportunities in their organisation because of these awards and other initiatives as the winning of such awards can be used to market the company image in a positive way towards customers, employees and other stakeholders.

3.4.3 The cost element
Finally, the cost element can be checked. If the positive human resource- and marketing advantages cannot convince the organisation to initiate a gender mainstreaming process maybe the downside risks and impacts of turnover costs, poor training return-on-investment (because employees leave shortly after arrival), poor overall brand image, failing community image as a good place to work for all employees, and many other negative impacts may convince the organisation to do so. Companies which promote equal opportunities can achieve competitive advantages because they are able to avoid the following:

- *Fines for discrimination*
Even though, as Krell mentions, the fines for discrimination of women in business are not yet very high in Europe the increase in attention for this issue on a legal level might lead to changes of this in the near future (translated from Krell, 2004). Increases in litigation charges can lead to negative publicity for an

organisation and therefore can damage the corporate image heavily. Examples of gender discrimination cases in the United States have shown already that high fines can be given to organisations and some examples are: State Farm ($250 million), Home Depot ($110 million) and Lucky Stores ($107 million) (Hubbard, 2004, 20).

- *Loss of motivation of workforce & reduced productivity*
Higher costs will be incurred from loss of motivation of the workforce (translated from Krell, 2004). An unmotivated workforce will lead to a decrease in productivity and can therefore lead to much higher costs for the organisation. Especially, since low productivity can lead to an increase in dissatisfied customer costs. Productivity does not only relate to direct effort but also to discretionary effort (i.e. extra effort employees undertake) and in today's workplaces, discretionary effort can make the difference between getting and not getting a client and between keeping and losing a client (Hubbard, 2004, 16). Demotivated and undervalued employees will rarely expend the extra effort that may be required to win over customers and gain a competitive advantage (Hubbard, 2004, 16).

- *High retention costs*
"If you consider that it can cost as much as $112,000 to recruit and train a full-time sales employee with a salary of $100,000 per year it becomes clear that the costs of high turnover of employees can be huge. This leads to poor training return-on-investment due to short tenure of employees. Also the costs of recruitment and selection of new employees and the process of settling in the new employees cost time and therefore money for the organisation. Typically, replacement costs are at least 1.5 times the yearly salary of employees (Hubbard, 2004, 13)."

- *Price of rebuilding a corporate image*
"Also the damage lack of equality can cause to the image of the organisation will lead to substantial losses for the organisation (translated from Krell, 2004, 15)." If the company image is affected also the overall brand image will be negatively influenced which results in negative economic impact for the organisation. A negative community image, whether or not the community perceives the organisation as a good place to work, has become a more important point for organisations to take into account when they review or decide whether to undertake gender equality management initiatives or not.

3.5 Organisational readiness to implement gender mainstreaming

It is important to realise that companies can follow two different paths with regards to how they decide to manage the gender mainstreaming issue. They can decide to be *reactive*, i.e. defensive, and state that gender equality is only necessary for compliance and to avoid discrimination complaints. Another option is to be *proactive* using the argument that diversity and gender mainstreaming is very valuable to the organisation and provides the organisations with such benefits that the positive impact makes it worth investing in this process. The advantages of gender mainstreaming show why a proactive approach to dealing with the gender mainstreaming challenge could provide organisations with a competitive advantage. But it is important to realise that every organisation is unique and therefore the opinions about investing in gender mainstreaming vary greatly between organisations.

3.5.1 Different levels of maturity

To establish the organisational readiness for a proactive approach towards gender mainstreaming it is important to discover what the level of maturity is of top management concerning this issue. Especially, since the critical factor for the readiness of the whole organisation towards tackling the challenge is the motivation of top management. The level of maturity in the heads of top management will have to go through the steps which are described in table 3 until the management is convinced that it is a strategic focus which would be beneficial for the organisation as a whole, including stakeholders and also external society. Then the last question in table 3 can be answered, i.e. the question: 'how to motivate the organisation towards accepting and implementing a new gender mainstreaming strategy'. Bonuses or other incentives will have to be put into place to ensure high motivation. Table 3 shows at which levels of maturity the top managers can be and therefore how mature the organisation would be for the implementation of gender mainstreaming incentives.

Steps	Action	Phase
1	I listen	Basic awareness
2	I gather information	Basic interest
3	I start to think about the issue	Interest
4	I start internal discussions around the subject in the organisation	Action plan
5	I ask the question: How would I be able to implement this in our company culture?	Action plan
6	I ask the question: How do I convince the other stakeholders of the organisation?	Completion of action plans
7	Finally I ask the question: How do I motivate the employees towards successful implementation?	Maturity phase / Implementation

Table 3: Seven steps for top management to go through towards organisational readiness for a gender mainstreaming initiative

In order to establish how high the level of maturity of individual employees is towards accepting diversity measures several questions could assist; some examples include:

- Am I comfortable with the evaluation of data on the basis of gender?
- Do I have biases towards female managers/employees?
- Have I thought of ways to overcome my biases?
- Do I have problems with accepting measurement systems which include and specifically focus on recognising gender differences in the organisation?
- Do I really want to do the work needed for the implementation of gender mainstreaming measures?

The answers to such questions will show the level of maturity at the employee level and at the same time it will also show the level of resistance that could exist in the organisations towards the gender mainstreaming process. The resistance to change and therefore to new measurement systems will be considered in further detail in chapter 5.7.2 (page 108).

It is very important that it is clear to everyone in the organisation that gender mainstreaming involves actions that can be beneficial to both female *and* male employees. For example men could start working part-time, especially when they are no longer judged for working fewer hours. Another example is, that top managers can easily state that they support gender equality without being laughed at. If this is communicated clearly it might also help to increase the level of maturity of the organisation towards implementing gender mainstreaming initiatives.

The attention gender mainstreaming receives from politicians and at European level has led to an increase in basic knowledge and awareness of the subject which is likely to grow even more. Many of the large multinationals are increasingly looking into implementing diversity and gender initiatives and by doing this they can serve as examples for other large internationally operating organisations. When more organisations implement initiatives in this field the general basic awareness level will increase and more people and organisations will become interested in gender mainstreaming initiatives.

3.5.2 Criteria to measure maturity level
To find out what the level of maturity of top management is in the organisation a number of criteria can be selected and reviewed. These criteria can be taken from social audits that review how social the organisation is or from total equality management initiatives. The work & family audit is a German non-profit organisation which was established on the initiative of the non-profit Hertie foundation and has developed the work and family audit as a management tool for business enterprises and organisations for the optimisation

of a family-oriented employment policy (www.beruf-und-familie.de, 2006). The organisation has now also commissioned the development of the European work & family audit which guides European companies through an internal process of defining and implementing goals and measures of a family-oriented employment policy (www.beruf-und-familie.de, 2006). The audits are performed by trained auditors or consultants and will be reviewed after three years. Such an audit could assist organisations with the review of their maturity towards equal opportunities and it is particularly helpful as the external auditor would also set aims and directions for improvements.

Total quality management within human resource strategy includes equal treatment of all employees. The gender initiatives under this policy can be called 'E-quality'. In Germany the organisation 'Total E-Quality Deutschland, E.V.' (a registered association) has developed a measurement instrument for gender equality. Using a list of criteria this organisation checks organisations and reviews how well they implement gender equality in the organisation. Those organisations that are doing very well receive an award (valid for three years) which they can use for marketing, public relations and company image purposes (www.total-e-quality.de, 2005). Deciding criteria for the award selection is that the organisations have reached a successful consensus between the interests of the organisation and the interests of the employees through a suitable human resources policy to realise equal opportunities (www.total-e-quality.de, 2005). The checklist they developed and use to examine the maturity of organisations towards gender equality can be very helpful to review the maturity of the top management and also of the overall organisation. The checklist contains seven fields of activity which show the effort towards equal opportunities (www.total-e-quality.de, 2005):
1. Personnel recruitment and staffing
2. Career and staff development
3. Work-life balance
4. Institutionalisation of gender equality policies
5. Planning and steering instruments in organisational development
6. Organisational culture
7. Research, teaching and academic study course
The results of the checklist can provide the basis for comparisons and other benchmarking activities (www.total-e-quality.de, 2005).

Another initiative which was developed by the Helmut Schmidt University in Hamburg, Germany, is the genderdax (www.genderdax.de). The genderdax gives an overview of the top organisations for career-oriented women. The organisations that successfully apply will be included in the genderdax which shows that they focus on equal opportunities (www.genderdax.de). The organisations can use the platform to target career-oriented women. Just like the checklist developed by the total E-Quality Deutschland E.V. the application form of the genderdax can help the organisation to review their maturity level toward equal opportunities, and more specifically, with regards to the level of assistance they provide for female employees with high potential.

Audits and total e-quality initiatives can be very helpful for organisations when they try to establish at which level of maturity they actually are with regards to gender equality, i.e. they assist with answering the question: 'where are we now?' But it is important that the organisations make continuous improvements in this area and therefore also look at the question: 'where do we want to be?' The total E-quality award and the work & family audit are only valid for the duration of three years after which re-evaluation will take place to review improvements in the equal opportunity field. How can progress and improvement in the level of maturity actually be measured? The total E-quality Deutschland E.V. uses checklists to monitor developments and also most actions other organisations undertake are employee questionnaires, interviews but also reviewing facts and figures regarding the salary level of men compared to women, level of education and development received for both parties, etc. Here it is also important to review and measure regularly how mature the employees are towards the gender mainstreaming initiatives. Gender mainstreaming is an idea that really has to go into the heads of all the people, the way they think has to change. As a consequence also the organisational culture will change. The impact on organisational culture will be discussed in further detail in chapter 4.3 (page 66).

In this part a number of questions for organisations with regards to their readiness for gender mainstreaming initiatives were looked at. The first question: 'where are we now?' was answered by reviewing the steps towards maturity of top management and thus the organisational readiness for implementation of gender mainstreaming initiatives (see also table 3 on page 53). The next question: 'where do we want to be?' or 'where should we be compared to our competitors?' was analysed by looking at total e-quality initiatives and social audits which can provide organisations with lists of criteria to review their performance in this specific field. This can also help them when they are developing a benchmark to compare their own performance in this area to that of their competitors. The final question is 'how do we actually get where we want to be?' In the next part some of the existing methods and tools to implement gender mainstreaming will be reviewed.

3.6 Existing methods and tools to implement gender mainstreaming

The advantages mentioned in chapter 3.4 (page 44) show why it is important for organisations to focus on the issue of gender mainstreaming and why research that can add to the successful practical implementation of gender mainstreaming is very relevant. Even though, a number of measures are available, some developed by the government and some by private organisations, which aim to encourage women in business life and which are developed to support them with the organisation of family life, only few methods have been developed specifically to assist organisations with the implementation of gender mainstreaming in their organisational culture.

Some of the existing measures governments and private organisations focus on (usually implemented in the personnel policies) aimed at supporting women in business-life include the following (translated from: Domsch, Hadler and Krüger, 1994, 47-127):

1. Being more woman friendly when hiring new employees – e.g. how is the position described in the announcement, is this woman friendly?
2. Improving selection policies for new employees
3. Stimulating female apprenticeships/internships (which is especially the case in Germany but less in other countries as it is not common for organisations in all countries to have apprenticeships)
4. Offering educational opportunities
5. Improving career planning and opportunities to be promoted for women
6. Offering flexible working hours
7. Stimulating measures to combine business life with family life successfully
8. Implementing special organisational measures, for example, to have a women's representative in the organisation

Some of these measures can be called soft factors and others are hard factors (e.g. offering flexible working hours) (Assig and Beck, 1996) The results of a research study done by the Institute of the German economy in Cologne on family friendly measures include that almost half of the participating organisations recognise the need for family friendly measures (translated from: Bundesministerium für Familie, Senioren, Frauen und Jugend, 2003). The main reasons for family friendly measures include: to increase working satisfaction and to attract and maintain qualified employees. In third place the cost saving argument is mentioned (reduce fluctuation and reduce illness). The family friendly measures that companies implement include on the first place working hour flexibility. Over 75 percent of all organisations in Germany offer flexible working hours in some form. Almost 42 percent offer support with the children by allowing breaks from work also on short notice (translated from: Bundesministerium für Familie, Senioren, Frauen und Jugend, 2003).

Most measures undertaken by organisations focus on immediate actions the company can implement, however, to change the long-term view and thereby the organisational culture has not often been the focus of research. Bendl writes: "organisational gender measures should be integrated into a goal oriented and *long term* organisational strategy" (translated from Bendl, 1997, 22). The following two are examples of research which has been conducted in this area:

1) Benchmarking
Wellington describes benchmarking as a tool to foster women's advancement (Wellington, 1998). In the book she wrote for the catalyst organisation (of which she is the President) she reviews best practises from corporate leaders (Wellington, 1998). According to Wellington benchmarking is: "a three-step programme that begins with an organisation's learning about its own practices and outcomes, learning about the best practices of others, and making changes that will enable it to compete with the best in the world. The goals of benchmarking women's advancement are twofold: to improve a company's competitive advantage in recruiting, retaining, and developing diverse talent so as to enhance business results, and to provide a corporate culture and work environment where everyone has equal access to opportunities and equal encouragement to contribute and succeed (Wellington, 1998, 40)." This means looking at the key performance areas of recruitment, retention, development and advancement outcomes such as employee job satisfaction, optimism about future opportunities for advancement and other measures of morale and commitment to the employing organisation (Wellington, 1998). Specific objectives of benchmarking women's advancement include (Wellington, 1998, 40):
- Creating the business case for gender diversity
- Tying diversity strategies to short- and long-term business imperatives and strategic business plans
- Identifying and recruiting the best and brightest talent
- Eliminating barriers to success
- Enhancing access to opportunities

The first step in gender diversity benchmarking would be to look at internal benchmarking, i.e. the process of gathering information on practices and outcomes within the organisation. This step is relatively easy. However, the problems with benchmarking arise when the second step needs to be taken, namely the external benchmarking. External benchmarking is very costly in terms of both financial and people resources, requiring a considerable degree of commitment from the organisation (Wellington, 1998). This is the main disadvantage of benchmarking as a tool to foster women's advancement. To collect all the necessary data is very costly and also difficult as it could be sensitive information that might have to be collected from competitors.

Finally, also the third step of making the actual changes is a very difficult step as there could be resistance to change from within the organisation and the actual change process requires a considerable amount of commitment from the top down through the organisation. This shows that even though benchmarking aims at changing the corporate culture it is also a very costly, human resource intense and difficult change mechanism to implement.

2) Business Process Reengineering

Osterloh and Wübker look at the possibilities of Business Process Reengineering for reaching equality (translated from: Osterloh and Wübker, in Krell, 2004). Business Process Reengineering has the following aim: to create transparent processes, which will allow for a problem-free and customer oriented total treatment from the supplier to the customer (translated from: Osterloh and Wübker in Krell, 2004, 234). Business Process Reengineering revolves around three new ideas: the process idea, the idea of horizontal segmentation and the idea of information connections (translated from: Osterloh and Wübker in Krell, 2004, 234). To be able to implement the process idea the company should have transparent processes and to do so the core processes must be separated from the support processes. When this is done the process owner (a person or a team) can change the process into a customer oriented process. The horizontal segmentation idea is the way to divide the work. This segmentation of the core and support processes can be done according to functions, expectations about the level of problems involved or according to customer groups (translated from: Osterloh and Wübker in Krell, 2004). The third idea of informational connections involves the new information technologies and communication mechanisms which allow for an organisation and its employees to be connected into a network which allows information to flow. The outcome of these three ideas will be the process organisation as Osterloh and Wübker describe it. According to Osterloh and Wübker the actual process of Business Process Reengineering can help to create organisational structures which would be both efficient and innovative and also help to create equality for women (translated from: Osterloh and Wübker in Krell, 2004, 234). To achieve this there will have to be women in the reengineering team to assist in renewing the processes from the beginning.

The main problems with achieving gender equality with Business Process Reengineering is that it is a complex and difficult tool to implement and it does not aim to change the organisational culture. It focuses on including more women in designing the processes and the work that is being done in an organisation but it does not necessarily change the way the employees in the organisation think about equality. Furthermore, one other danger with reengineering is that it can become a strategy of cost-cutting and reducing the number of employees. Especially, without the strategy focus of, for example the balanced scorecard, the default measure for reengineering programs ends up being cost savings.

The methods described above do not offer the balanced overview that the balanced scorecard can provide. Besides this, the balanced scorecard is also already wide-spread and implemented in organisations around the world as strategic management tool. Therefore, the balanced scorecard could be a very valid practical management tool to assist organisations in achieving gender mainstreaming in their organisational culture.

3.7 Conclusion

In this chapter the gender mainstreaming foundation has been described in detail. After a brief historical overview the definitions of gender, gender equality and equity and gender mainstreaming were given. Then, the advantages that the implementation of gender mainstreaming can offer organisations were mentioned. Furthermore, organisational readiness and maturity towards the issue of gender mainstreaming initiatives were described. To finalise, some existing methods and tools which can be used to implement gender mainstreaming were reviewed. In the next chapter the third theoretical foundation will be analysed namely the organisational culture and the organisational ability to change culture.

4. Organisational culture

4.1 Introduction

In this part the third and final theoretical foundation will be introduced namely organisational culture and the possibilities for organisations to change their organisational culture into an 'engendered culture'. However, it has to be noted here that the subjects of organisational culture and change are complex research areas by themselves. Here only a very brief overview will be provided which relates directly to the overall aims of this research. Therefore, it is very important to first define briefly what organisational culture means and how it can be analysed. Secondly, it is necessary to analyse how organisational culture can be changed as this would be the prerequisite to be able to develop an engendered culture. And, in the third part of this chapter characteristics of an engendered culture will be looked at in more detail.

4.2 Organisational culture defined and analysed

The first question that needs to be answered here is the question how organisational culture can be defined. According to Wellington the mission, beliefs, value system, policies, rituals, tools and philosophies of a corporation make up its culture (Wellington, 1998, 61). Mintzberg, Ahlstrand and Lampel (1998, 265) associate organisational culture with collective cognition; "it becomes the "organisation's mind", the shared beliefs that are reflected in traditions and habits as well as more tangible manifestations – stories, symbols, even buildings and products." Hofstede defines organisational culture as: "the differences in collective mental programming found among people from different organisations, or parts thereof, within the same national context (Hofstede, 2001, 373)." As Hofstede mentions culture is what differentiates one organisation from another, one industry from another, one nation from another. Trompenaars and Woolliams (2003, 3) define organisational culture as: "a series of rules and methods, which an organisation has evolved to deal with the regular problems that it faces."

Organisational culture is a relative recent phenomena and the term organisational culture first appeared casually in English literature in the 1960s as a synonym for 'climate' (Hofstede 1994). The term corporate culture started to become popular in the 1970s. The term became even more popular after the best-selling book 'In Search of Excellence' by Peters and Waterman was published in 1982. In this book Peters and Waterman wrote the following about corporate culture: "without exception, the dominance and coherence of culture proved to be an essential quality of the excellent companies. Moreover, the stronger the culture and the more it was directed towards the marketplace, the less need there was for policy manuals, organisational charts, or detailed procedures and rules. In these companies people way down the line know what they are supposed to do in most situations because the handful of guiding values is crystal clear" (Peters and Waterman, 1982). The focus on organisational culture also increased because of changing organisational structures. When organisations become flatter and less bureaucratic and hierarchical there is an increased need for a strong organisational culture to make the organisation successful. Hofstede (2001, 391) mentions several characteristics of organisational culture, as being:

1. Holistic; referring to a whole which is more than the sum of its parts
2. Historically determined; reflecting the history of the organisation
3. Related to the things anthropologists study; like rituals and symbols
4. Socially constructed, created and preserved by the group of people who together form the organisation
5. Soft
6. Difficult to change, although authors do not agree on how difficult!

As organisational culture becomes increasingly important for organisations it is also necessary to find ways to analyse the corporate culture. Hofstede mentions six most identified dimensions of organisational culture as being (Hofstede, 2001, 397):

1) process oriented (concerned with means) versus results oriented (concerned with goals)
2) employee oriented (concerned with people) versus job oriented (concerned with completing the job)
3) parochial (employees derive their identity largely from the organisation) versus professional (employees identify with their type of job)
4) open system (almost anyone would fit in the organisation and it takes only few days to feel at home) versus closed system (only special people fit into the organisation, and new employees need more than a year to feel at home)
5) loose control (no-one thinks about costs, meeting times are kept only approximately, jokes about the job and the company are frequent) versus tight control (cost conscious, punctual meeting times, jokes about job or company are not common)
6) normative (perceive their task towards the outside world as the implementation of inviolable rules) versus pragmatic (market driven)

These six dimensions can be analysed to describe a culture, however, there are no good or bad dimensions. These dimensions can often be connected to the organisational structure the organisation has adopted. For example, flatter organisations tend to be more result orientated and more negative towards specialisation and formalisation. Whereas process oriented cultures seem to value more specialised and formalised units like under the bureaucratic form of organisation (Hofstede, 2001).

Another way to analyse organisational culture is offered by Trompenaars and Woolliams. Trompenaars and Woolliams (2003, 107) identify four competing organisational cultures that are derived from two related dimensions:
1. Task or person (high- versus low formalisation)
2. Hierarchical or egalitarian (high- versus low centralisation)
Combining these dimensions led to four possible organisational types as shown in figure 6 (Trompenaars and Woolliams, 2003, 106).

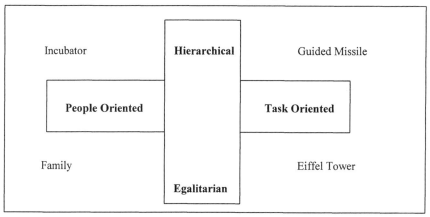

Figure 6: Four culture types (source: Trompenaars and Woolliams, 2003, 106)

In table 4 the main characteristics of these four culture types can be found.

The Incubator:	The Guided Missile:
➤ Person oriented	➤ Task orientation
➤ Power of the individual	➤ Power of knowledge/expertise
➤ Self-realisation	➤ Commitment to tasks
➤ Commitment to oneself	➤ Management by Objectives
➤ Professional recognition	➤ Pay for performance
The Family:	**The Eiffel Tower:**
➤ Power-orientation	➤ Role-orientation
➤ Personal relationships	➤ Power of position / role
➤ Entrepreneurial	➤ Job description / evaluation
➤ Affinity / trust	➤ Rules and procedures
➤ Power of person	➤ Order and predictability

Table 4: Characteristics of the four culture types from Trompenaars and Woolliams (source: Trompenaars and Woolliams, 2003, 107-111)

Measurements and assessment using this model of four cultures have been based on the corporate culture assessment profile questionnaire which was developed by Trompenaars and Woolliams (2003). Hofstede's cultural dimensions and/or Trompenaars and Woolliams four culture model are two possible ways to analyse the organisational culture and to establish the current situation.

As soon as management is able to analyse their organisational culture they can also assess whether this culture actually fits their organisational structure and their strategy. Other reasons why organisations need to analyse and review their organisational culture include (Hofstede, 2001):

1. to identify subcultures in one's own organisation
2. to test whether the culture fits the strategies set out for the future
3. to check whether the cultures would fit in case of mergers and acquisitions
4. to measure the development of organisational cultures over time (this can also help to determine if attempts to change organisational culture have been successful)

If the organisation decides that gender mainstreaming should be part of their organisational culture the management team will need to start of with an analysis of the existing culture. It can be expected that gender initiatives will be easier implemented in certain types of cultures than in others. For example in cultures with closed systems, tight control and hierarchical structures it could be difficult to change the culture. On the contrary, open systems, loose control and flat structures could be a more flexible culture to change into an engendered culture. When the current state, i.e. the actual situation, is determined only then the change process can be initiated as the next step. The final stage would then be to arrive at the desired culture, i.e. the engendered culture. The next step now is to look at the change process involved in changing organisational culture.

4.2.1 Is it possible to change organisational culture?

The second question that this chapter tries to answer will now be the main focus. The question is: *are organisations actually able to change their organisational culture?* According to Hofstede (1994) there are several steps and considerations when managing and changing corporate culture:

- This is a task of top management which cannot be delegated
- Should start with a cultural map of the organisation
- Demands strategic choices
- Create a network of change agents in the organisation
- Design the necessary structural changes
- Design the necessary process changes
- Revise personnel policies
- Continue monitoring development of organisational culture

Extensive debate has arisen on how to define the critical features of successful change and examples here are: Douglas Smith who identifies ten characteristics of change leaders, John Kotter who suggests eight keys to successful leadership of change or Michael Beer's change model which features five core factors (Becker, et all, 2001, 185). However, according to Becker, Huselid and Ulrich (2001) using a checklist – any checklist – is more important than choosing one particular checklist over another and for this reason they developed a checklist of seven key success factors and processes for change and different processes for making things happen. In table 5 below these can be found. They recommend that change leaders routinely assess the progress they are making on each of the dimensions of the change process using a profiling system that can be similar to the one in table 5 and by plotting scores to the dimensions from 0 through 100 (Becker, et all, 2001).

Key success factors for change	Questions for assessing and accomplishing change
1) *Leading change* (who *is responsible*)	Do we have a leader ... ■ Who owns and champions the change? ■ Who demonstrates public commitment to making it happen? ■ Who will garner resources to sustain it? ■ Who will invest personal time and attention to follow it through?
2) *Creating a shared need* (why *do it*)	Do employees ... ■ See the reason for the change? ■ Understand why the change is important? ■ See how it will help them and the business in short and long term?
3) *Shaping a vision* (what *will it look like when we are done*)	Do employees ... ■ See the outcomes of the change in behavioural terms (i.e. what will they do differently as a result of the change)? ■ Get excited about these outcomes? ■ Understand how the change will benefit customers and other stakeholders?
4) *Mobilising commitment* (who else *needs to be involved*)	Do the sponsors of the change ... ■ Recognise who else needs to be committed to the change for it to happen? ■ Know how to build a coalition of support for the change? ■ Have the ability to enlist the support of key individuals in the organisation? ■ Have the ability to build a responsibility matrix to make the change happen?
5) *Building enabling systems* (how *will it be institutionalised*)	Do the sponsors of the change ... ■ Understand how to sustain the change through modifying HR systems (e.g. staffing, training, appraisal, rewards, structure, communication)? ■ Recognise the technology investment required to implement the change? ■ Have access to financial resources to sustain the change?
6) *Monitoring and demonstrating progress* (how *will it be measured*)	Do the sponsors of the change ... ■ Have a means of measuring the success of the change? ■ Plan to benchmark progress on both the results of the change and the implementation process?
7) *Making it last* (how *will it be initiated and sustained*)	Do the sponsors of the change ... ■ Recognise the first steps needed to get started? ■ Have a short- and long-term plan to keep attention focussed on the change? ■ Have a plan for adapting the change over time to shifting circumstances?

Table 5: Keys and processes for making things happen (Becker, Huselid and Ulrich, 2001, 186)

The steps involved in change that Hofstede mentioned are very similar to the comprehensive checklist developed by Becker, Huselid and Ulrich (see table 5). It is very important that the leader (i.e. top management) is the driving force behind the gender initiative. As a next step it is important to establish were the organisation is currently, i.e. draw the cultural map of the organisation, to see which changes are needed to arrive at the desired engendered culture. Also Hubbard (2004) agrees that no change effort will get far without some form of organisational diagnosis of climate and/or culture. A formal measurement of the current state is necessary, both to guide action planning and to set a baseline for assessing progress (Hubbard, 2004). One problem that can occur when an organisational culture is changed is that also the structure of the organisation needs to be changed accordingly. An organisation may become gender-aware and yet have difficulties achieving gender equality because it is still structured as before. Changes in structure and culture must go hand in hand (MacDonald, Sprenger and Dubel, 1997, 26).

However, the main problem with changing an organisational culture is resistance to change from the employees. As Mintzberg, Ahlstrand and Lampel mention: "it is culture's very deeply held beliefs and tacit assumptions that act as powerful internal barriers to fundamental change" (Mintzberg, Ahlstrand and Lampel, 1998, 269). Furthermore, they mention that before 'strategic' learning can occur the old logic must be unlearned (i.e. forgotten) by the organisation (Mintzberg, Ahlstrand and Lampel, 1998, 269). In the process of changing organisational culture it becomes really important that the way people think is changed. This is the basic requirement that needs to be met to be able to change culture in an organisation. Hofstede insists that the change process starts at the top of the organisation and that a network of change agents is placed within the organisation as these agents can overcome the resistance to change. A problem with the leader of change might be that even though the leader sees what the future might look like after the change but that he or she has not been effective at communicating this engendered culture vision to the rest of the organisation. For the specific aim of engendering the corporate culture a team of change agents in the organisation could be crucial as shall be described in more detail in the next part.

4.3 Gender mainstreaming in organisational culture
Every organisation has a unique organisational culture. Even though there are a number of ways to identify and analyse organisational culture (see chapter 4.2, page 61) each culture is unique and this is also what makes it even more difficult to implement changes. For example, if the six dimensions developed by Hofstede are reviewed, it becomes clear that changing an open system with loose control could be an easier job than a closed system with tight control.

However, the changes in culture will need to be adopted by the employees as they are the persons who live the culture. Therefore, change agents could be essential in introducing changes to organisational cultures. But the process needs to start with top management as they need to be the persons who actually see the strategic need for a change in the culture to be more effective as a company. So, if the top management decides that they want to make use of the opportunity gender mainstreaming offers they can start the change process which can lead to the embracing of gender mainstreaming at all levels in the organisational culture.

4.3.1 How to initiate the change in organisational culture

Based on table 5 'the keys and processes for making change happen' (see page 65) also the guidelines for implementing a gender balanced scorecard (or other gender initiatives) and for guiding the sponsors of the change process (who automatically will be involved with the implementation of a gender balanced scorecard) can be developed. These guidelines can be found in table 6.

Table 6 shows an extensive checklist that can be followed to initiate the change process for creating an engendered culture either by implementation of a gender balanced scorecard or other gender initiatives. The steps can help to make the current situation of the organisational culture clear and it can then assist in creating the vision that needs to be achieved and the plan to get there. Four key steps involved with mainstreaming gender in the organisational culture which can be derived from table 6 would include:

Step one: Gather all data concerning gender roles and ratios at the various levels of the organisation in order to get a clear picture of the organisation's current culture (i.e. draw the so-called cultural map from Hofstede but then specifically for women)

Step two: Identify possible gender gaps and inequalities

Step three: Assess the strategic needs for short-term and long-term changes and plan how to meet these needs

Step four: Identify and allocate resources (i.e. roles for both men and women) to the plan in order to be able to implement it (i.e. put the team of change agents into place).

Key success factors for change	Guiding questions for change sponsors
1) *Leading change* (who *is responsible*)	✓ Is the leader fully committed to implementation of the gender balanced scorecard (or other gender initiative) ✓ Who else will sponsor the change process, i.e. the team of change agents ✓ Are there resources made available for the change effort, i.e. the budget for gender measurements
2) *Creating a shared need* (why *do it*)	✓ Why develop the gender balanced scorecard (or other gender initiative) ✓ How does it fit to our business ✓ Do employees see the reason for the change and understand why gender mainstreaming in the culture is important and beneficial ✓ Do employees see how it will help them and/or the business in the short and long term
3) *Shaping a vision* (what *will it look like when we are done*)	✓ What is the outcome we want to achieve with the gender balanced scorecard (or other gender initiative) ✓ Do employees see the outcomes of the change in behavioural terms (i.e. what will they do differently as a result of gender mainstreaming) ✓ Do employees understand how gender mainstreaming will benefit customers and other stakeholders
4) *Mobilising commitment* (who else *needs to be involved*)	✓ Who else needs to be committed to support the project ✓ Who else will need to take responsibility for the gender balanced scorecard/gender initiative
5) *Building enabling systems* (how *will it be institutionalised*)	✓ How do we build the systems needed to sustain gender mainstreaming (changing the way people think in the long term) in our culture ✓ Which departments will need to be involved (e.g. the personnel department with staffing, training, appraisal, rewards and structure or the marketing department with communication and image building to external stakeholders) ✓ Which technology investment (if any) would be required to implement the gender balanced scorecard/gender initiative ✓ Are there enough financial resources available to sustain the change in the culture?
6) *Monitoring and demonstrating progress* (how *will it be measured*)	✓ What will we use to track the implementation process (regular monitoring meetings of the gender balanced scorecard/gender initiative development) ✓ Is there a good way to measure the success of the gender balanced scorecard/gender initiative (i.e. how do we monitor, analyse and show the organisational cultural changes)
7) *Making it last* (how *will it be initiated and sustained*)	✓ Is there a short- and long-term plan to keep attention focussed on the gender balanced scorecard/gender initiative

Table 6: Checklist for implementation of a gender balanced scorecard or other gender initiative in the organisational culture (adapted from: Becker, Huselid and Ulrich, 2001, 186 and Hubbard, 2004, 333)

4.3.2 Characteristics of an engendered organisational culture

Changes in corporate cultures to ones in which gender equality is valued, managed and embraced is a difficult process. As Davidson and Burke mention: "organisational life is still too often imbued with 'male values' of dominance, aggression, competition and 'transmitting' rather than 'receiving' information. Corporate cultures need to change to encourage listening skills, problem resolution, support co-operation, participation and negotiation as the evidence is mounting that confrontation, competition and the 'macho' management style are producing more workplace stress and less productivity (Davidson, Burke, 2004, 12)." A number of other authors agree that 'male-oriented' organisational cultures, which are characterised by hierarchical authority, independence, autocratic leadership styles and top down communication (e.g. Klenke, 1996, Maier, 1999) are barriers to women's progress (e.g. Hofstede, 2001, Marshall, 1993, Bajdo 2002). The results of a major study conducted by Catalyst, the US national foundation for women business owners, in 1998 showed that high-powered women stated four reasons for leaving their firms to start their own companies: the need for more flexibility (51 percent), the glass ceiling (29 percent), unhappiness with the work environment (28 percent) and lack of challenge (22 percent) (Solomon, 2001). In the report the women defined the construction of the glass ceiling: their contributions were not recognised or valued, they were not taken seriously, they felt isolated as one of few women or minorities, they were excluded from informal networks, they were excluded from training opportunities and many said they faced inhospitable corporate cultures (Solomon, 2001). This was also the outcome of a study by Lyness and Thompson (2000), in which they found out that female executives reported greater barriers to their advancement including lack of culture fit and exclusion from informal networks than did male executives. According to Hubbard (2004, 139) there are a number of key components which make up a diversity climate or culture and these can be seen in table 7.

Hubbard states that all of these components (see table 7) are important but to create a usable diagnosis of the organisation's culture not all need to be included (Hubbard, 2004, 139). Some components are easier to measure than others for example how many women are in management, i.e. power positions is straightforward. But the openness to women and the level of informality of the social and communication networks in the organisation is more difficult to measure. Some statistical information like recruitment figures (women and men hired) or compensation gaps between men and women in similar positions can help to determine what sort of organisational culture is present and the role gender equality plays in this culture. When the current situation and the role of gender equality in the current culture are determined the desired results after the change process should be projected.

Individual-level measures	Definition
1) Amount of identity-group prejudice	Predisposition to dislike or have a negative attitude toward someone
2) Amount of stereotyping	Assuming that individuals have limited abilities or negative traits based on membership in a group
3) Amount of ethnocentrism	Preference for members of one's own 'in-group'
4) Diversity-relevant personality traits	Examples: tolerance for ambiguity; authoritarian personality
Work group-level measures	**Definition**
1) Level of intergroup conflict	Conflict that is explicitly related to sociocultural group differences
2) Group identity strength	The extend to which a person feels a strong bond with his or her group
3) Quality of intergroup communication	Frequency and effectiveness of communications across groups
4) Diverse work team productivity	Amount or rate of increased output produced versus traditional team output
5) Diverse work team innovation	Amount or rate of increased new product or process output produced versus traditional team product or process output
6) Cultural differences and similarities	Amount of cultural distance versus overlap between cultures of groups
Organisation-level measures	**Definition**
1) Identity profile of workforce	Demographics of key differences in a defined work group or organisation
2) Mode of acculturation	Method of handling cultural differences (assimilation vs. pluralism)
3) Content of organisational culture	Key norms, values and beliefs
4) Power distribution among groups	Extend to which people of different identity groups have authority or power
5) People management practices and policies	Recruiting, promotions, compensation, physical work environment, member development, work schedules
6) Openness of informal networks	Extend to which people of all identity groups have access to social and communication networks
7) Adaptability to change	Rate of absorption and integration of new environmental demands and content from internal and external sources

Table 7: Key components of diversity climate (source: Hubbard, 2004, 139, partly adapted from Cox, 2001)

To determine what the culture should look like when it is a culture where gender mainstreaming is implemented it can be helpful to review some best practices that were researched in the United Kingdom by Rajan et al. When Rajan et al. (2003) researched best practices among UK companies regarding diversity management they found that they implemented these best practices by driving major changes in HR processes, business conduct and leadership actions. The nature of drivers has varied between four overlapping business cultures that prevail in most of these companies (see figure 7):

- Some have set overt targets, some have relied on gradual evolution
- Some focus on management style, some on HR processes

Management Style	
Culture of leadership Driven by chairman or CEO Creation of diversity council Performance metrics include diversity & inclusion	**Culture of inclusion** Strong participative culture Managers engage by walking the talk Teams are required to have diverse styles
Targets —————————————————— *Osmosis*	
Culture of customer primacy Direct pressures from customers Strategic targeting of new customers Involvement of public sector in the supply chain	**Culture of compliance** Explicit stipulations in business contracts and mandates Threat/experience of legal action Compliance with laws and regulations
HR Processes	

Figure 7: Key drivers of a diverse workforce (Source: Rajan et al., 2003, 4)

The key drivers of a diverse workforce (see figure 7) can be specified for the gender purposes of this research as gender is one smaller part of the overall diversity workforce. Many of these best practices of the business cultures fitting to a diverse workforce also apply to gender initiatives. For example the business culture of organisations that are looking to include gender mainstreaming into their culture can achieve this when it is driven by the chairman or CEO, supported by a team of change agents or gender specialists and managers that engage by walking the talk. Increase in the number of female customers or other direct pressure from customers can be key drivers for a gender initiative. A culture of compliance is not very acute in most European countries currently, however, there is an increase in the legal focus on gender mainstreaming on a European level. In a culture with gender mainstreaming it should be possible to identify the best practices mentioned above, and achieve these by driving major changes in HR processes, business conduct and leadership actions.

Rajan, et al. (2003, 4) state that these key drivers together will amount to:
1) Creating a level playing field
   ✓ reflecting fairness and openness in HR practices
   ✓ combining meritocracy with sensitivity
   ✓ reconciling corporate needs with family responsibilities
   ✓ providing individualised support to meet demanding targets
   ✓ using conventional and unconventional recruitment channels

2) Embedding diversity and inclusion into everyday business practices
   ✓ seeking new ideas
   ✓ creating support networks
   ✓ building diversity into sales and marketing campaigns
   ✓ getting a buy-in from clients
   ✓ observing national laws
   ✓ forging links with disadvantaged business suppliers

3) Creating a culture of leadership
   ✓ setting indicative targets for different employee groups in some cases
   ✓ enabling managers at all levels to develop a style that shows sensitivity to different employee groups, their specific needs and their work approaches
   ✓ reflecting diversity in business pursuit teams
   ✓ putting diversity and inclusion on leaders' performance scorecards
   ✓ creating diversity councils, comprising top executives, to monitor corporate actions and business results

Even though Rajan, et al. focussed on managing diversity in the broader sense their arguments and findings also apply when managing gender equality is the specific focus. Changing corporate culture is a very complex process which involves support from all levels in the organisations but, as most experts agree, it should be initiated at the top. More specific, Rajan, et al. found out, that it is important that the leaders put the diversity/gender objective on their personal performance scorecard or that they receive bonuses and/or other initiatives based upon achieving the desired results. Besides the leader many employees at different levels are involved in the change process. These include the agents for change, and as best practices in the UK show, also the creation of diversity councils (Rajan, et al., 2003). A study from Bajdo (2002) also mentions that characteristics of organisational culture typically associated with women are related to opportunities for women in management. In particular, organisational cultural practices reflecting high humane orientation, high gender equity, high performance orientation, and low power distance are related to women's advancement (Bajdo, 2002). This would mean that the organisational cultural change into a gender mainstreaming culture could be easier achieved if more women are in management positions in the organisation and therefore act as agents of change. Thus it can be stated that organisations seeking to create a culture supportive of diversity ought to increase the number of women at management levels (Bajdo, 2002). The lower level employees may have a feeling that the organisation is always changing and that there is no stability. However, according to Hubbard this is not the actual change but the transitions. Hubbard (2004) mentions that change is situational and may involve a new boss of a gender different than the last, new diverse work teams or new policies. However, transition is the psychological process people go through to come to terms with the new situation (Hubbard, 2004). Change is external but transition is internal. For organisational culture to change in a gender sensitive culture it is critical that the way people think is changed!

4.3 Conclusion

In this chapter organisational culture was defined and analysed. Secondly, the question whether organisational culture can be changed was reviewed. This was followed by an examination of the changes required to embrace gender mainstreaming in the organisational culture. It can be concluded that changing an organisational culture into a gender equality culture is a very complex and difficult process that involves support at all levels of the organisation but it needs to be initiated at the top. In the next chapter the focus will be on building the gender balanced scorecard.

5 The gender balanced scorecard

5.1 Introduction

In this chapter the three theoretical foundations, i.e. the balanced scorecard, gender mainstreaming and changing organisational culture, will be put together into the gender balanced scorecard. First of all, the reasons for developing a management tool to achieve gender mainstreaming will be analysed. Then, the balanced scorecard will be reviewed with regards to several new applications for use, namely, as human resource tool or as a tool to achieve diversity objectives for companies. Thirdly, it is necessary to review why the balanced scorecard should be the tool for companies to use when they attempt to implement gender mainstreaming in their organisational culture.

The next step is the actual design of a gender balanced scorecard. The different perspectives that should be part of a gender balanced scorecard will be reviewed and possible indicators and critical success factors will be analysed. The implementation of the gender balanced scorecard will follow with a review of who should be responsible for implementation. Also the process of change and the resistance that is inevitably connected to this process will be considered. Finally, an explanation will be given of how the gender balanced scorecard can be put into action as controlling tool to assess the results.

5.2 Why do organisations need a management tool to implement gender mainstreaming?

The question why gender mainstreaming leads to competitive advantages for organisations nowadays has already been answered and addressed in chapter 3.4 (page 44). Especially, the changing pressures of stakeholders on organisations has demanded from many organisations that they change their strategies and that they also focus on becoming a more social organisation that takes notion of the community surrounding it. Regulatory and social processes help organisations to earn the right to operate in the countries in which they produce and sell their products. National and local regulations – on the environment, on employee health and safety, and on hiring and employment practices – impose standards on companies' practices (Kaplan & Norton, 2004).

However, many companies try to go beyond just complying with the minimal standards established by regulations. They wish to perform better than the regulatory constraints so that they develop a reputation as an employer of choice in every community in which they operate (Kaplan & Norton, 2004). This company image has become a very important point for organisations and will be able to provide them with a competitive advantage in the longer run.

As was described in chapter 3.4 (page 47) in the Harris-Fombrun corporate reputation quotient many drivers of the organisation's reputation are measured and those organisations that are most reputable and/or visible are placed on a list for potential employees and other stakeholders to review (Fombrun, van Riel, 2003).

Because companies become more social and focus on becoming an 'employer of choice' they also realise that offering equal opportunities for men and women has become an issue that should be focussed on and dealt with in detail. But, the biggest issue is that to achieve gender equality the minds of the employees have to change, i.e. the way people think has to change, and this can only be achieved by a change in organisational culture/climate. Changing organisational culture is a major change process and this can not easily be managed as was discussed already in chapter 4.2.1 (see page 64). For this reason, it is important to design a management tool that can assist organisations with managing this major change process and thus achieving gender mainstreaming in their culture. The management tool that is selected to achieve this is the gender balanced scorecard and the development of this new management instrument will be discussed in this chapter.

5.3 From 'holding' balanced scorecard to gender balanced scorecard – new uses for the balanced scorecard
As was pointed out earlier the balanced scorecard has been a huge success as management tool and is nowadays used by many organisations around the globe. It can support companies in a number of ways (see also chapter 2.3, page 29). However, there are more purposes that the balanced scorecard in an adapted form could serve.

Several researches have been done in the field of personnel management to develop a specific human resources scorecard. Recently, also more information has been published about the possibilities to use the balanced scorecard for diversity management in organisations. Based on this diversity management scorecard the next stage could be to further develop the scorecard into a gender balanced scorecard as shall be shown later in this chapter.

In figure 8 the steps from holding balanced scorecard (i.e. the organisational balanced scorecard) to the gender balanced scorecard can be found.

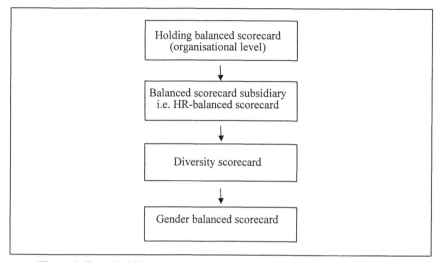

Figure 8: From holding balanced scorecard to gender balanced scorecard.

5.3.1 The HR-balanced scorecard

To put a human resource focus in the balanced scorecard was already mentioned in the same year that Kaplan & Norton actually first published about the balanced scorecard in the Harvard Business Review. Maisel's Balanced Scorecard, which was first introduced in the Journal of Cost Management in 1992, not only has the same name as the Kaplan & Norton model but it also defines four perspectives from which the business should be measured (Olve, et al., 2000). Instead of a learning and growth perspective, Maisel uses a human resource perspective in his model (Olve, et al., 2000). Maisel's balanced scorecard model can be seen in figure 9.

Maisel's balanced scorecard model was probably the first HR balanced scorecard model but a number of authors have continued to develop scorecards specifically for HRM purposes. Becker et al. published a book in 2001 called the 'HR Scorecard', which entails a step wise approach to HR measurement. Most important in their approach is the linkage between business strategy and the way in which HRM helps to add extra value. Becker et al. call these strategic HR deliverables, meaning those outcomes of the HR architecture or HRM system that serve to execute the firm's strategy (Becker, Huselid and Ulrich, 2001, 30). These strategic HRM deliverables come in two different shapes. One category are the so-called performance drivers, for example employee productivity and innovativeness. The other category is called enablers, which reinforce the performance drivers like training programmes and performance appraisal systems. These are HRM activities or practices.

Becker, Huselid and Ulrich (2001, 36-52) outline seven steps in order to develop the HR scorecard and as a model for implementing HR's strategic role:

1) Clearly define business strategy
2) Build a business case for HR as a strategic asset
3) Create a strategy map
4) Identify HR deliverables within the strategy map
5) Align the HR architecture with the HR deliverables
6) Design the strategic HR measurement system
7) Implement management by measurement

Once the HR Scorecard is developed along these seven steps it will result in a new management tool. However, this is a complex and long process and therefore companies may hesitate to adopt this model.

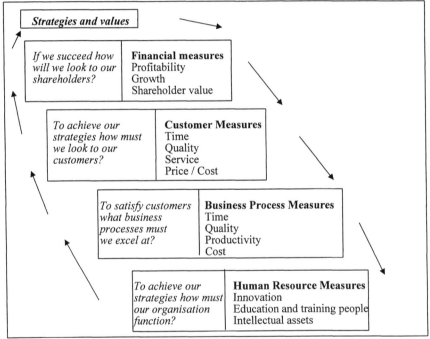

Figure 9: Maisel's balanced scorecard model (adapted from: Olve, Roy & Wetter, 2000, 20, original source: Lawrence S. Maisel, Performance Measurement, The Balanced Scorecard approach, Journal of Cost Management, Summer 1992, 50)

Pauwe (2004, 195-196) developed the 4logic HRM scorecard which focuses on different stakeholders and dimensions and represents these in four perspectives or 'logics': the strategic logic, the professional logic, the societal logic and the delivery logic.

The strategic logic focuses on the expectations of boards of directors, CEOs, shareholders and financial institutions. The professional logic focuses on the expectations of line managers, employees, works councils, and colleagues of HR departments. The societal logic emphasizes moral values and focuses on the expectations of works councils, trade unions, government, and other interest groups, both inside and outside the company. The fourth logic is the delivery logic which is based on cost effectiveness and works through the following delivery channels: HR departments, line management, outsourcing, teams and employees themselves and self service through e-HRM (implies web-based delivery). As with the balanced scorecard also Pauwe's four logic scorecard has its own distinct set of criteria, which helps management to make choices and to monitor and evaluate the actions chosen. Later the chosen indicators are linked to HR practises. Even though, Pauwe's approach looks very different it actually does show considerable overlap with the traditional balanced scorecard and its perspectives and indicators. For example, for the stakeholders in the first logic (the strategic logic) the traditional financial indicators will be important and the professional stakeholders will mainly focus their expectations and indicators on the balanced scorecard learning and growth perspectives.

Some other human resource specific scorecards and HR effectiveness measurement systems that have been developed include the following: Phillips et al. with the human resources scorecard, Mayo with his Human Capital Monitor, Watson Wyatt's Human Capital Index, William Mercer's Human Capital Wheel, the Skandia Navigator (based upon the Scandinavian Skandia company and their inclusion of intellectual capital, i.e. human capital within the profit & loss reporting) and Sveiby's Intangible Assets Monitor. There are more approaches available, however, the general human resource scorecard idea is only one step towards the development of the gender balanced scorecard which is the purpose of this project. The next step from holding balanced scorecard to gender balanced scorecard is the development of a specific diversity scorecard. Therefore, the diversity scorecard idea developed by Hubbard will be described in the next part.

5.3.2 The diversity scorecard
In 2004 Hubbard published a book called 'the diversity scorecard' in which he describes a diversity scorecard as: "a balanced, carefully selected set of objectives and measures derived from an organisation's strategy that link to the diversity strategy (Hubbard, 2004, 132)." As described before, more and more companies see the need for a strategy that focuses on successfully managing diversity, also sometimes referred to as inclusion, in the organisation. The purposes of such strategies are to overcome gender biases, to promote multicultural workforces and to include disabled people in the workforce.

As with the balanced scorecard also diversity scorecards are unique to each organisation that develops it. Nonetheless, according to Hubbard the basic objectives and measures of a diversity scorecard will generally view the organisation's diversity performance from six perspectives as can be seen in table 8 (Hubbard, 2004, 132).

Six perspectives	Description
Financial impact	Shows many of the traditional instruments of management control in the form of financial measures and key ratios.
Diverse customer/community partnership	Shows the ways in which value is to be created for diverse customers, how diverse customers' demand for this value is to be satisfied, which operational excellence is required to achieve this value, and why these diverse customers will be willing to pay for it. It also describes the degree to which the community views the organisation as a strategic partner and sees its presence as value added, therefore it needs to reflect the organisation's effort as a good corporate citizen to all external constituent and stakeholder communities represented in its marketplace.
Workforce profile	Reflects the recruitment, selection and retention efforts of the organisation beyond the normal affirmative action reporting.
Workplace climate/culture	This perspective is structured to provide feedback on the degree to which the organisation has created a diverse, inclusive environment that fosters employee satisfaction and performance.
Diversity leadership commitment	Shows the degree to which the organisation's leaders are utilising behaviours that set the vision, direction, policy, and a personal model for the diversity effort through demonstrated actions.
Learning and growth	This perspective assesses the degree to which key strategic capabilities are being developed among all segments of the diverse workforce.

Table 8: Six perspectives to review diversity performance on a diversity scorecard (source: adapted from Hubbard, 2004, 132-143)

All of the measures on the diversity scorecard serve as translations of the organisation's strategy and link them to the diversity strategy. According to Hubbard the diversity scorecard is rooted in the organisation's vision and is driven by its leadership.

The holding balanced scorecard (i.e. the traditional organisation's balanced scorecard) is the scorecard widely used in organisations to translate and communicate the vision and the strategy to all employees. The human resource specific balanced scorecard, which can take many different outlooks, is developed usually to provide the organisation with more specific HRM strategic objectives. The diversity balanced scorecard, as described above is already more detailed with its focus on the implementation of the diversity objectives of the organisation. The next step down is to look at an even more specific balanced scorecard development namely the gender balanced scorecard.

5.3.3 The gender balanced scorecard; Why align gender mainstreaming to the balanced scorecard?

As a first step towards developing a gender balanced scorecard it is important to answer the question why gender mainstreaming should actually be aligned to the balanced scorecard? In chapter 3.4 (page 44) the advantages of implementing gender mainstreaming measurements for organisations were already described. These advantages have shown that companies nowadays have to think more about their company image and that they are more often concerned about the value they bring to the society and communities surrounding them. However, also demographic changes and changes to the market place have forced companies to look at finding the best personnel among all the available groups of men, women, minorities and disabled people. For these reasons companies have started to adopt more and more programmes which focus on dealing with diversity (also referred to as inclusion) and also more specifically to achieve gender equality and to become an equal opportunity employer.

The development of such programmes can take different forms and different measures can be selected by the organisation. However, to make use of the well-known and widespread used and therefore tested balanced scorecard framework could be an opportunity that enables organisations to effectively create a balanced and all inclusive method to achieve gender mainstreaming. At the same time the balanced scorecard is used as a tool to achieve change and to achieve gender mainstreaming a process of change is inevitable. Therefore, the combination of gender mainstreaming and the balanced scorecard seems like a logical connection. For organisations that are familiar with the traditional balanced scorecard it could be a logical and easy extension and for organisations that do not have the experience but that are looking to implement gender mainstreaming measures it could be developed as an independent tool.

The gender balanced scorecard will have as main aim to achieve gender mainstreaming in the organisational culture. Therefore, it has to be developed in such a manner that it achieves gender equality and that it is suitable for implementation in the specific organisational culture. As with all the other balanced scorecard ideas the gender balanced scorecard is unique to the organisation that develops it and each organisation will have their own set of objectives and aims for implementing the gender balanced scorecard.

The following points are relevant in answering the question why gender mainstreaming initiatives should be aligned with the balanced scorecard:
> The balanced scorecard is intended to provide a balanced process towards performance improvement which goes beyond pure financial measures. The gender balanced scorecard will offer a similar approach but with an

even higher people dimension and then, even more specific, a focus on achieving the gender mainstreaming and gender equality initiative of the organisation.

➢ The aims of the gender balanced scorecard can be fitted to the perspectives of the balanced scorecard:

  ▪ Training, learning & competence measurement *fits to* learning & growth perspective
  ▪ Employee actions and behaviour *fits to* customer perspective
  ▪ Productivity, performance & change *fits to* internal business processes perspective
  ▪ Organisational effectiveness *fits to* financial perspective

➢ The balanced scorecard has proven its use as management tool to achieve change which is exactly what the gender balanced scorecard would aim to achieve

➢ The balanced scorecard is a proven tool to communicate strategy throughout the organisation to all employees which is also needed to implement a gender mainstreaming initiative

➢ The balanced scorecard is widely used, understood and accepted in the business world which would make it easier to adapt it and use it for different purposes without having to invest extensively in teaching top management and employees about this new management initiative

Even though the gender balanced scorecard is similar in its basic aim to the diversity scorecard it goes further into detail with the specific focus on achieving gender mainstreaming. This means that the gender balanced scorecard ignores the other groups that are included under the diversity approach (i.e. the disabled and other minority groups) and focuses specifically on gender measurements. Besides this the gender balanced scorecard also has the specific aim to include gender mainstreaming into the organisational culture which shows the important role of the climate and culture of the organisation.

The holding balanced scorecard and the gender balanced scorecard should be aligned in order that they both aim to fulfil the ultimate strategic objectives of the organisation. The gender balanced scorecard should not be a stand-alone strategy but should show familiarity and connection to the overall strategy and vision of the organisation. In this way it can be a tool that aims to fulfil its own specific aims and objectives within the total organisational vision. How the gender balanced scorecard could be connected into the holding balanced scorecard can be seen in figure 10. This connection can actually be made with only one or two criteria/indicators of the gender balanced scorecard into the perspectives of the holding balanced scorecard.

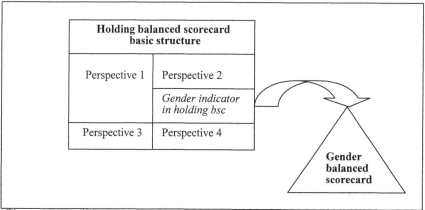

Figure 10: Possible connection between a gender balanced scorecard and a holding balanced scorecard

In the next part of this chapter the gender balanced scorecard will be developed from policy and design to implementation issues and finally to acceptation within the organisation. But, first of all, a marketing plan should be developed that can assist the gender balanced scorecard team with the communication for- and the positioning of the gender balanced scorecard within the organisation.

5.4 A sample marketing/communications plan for the gender balanced scorecard

The advantages of gender mainstreaming should be communicated throughout the organisation as they will show the necessity for the gender mainstreaming initiative to be implemented. For this reason the first step before the actual development and implementation of the gender initiative should be the development of a clear marketing/communications plan. This section will try to review some practical steps involved in the marketing plan that should be developed before the actual implementation of the gender initiative (like the gender balanced scorecard) takes place. The main question it tries to answer is: how should the gender initiative, i.e. the gender balanced scorecard instrument, actually be marketed and communicated within the organisation? The marketing/communications plan for the gender balanced scorecard should:

1. Provide the focus for the actual message/instrument throughout the organisation.
2. Help to identify how the message can best be delivered to the employees and other stakeholders.
3. Help to evaluate the time frame and stages that the project goes through.

The following parts could be included in a marketing/communications plan for a gender balanced scorecard or another gender initiative:

Part I. Purpose and mission
The purpose and mission for the gender balanced scorecard would be: *to achieve gender mainstreaming in the organisational culture.*
- Set the objectives the gender balanced scorecard should achieve:
  What needs to be achieved?
  What would be beneficial to achieve?
  What should be done to get there?
- What are the key messages for the employees and other stakeholders of the organisation, i.e. which advantages of the new management instrument should be communicated to the different audiences?

Part II. Situational analysis
In this part the review of the actual situation (regarding gender equality) and the desired outcome of the gender initiative (e.g. the gender balanced scorecard) should be done. Here an analysis can be provided of the actual maturity and awareness levels in the organisation towards the subject. This analysis can also include: a competitor analysis (benchmarking), a financial analysis, a customer analysis or any other relevant analysis (which could be relevant to the particular business surroundings of the individual organisations).

Part III. Strategy and objectives
The marketing/communications strategy for the gender balanced scorecard should describe the strategies that will help to position the organisation in such a way that the desired outcome (i.e. the engendered organisational culture) will be achieved within the set time limits. The objectives and goals that the gender balanced scorecard tries to achieve can be more specific than the general strategy, such as increasing the number of female members of the board, or increasing the number of female new hires, etc.

Part IV. Vehicles/tactical programmes
What is the best way of communicating your key messages? How many and which communication methods are suitable? In this part of the plan a list of specific projects and activities that are required to achieve the strategic objectives should be developed. Example of tasks could include the development of a newsletter, website (internally in the organisation), events, brochures, etc.

Part V. Resources and timescale
- Research and allocate resources: people, equipment and budget.
- Sort your tasks into a timeline which will help you to keep the overview over the complete project.

Part VI. Performance analysis, measures of success and implementation
- Regular *performance reviews* of the project and the improvements that happen with regards to gender mainstreaming have to take place. The implementation of a gender balanced scorecard is an ongoing project.
- *Measurement of success* is very important to find out whether the communication actually reached the intended audience (i.e. employees, stakeholders, top management). Some criteria that can be looked at here include: relevance i.e. was the message clear, credibility, i.e. was the message trustworthy and responses to the message. Especially, the response is very important as this could help to identify potential resistance to the new management instrument and initiative. If there are many negative responses this could lead to high resistance in the organisation when the implementation of a gender balanced scorecard takes place.
- The *actual implementation* team and the activities and projects they need to do can be listed here.

Such a marketing/communications plan could assist the gender balanced scorecard implementation team with their initial tasks of communicating the new gender initiative to all employees and stakeholders of the organisation and by doing so raising the general awareness levels. It will assist with the communication of the advantages of the initiative and it will show where the initiative exactly fits in the organisation. Furthermore, the communication activities (like newsletters, brochures, etc.) which explain the gender balanced scorecard can already help to identify resistance to the change that might occur when the gender balanced scorecard is actually put to work.

This marketing/communications plan actually could serve as a pilot plan before the actual development/design and implementation of the gender balanced scorecard happens and could be a good starting point for the change initiative. It will show everybody involved where the gender balanced scorecard fits in the organisation, where it would be effective and why it is important to make it a success. It can identify critical success factors for each individual organisation, especially, when responses to the communication activities are allowed for example at events and training sessions to raise awareness for the initiative. A critical factor that could influence the success could be the level of resistance that may have to be dealt with.

5.5 The initial policy; designing the gender balanced scorecard

When the positioning of- and the reasoning behind the new gender initiative are clearly communicated to all stakeholders involved the actual design of the new management instrument is the next step. There are several approaches possible to design a gender specific balanced scorecard, which include the following options:

1. Add specific gender mainstreaming measures to the traditional four balanced scorecard perspectives
2. Add one separate perspective to the four traditional perspectives, i.e. the gender mainstreaming perspective and place all gender measures into this fifth perspective
3. Develop a number of new perspectives (like Hubbard proposed for the diversity scorecard (Hubbard, 2004))
4. A combination, i.e. use the traditional four perspectives and add specific gender measurements to each of these perspectives and add one or two additional perspectives to the scorecard

1. Use the traditional balanced scorecard and add gender mainstreaming measures

This option has as main advantage that organisations which already use the balanced scorecard can continue to use it and only add in this traditional scorecard new measures which focus on achieving gender mainstreaming. This option would be the least costly for the organisation as they do not need to develop a complete new management scorecard. However, at the same time it would probably be the least effective as it does not create the necessary support and focus on gender mainstreaming. The aim and objectives of achieving gender mainstreaming might get lost in the bigger picture of the overall aims and objectives. Another disadvantage is that this option does not focus on implementing specific changes into the organisational culture which is a requirement for successfully implementing gender mainstreaming in the long run into any organisation.

2. Add a perspective to the four traditional perspectives, i.e. the gender perspective and place all gender measures in this fifth perspective

This option would achieve the focus on the gender mainstreaming aim of the organisation. However, the main negative point is that all gender measures would be placed in one perspective whereas some gender mainstreaming measures would fit better to the other four perspectives (e.g. financial measures, etc.). Also under this option there is no specific focus on implementing changes into the organisational culture which is a requirement for successfully implementing gender mainstreaming in the long run into any organisation.

3. Develop a number of new perspectives (like Hubbard proposed for the diversity scorecard (Hubbard, 2004))
Under this option the organisation designs a complete new balanced scorecard with unique gender perspectives only. The main advantage would be that this option could also be interesting for organisations which have no experiences with the balanced scorecard yet. This option would lead to the development of a completely new management tool which has no connection to the original balanced scorecard. This is also immediately a disadvantage for organisations that already use the balanced scorecard and now need to implement a completely new scorecard. This leads to high costs and a complexity in implementation as the employees need to work with two different scorecards, i.e. two different management tools. Especially, since all balanced scorecards (also diversity scorecards) need regular adaptations and reviews to keep up with the changing environment it would be difficult for organisations to pursue two different scorecards for the total organisation. This option would be costly and time consuming for organisations.

4. A combination, i.e. use the traditional four perspectives and add specific gender measurements to each of these perspectives and add one or two additional perspectives to the scorecard
The fourth option includes a combination of the above. Organisations that already use the balanced scorecard can redesign and adapt their scorecard to include gender measurements under the traditional perspectives. As was shown in figure 10 this might be only one or two gender criteria but these would provide the connection to the new gender balanced scorecard. The additional perspectives needed for achieving gender mainstreaming in the organisational culture can be added. These new perspectives could focus especially on changing the organisational culture towards an engendered culture. For those organisations that are familiar with using the balanced scorecard this option would be time- and cost effective. For organisations that have not used the balanced scorecard before it would mean that they would implement one new management tool which gives them two main results, namely the result of the traditional balanced scorecard of communicating and implementing the company strategy throughout the organisation and this is immediately combined with the gender mainstreaming objective.

5.5.1 The gender balanced scorecard: a combination of the traditional balanced scorecard and additional perspectives
The fourth option seems to offer the most advantages for organisations that have experience with the balanced scorecard. For organisations without prior experience all four options require the implementation of a new management tool but, only the fourth option would offer two results simultaneously.

Therefore, the logical choice will be to design the gender balanced scorecard according to the fourth option, i.e. as a combination of the traditional balanced scorecard perspectives and additional gender perspectives. *So, what should be part of this gender balanced scorecard?*

To answer this question it is good to look at the steps organisations would go through when they decide to develop a gender balanced scorecard.

Step one: Define the vision

Step two: Develop strategies for the perspectives to achieve this vision

Step three: Define indicators under the perspectives to be able to measure the results of the actions

Step four: Collect the data for the indicators and convert the contributions to money/tangible value

Step five: Identify the critical success factors

Step six: Develop the message-scorecard/action plan

Step seven: Feedback & learning

If the mission/vision (step one) of the gender balanced scorecard is to achieve gender mainstreaming, then examples of strategies (step two) for the four traditional perspectives can be seen in table 9.

Perspective	Specific gender mainstreaming strategies:
Financially	Achieve better business results, i.e. increase profit. To achieve gender mainstreaming specific financial results from female employees could be monitored to see whether the employee is in the right position and performs to her best ability.
Customer perspective	For the customer it could be very valuable when the organisation can communicate that it has implemented the policy of gender mainstreaming, especially, when the main part of the customer base is female. This could positively influence their buying decisions and thereby improve overall business results.
Internal business process	When female employees are satisfied with their position they will automatically optimise the internal business processes and achieve better business results.
Learning and growth	The organisation should aim to be a learning organisation and therefore stimulate the educational development of female employees. Furthermore, the amount of new female employees hired and the number of female leaders in a company can have important impact on the organisational culture and thereby on the ability of an organisation to be innovative and open to change.

Table 9: Examples of strategies for the traditional balanced scorecard perspectives to achieve the mission of a gender balanced scorecard

The next step (step three) is to develop the additional perspectives which are needed for achieving the mission. One additional perspective will need to be **organisational culture**. This new perspective should be included on all gender balanced scorecards by all organisations that want to achieve the gender mainstreaming objective. The main reason for this is that changing the organisational culture is critical for achieving gender mainstreaming.

The way the people think and behave needs to be changed and this is a fundamental change in culture and climate. Even though the gender balanced scorecard will be unique for each organisation the focus on this perspective will be the same for all organisations. The measures and indicators they include under this perspective may vary between organisations. Other additional perspectives may vary between organisations but, examples could be community, leadership commitment or workforce profile.

5.5.2 The gender balanced scorecard indicators

The third step in the development of a gender balanced scorecard is to define indicators under the perspectives to be able to measure the results of the actions. In figure 11 the gender balanced scorecard perspectives can be seen. The optional additional perspectives are included but these may vary between organisations. Another adaptation from the holding balanced scorecard is that the gender balanced scorecard adds an additional sub-objective to the main vision of the organisation, namely to achieve gender mainstreaming in the organisational culture.

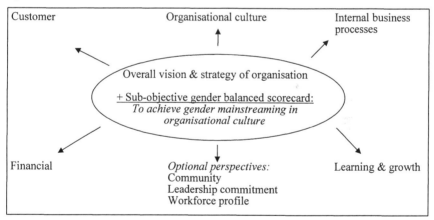

Figure 11: The gender balanced scorecard perspectives

Now it is important to determine which indicators are likely to be included under the different perspectives. The gender balanced scorecard should include a good mixture of leading and lagging indicators. The data for the indicators can be collected from interviews and surveys with employees, from focus groups and special project assignments, from performance monitoring and performance contracts (e.g. individual development plans), etc. The number of metrics that the organisation needs is difficult to predict and there is no right amount or wrong amount.

But it is necessary that the employees are able to implement the amount of measures and therefore too many might lead to difficulties with this process. Another question is how often measurement should take place and here the guidelines from Frost can be of assistance (Frost, 2000):
➢ It depends on the nature of work, but other things being equal measurements are done according to the rate of change expected in the results
➢ The more there is at stake, the more often measurements are taken
➢ The longer it takes to respond, the more often measurements need to be done and the more fine-tuned the metrics must be
➢ The more short-term variability in the results, the more one needs to average over time to separate what's really happening from the short-term changes
➢ Then there are administrative and political factors

The following are examples of general indicators that could be included on a gender balanced scorecard under the different perspectives.

Financial perspective
Under the financial perspectives the traditional finance indicators can be adapted to show the effects of the gender initiatives and can include the following indicators (adapted from Hubbard, 2004):

- Return on investment for the gender initiatives
- Amount of money saved as a result of gender initiatives
- Benefits costs as a percentage of payroll or revenue
- Turnover; using a base year and taking the external economic development of the year into consideration
- Turnover per employee, differentiating between men and women

- Gender initiative expenses per employee or as percentage of total expenses
- Amount of money incremental increase generated from diverse market share penetration
- Gender initiative budget as a percentage of sales
- Reduced litigation costs
- Human capital value added
- Amount of money revenue improvement

Customer perspective
The customer perspective on the gender balanced scorecard includes measures that show in detail how the female employees can have impact on the customers of the organisation. Customer satisfaction is one of the most important issues for many organisations as they depend upon repeat business from their customer base. Potential customer indicators can include some of the following (adapted from Hubbard, 2004):

- Market share division between female and male customers and the representation in the workforce of male and female employees
- Percentage diverse (i.e. male and female) customer satisfaction
- Number of new customers attracted by male and female employees
- Percentage customer retention by male and female employees
- Number of solutions offered per client by male and female employees

- Number of hours spent with male and female customers
- Percentage on-time delivery rating of male and female employees
- Percentage customer loyalty (i.e. male and female customers)
- Profitability of male and female customers
- Level of spending per customer group (male vs. female)
- Number of customer complaints successfully dealt with by male and female employees
- Number of customer awards received

Internal business processes

The measures that are placed under the customer perspective are very important but they must be translated into measures which the company should take internally to meet the expectations of its customers. The internal measures for the gender balanced scorecard should be derived from those business processes that impact the customer satisfaction. Important here is also that the organisation identifies the core competencies it must excel at and design measures for these competencies. Possible internal business process indicators can be:

- Throughput time per business action (male vs. female employees)
- Compare costs and achievements (per department or comparing female & male employees)
- New product introduction and design (male vs. female employees)
- Number of awards received for equality/diversity initiatives

- Employee satisfaction and female employee satisfaction to be assessed with questionnaires
- Number of customer complaints (e.g. about service of female vs. male employees)
- Social audit results
- Selection of critical core competencies/technologies (e.g. human capital as core competence)

Learning & growth perspective

Under the learning & growth perspective key is to review the organisational ability to maintain and enhance the capability of its diverse intellectual assets (Hubbard, 2004, 222). Measures that could be included under this perspective might include some of the following (adapted from Hubbard, 2004):

- Number of female employees
- Number of female managers/leaders
- Number and percentage of gender-competent employees
- Comparison of educational budget spend on women and men
- Motivation index
- Productivity (male vs. female)
- Satisfaction (male vs. female)
- Cross-functional assignments (male vs. female employees)
- Innovation index (male vs. female employees)

- Personal goal achievement (male vs. female employees)
- Number of male and female employees with computers
- Empowerment index
- Timely completion of performance appraisals for male vs. female employees
- Ethic violations against male vs. female employees
- Percentage of male vs. female employees with advanced degrees
- Employee suggestions (male vs. female employees)

Organisational culture perspective

The organisational culture perspective will show how the employees perceive the climate they work in. Therefore employee satisfaction (in particular for female employees) would often be reviewed under this perspective. However, this can also be included under the internal business processes perspective. Measures under the organisational climate perspective may include some of the following (adapted from Hubbard, 2004, 209):

- Percentage favourable ratings on cultural audit for female vs. male employees
- 'Employer of choice' ratings versus top 5 to 10 competitors
- Perception of consistent and equal treatment of all employees
- Gender equity tied to management compensation
- Number and type of policies and procedures assessed and changed for gender impact
- Absence rate/percentage absenteeism (male vs. female)
- Absenteeism cost (male vs. female employees)
- Possible costs of lawsuits
- Workplace flexibility index ratings

- Retention rate of critical human capital
- Percentage gender initiatives fully implemented
- Percentage favourable ratings on climate surveys (male vs. female)
- Average time for dispute resolution
- Cost per grievance
- Employee referral rate (male vs. female employees)
- Percentage gender-based pay differentials
- Percentage work-life balance benefits utilised
- Organisation's 'openness' ratings
- Percentage managers receiving gender-related incentives by department

Optional perspectives:

Community

If the community perspective is relevant for the organisation implementing the gender balanced scorecard it could include measures which show how the community surrounding the organisation views and values the company as member of this community. Not all organisations are aware of- or involved with the community they operate in. Under the community perspective some of the following indicators could be analysed (adapted from Hubbard, 2004, 256):

- Percentage subcontracting euros to women-owned businesses
- Money given to the community
- Awards received from the community

- Number of sponsored community events
- Company image (e.g. being an 'employer of choice' for female potential employees)

Leadership commitment

As change usually needs to be initiated at the top the leadership commitment to the gender initiatives is an important issue to review. Examples of data collected under the leadership commitment perspective could include the following (adapted from Hubbard, 2004):

- Leadership participation in designing the vision and strategies for achieving gender mainstreaming
- 360-degree feedback assessment about the commitment and accountability of the leader to gender equality management
- The degree in which leaders support female employees in achieving their individual development plans in the set time limits for their performance reviews
- The number of female employees in formal mentoring programmes with the leader
- The number of female employees personally selected by the leader for special assignments

- The degree of personal participation in creating an inclusive organisational culture
- The ability of the leader to overcome tension when it arises in the change process
- Money and other resources allocated by the leader to the gender mainstreaming initiative
- Level of priority the leader assigns to achieving the gender mainstreaming initiative will impact the priority it gets throughout the organisation
- Amount of real policies and procedures that are created from the vision to achieve gender mainstreaming
- The representation mix on the organisation's board of directors

- The percentage of gender objectives that are tied to key strategic business objectives connected to the bonus and compensation of the leader
- Leadership representation on the gender steering committee and advisory boards

- The number of executives and managers that are competent due to training in dealing with gender mainstreaming issues
- Leadership behaviour towards work–life balance issues (such as flexible working hours, glass-ceiling issues and family leave policies)

Workforce profile

According to Hubbard the diverse workforce profile would reflect a statistical summary of the organisation's personnel makeup sorted by key demographic groups and for the specific gender perspective this could include an analysis of personnel by gender, length of service, voluntary/involuntary turnover and organisational level. This information can then be compared to the demographic dimensions of the community and/or the customer base (Hubbard, 2004). Examples of indicators under the workforce profile perspective can include the following (adapted from Hubbard, 2004, 190):

- Percentage female managers and officials
- Percentage female survival and loss rate
- Percentage turnover by length of service (male vs. female)
- Percentage absenteeism (male and female)
- Percentage involuntary turnover: exempt and non-exempt
- Percentage voluntary turnover: exempt and non-exempt

- Percentage female new hires
- Number of employee referrals (male and female)
- Number of offers made to female interviewees
- Cost per hire (male and female)
- Number of male and female employees returning from leave
- Average tenure for male and female employees
- Percentage hired versus applicant flow (male and female)

The data that would need to be collected for the workforce profile perspective can come from many different sources like the internal recruitment process, the external recruitment processes, affirmative action and equal opportunities statistics and from other external databases for comparative statistics.

Now that the general gender balanced scorecard has been designed and possible strategies and indicators have been identified the next step (step four) in the development of the gender balanced scorecard has to be dealt with: i.e. how can the results of gender mainstreaming initiatives actually be measured in financial terms (i.e. how can measurable value be aligned to these gender initiatives).

5.5.3 How can an intangible asset like gender mainstreaming create tangible results?

It doesn't matter what aim the company pursues, whether it is culture change, total quality management, innovation, organisational learning, gender mainstreaming or any other initiative, the organisation will have to be able to demonstrate a payback in a certain period of time because otherwise they are wasting time and resources. For this reason it is critical to find a way to put value and return on investment results towards the gender mainstreaming initiative of the organisation.

To create value from intangible assets is different from creating value from tangible assets especially because (Kaplan & Norton, 2004, 29):

- *Value creation is indirect.* Intangible assets seldom have a direct impact on financial outcomes such as increased revenues, lowered costs, and higher profits. Improvements in intangible assets affect financial outcomes through chains of cause-and-effect relationships (for example increased customer loyalty because of specific employee training can lead to improved sales).
- *Value is contextual.* The value of an intangible asset depends on its alignment with the strategy.
- *Value is potential.* Intangible assets have potential value but no market value.
- *Assets are bundled.* Intangible assets seldom create value by themselves. Maximum value is created when all the organisation's intangible assets are aligned with each other, with the organisation's tangible assets and with the strategy.

The measurement of intangible assets is thus one of the main difficulties one has to deal with when evaluating the success of gender equality/mainstreaming policies. In figure 12 the impact organisational initiatives can have on employee behaviour and therefore on human capital value added to organisational results can be seen.

Intangible assets – those not measured by a company's financial system – account for more than 75 percent of a company's value. The average company's tangible assets – the net book value of assets less liabilities – represent less than 25 percent of market value (Kaplan & Norton, 2004, 4). One of these intangible assets of an organisation is the intellectual capital which is cultivated in part by hiring and developing the right kind of employees, in other words, by increasing human capital. But since this resource is volatile, the need for stability must be met by tying accumulated competence and capability to the company in a more lasting way.

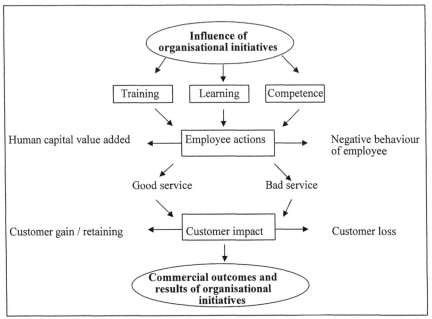

Figure 12: Impact of organisational initiatives on employee behaviour and therefore
on human capital value added to organisational performance
(Adapted from: EP-First, 2003/2004, 4)

The development of structural capital has external aspects: investing in
customers' image of the company, e.g. by making the company known to more
customers, by presenting them with a more favourable image, or in some other
way making them more inclined to patronise the company (Olve, Roy & Wetter,
2000, 28). Structural capital is also closely related to internal processes,
knowledge and capabilities. According to Olve, Roy and Wetter intellectual
capital will become increasingly important, however, it is still extremely
difficult to determine the value of intellectual capital (Olve, Roy & Wetter,
2000). Investors and organisations such as the Swedish firm Skandia have made
it clear that intangible assets are important as they actually include intellectual
assets as a normal part of their profit and loss (P&L) reporting (Hubbard, 2004).
Also Gehringer and Walter agree that human capital as resource of the future is
becoming increasingly valuable and important (Gehringer, Walter, 2003).
According to them creative, highly educated and highly motivated employees
will be the key for maintaining an organisation and economy which is
innovative and competitive (Gehringer, Walter, 2003).

Because of the difficulties with measuring the added value gender equality programmes bring to the organisation it is also beneficial to use the balanced scorecard. As with the HR scorecards and with the diversity scorecard it is important that ways are identified which translate intellectual capital into values and figures that are tangible. The traditional way to look at human capital was to calculate the sales per employee. However, nowadays organisations employ their human capital in several new and different ways. According to Fitz-enz (2000) the calculation needs to include the fact whether the employees are full-time, part-time or employed on flexible working hour contracts. Fitz-enz therefore proposes to change the corporate denominator from employee to a full-time equivalent (FTE) (Fitz-enz, 2000). FTE represents then the total labour hours invested (Fitz-enz, 2000). FTE is a basic measure of human productivity as it shows how much time is spent to generate a certain amount of revenue and for our gender balanced scorecard this measure can be further developed to compare male and female employees.

How can the return on the investment for a gender mainstreaming measurement system be calculated? Hubbard has developed a diversity return on investment process in which he offers possibilities to calculate the return on investment for diversity programmes (Hubbard, 2004). The seven steps that are involved are the following (Hubbard, 2004, 45):

1. Initial analysis and planning
2. Collect data and analyse it
3. Isolate the diversity's contribution
4. Convert the contribution to money
5. Calculate the costs and benefits
6. Report it to others
7. Track and assess progress

Step one to three are also the starting point for the gender balanced scorecard development. However, the difficult part is step four where the contribution will be converted into money.

Phillips, Stone and Phillips describe ten different strategies to convert data to monetary value and the strategy selected depends on the type of data and the initiative which is reviewed (Phillips, Stone and Phillips, 2001):

1. Output data are converted to profit contribution or cost savings. Output increases are converted to monetary value based on their unit contribution to profit or the unit of cost reduction
2. The cost of quality is calculated and quality improvements are directly converted to cost savings

3. For diversity initiatives where employee time is saved, the participant's wages and benefits are used for the value of time
4. Historical costs are used when they are available for a specific variable. In this case, organisational cost data are utilised to establish the specific value of an improvement
5. When available, internal and external experts may be used to estimate the value for an improvement
6. External databases are sometimes available to estimate the value or cost of data items
7. Participants estimate the value of the data item
8. Supervisors of participants provide estimates when they are both willing and capable of assigning values to the improvement
9. Senior management may provide estimates on the values of an improvement
10. Diversity staff estimates may be used to determine the value of an output data item

For soft data the conversion is the most difficult but with the strategies mentioned above it should be possible in many cases. However, there may still be some exceptions and this soft data will have to be taken into account during the evaluation as data not money values. After the data are converted into money value wherever possible the next step is to calculate the costs and benefits and then finally to calculate the return on investment. Hubbard (2004, 49) developed the following formula for the return on investment for a diversity initiative:

DROI% = (Net diversity initiative benefits / Initiative costs) x 100

These steps developed to calculate the diversity return on investment can also be used to calculate the gender initiative return on investment. The outcome will give all stakeholders of the organisations a value and tangible result for their gender initiative.

5.6 Implementation of the gender balanced scorecard
Until now we have described steps one to four in the process of designing a gender balanced scorecard. In this part step five (i.e. identify the critical success factors) and step six (i.e. develop the action plan or the message scorecard) will be dealt with.

The actual implementation of the gender balanced scorecard is similar to the implementation of the 'holding' balanced scorecard and therefore, it would follow a similar pattern as was described in figure 4 (page 36) putting the balanced scorecard to work. The process of developing the gender balanced scorecard in an organisation can be seen in figure 13.

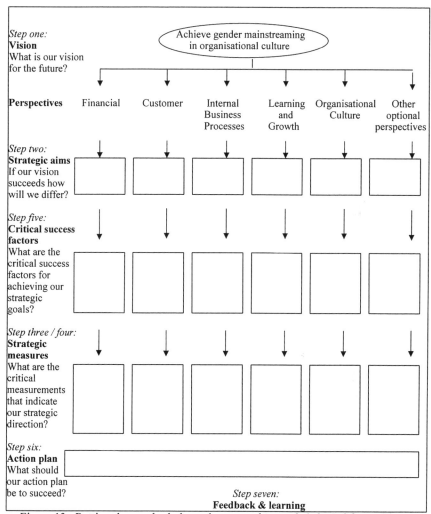

Figure 13: Putting the gender balanced scorecard to work (adapted from: Olve, Roy & Wetter 2000, 42 / Original source: Kaplan & Norton, Sept/Oct 1993, 139)

There are three principles that enable an organisation's balanced scorecard to be linked to its strategy (i.e. they assist in developing the measures on the scorecard) and these are (Kaplan & Norton, 1996, 149):

4) Cause-and-effect relationships
5) Performance drivers
6) Linkage to financials

A strategy is a set of hypotheses about cause and effect which can be expressed by a sequence of *if–then* statements (e.g. *if* we can achieve this, *then* this will happen) (Kaplan & Norton, 1996). All balanced scorecards use certain generic measures which tend to be the lag indicators. However, the performance drivers, i.e. the lead indicators are the ones that tend to be unique for a particular business unit and they reflect the uniqueness of the business unit's strategy (Kaplan & Norton, 1996). A good balanced scorecard should have a mix of outcome measures (lagging indicators) and performance drivers (leading indicators) (Kaplan & Norton, 1996). And, finally, causal paths from all the measures on a scorecard should be linked to financial objectives (Kaplan & Norton, 1996).

Selecting the right metrics and measures which help to achieve the objective of gender mainstreaming is actually much more than just deciding on what to measure. The indicators are part of the strategy that leads to success. To come up with the right measures which show the important cause-and-effect relationships, the performance drivers and linkage to financial results is a very difficult process. Especially, because there is a lack of practical experience in designing gender measures for a gender balanced scorecard this part of the implementation and design of the gender balanced scorecard is very difficult. Hubbard recommends for implementation of the diversity scorecard that organisations hire a diversity metrics consultant with these diversity metrics design skills to assist organisations (Hubbard, 2004). However, because the design of any scorecard involves some trial and error it may also be possible to do extensive research beforehand and then provide training and expertise to a designated expert in the organisation (or a team of experts) who then makes a proposal of the appropriate measures to top management. For the implementation of the gender balanced scorecard the complete organisation should be involved but the initiative should be taken at the top of the organisation.

5.6.1 The critical success factors
In figure 13 it can be seen that identifying the critical success factors is step five in the process of putting the gender balanced scorecard to work. When the critical success factors are identified they should be compared to the vision, mission and strategy to review to which extend it is a relevant factor to analyse and include on the gender balanced scorecard. In this section examples of critical success factors under the different perspectives are discussed.

Financial perspective
A recent study has shown that 49 percent of organisations give financial measures higher importance than any other indicators (Maisel, 2001).

This shows that it is very important to have the correct indicators under the financial perspective on the gender balanced scorecard as many leaders place high value on the outcome of these indicators. Critical success factor areas under the financial perspective will therefore focus mainly on profitability and return on investment for the gender initiative. An increase in profits and a positive return on investment is the ultimate aim of any organisation. Other success factor areas may include (adapted from Hubbard, 2004): benefits generated, market share increase (especially paying attention to increase in female customers' market share), cost reduction, expenses reduction, revenue improvement, changes in litigation costs, human capital value changes.

Customer perspective
One very important success factor is customer loyalty to the organisation. Under the customer perspective it will be important to review whether the gender initiatives have impacted the degree of loyalty of the customers. Other critical success factors might include (adapted from Hubbard, 2004): market share by male or female customers, new customers, diverse customer satisfaction, profitability, brand image and recognition, and customer intimacy.

Internal business processes
The critical success factors under the internal business processes perspective are to review whether the core competencies (e.g. human capital) of the organisation are being used correctly. Which internal business competence should be improved to increase customer satisfaction? The outcomes of social audits can assist with the identification of critical success factors under this perspective on the gender balanced scorecard. The data collected under the internal business processes perspective can come from a number of different sources such as: business technology systems, technology policies and procedures and productivity enhancement systems.

Learning & growth perspective
The critical success factors for the learning & growth perspective could include (adapted from Hubbard, 2004): career development, gender training, competency coverage, productivity, morale, learning gain, technology access and utilisation and innovation. The data for the learning & growth perspective can be collected from a number of sources including: career development policies & procedures, training and development systems, human resource planning, work-life benefit policies and procedures, and other processes to build morale (Hubbard, 2004).

Organisational culture perspective
According to Hubbard (2004) critical success factors under the organisational culture perspective might include outcome areas such as the following: employee commitment, organisational flexibility, employee complaints, grievances, discrimination, work-life balance, leadership behaviour and practices, teamwork, employee satisfaction and openness to change. Sources where all of the information under the organisational culture perspective can be collected from include: climate survey data, cultural audit data, employee complaints, grievances and gender discrimination complaints. All this information can assist in determining the level of commitment by the organisation to change the organisational climate into becoming a more inclusive and engendered organisational culture.

Optional perspectives:
Community
Community interaction is becoming more important for organisations as they strive to become the 'employer of choice'. Other critical success factors according to Hubbard could include corporate citizenship, adherence to environmental regulations, adherence to health and safety guidelines, and brand image and recognition.

Leadership commitment
The art of leadership is to delicately balance the tension between stability and change (Kaplan & Norton, 2001). According to Kotter successful transformation is 70 to 90 percent leadership and only 10 to 30 percent management (Kotter, 1996, 25). According to Kaplan & Norton's research the individuals who led the successfully adopting organisations felt that their most important challenge was communication. The balanced scorecard requires a participative, not authoritative, style of management. The lead executive creates the climate for change, the vision for what the change can accomplish, and the governance process that promotes communication, interactive discussions, and learning about the strategy (Kaplan & Norton, 2001). Without leadership and commitment from the top of the organisation the gender balanced scorecard project is doomed to failure. It is a critical success factor that the process of change is initiated and guided by top management. However, for the gender balanced scorecard specifically also the role of the change agents are very important as they possess the expertise and experiences to guide the project and to assist the top management with the decision making in areas where they may not have the relevant expertise. According to Hubbard a number of critical success factors that are part of the leadership commitment are: vision formulation, personal leadership accountability (walking the talk), vision communications impact, individual development plan achievement, mentoring,

succession management, compensation equity, board representation utilisation, litigation risk management, gender-focussed brand management, resource allocation (Hubbard, 2004). This last success factor was also recognised by MacDonald, Sprenger and Dubel as they wrote: "Whatever the readiness to change of the organisation and its managers, top management must be convinced of the need to devote the resources necessary to carry out the change process (MacDonald, Sprenger and Dubel, 1997).

Workforce profile
According to Hubbard (2004) a sample set of critical success factor areas for the workforce profile area might include outcomes such as: workforce demographic representation, workforce turnover, workforce profile of women, recruitment impact, cost per hire, workforce retention, workforce stability and workforce profile of new hires. In these critical success factor areas different data analyses can be done which show the strength of the female workforce for the organisation.

5.6.2 The action plan
Step six (see figure 13) is the actual action plan or the message scorecard. When the theoretical decisions are made, including decisions about the perspectives, the indicators that should be measured and the critical success factors the practical implementation has to be the next step. The final question: *'what should be our action plan to succeed?'* (see figure 13) should be answered here. The action plan or message scorecard should answer practical question like:

- Who will carry responsibility? The gender balanced scorecard team needs to be put in place.
- Who is the project leader?
- When does the project start? The planning of the project needs to be made.
- What will be included in the communication plan (i.e. as described in the marketing/communications plan: events, brochures, education and other ways of awareness raising)?
- When will reviews be made?
- What is the actual budget for the implementation?
- How will resistance be dealt with?

When these practical issues are taken care of the actual message scorecard can become reality in the organisation and the gender balanced scorecard can be put to work. However, one very large obstacle to the smooth implementation and working of the gender balanced scorecard is the potential resistance that might occur within the organisation. In the next part the actual change process and the possible resistance that grows with this change will be analysed.

5.7 Acceptance - the actual process of change

As Kaplan & Norton (2001) recognise a successful balanced scorecard programme starts with the recognition that it is not a 'metrics' project; it's a change project. Initially, the focus is on *mobilisation* and creating momentum, to get the process launched. Once the organisation is mobilised, the focus shifts to *governance*. Finally, and gradually over time, a new management system evolves – a *strategic management system* that institutionalises the new cultural values and new structures into a new management system (Kaplan & Norton, 2001). The balanced scorecard is most effective when it is part of a major change process in the organisation (Kaplan & Norton, 2001). Ongoing change has become a very important element of doing business nowadays and most organisations are fully aware that they need to manage this change process actively. The change equation of Beckhard and Harris (1987, 1992; attributed by them to Gleicher) is a simple, powerful tool that can be useful when organisational change should take place. Their equation is:

Change happens when: *Dissatisfaction x Vision x First steps > Resistance*

This means that change is likely to happen when there is enough dissatisfaction with the current situation, a clear vision of change (in this case the vision of an engendered corporate culture), and clearly described first steps to complete it. These three elements must be greater than the resistance that is present for the change to happen. The change equation shows that the following three components must be present to overcome resistance to the change:

- Dissatisfaction with the current situation
- Vision of what is possible in the future
- Achievable first steps towards reaching this vision

The implementation of a fundamental change process and the agents of change that are involved in such a process can be identified using the promotor model as will be described next.

5.7.1 Aligning all employees with the new strategy using the promotor model

As mentioned already before there are many people involved with the implementation of the gender balanced scorecard. The promotor model can assist with giving an overview of the roles that need to be played in order to get this process of change organised and implemented. The place of the promotor model in this fundamental change process can be seen in figure 14.

The promotor/champions model was initially developed by Witte in 1977. Witte introduced the expression 'promotor' to describe people who were actively and intensely supporting an innovation (Witte, 1973). Witte found that the technology promotor and the power promotor should overcome the barriers of unwillingness and ignorance together.

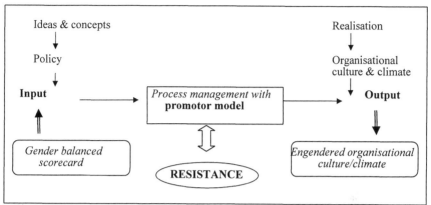

Figure 14: From initial concept to changing culture: using the promotor model to manage the process of change leading to acceptance of an engendered organisational culture

The promotor model was further developed by Hauschildt and Gemünden as a model for the management of innovation (Hauschildt and Gemünden, 1999). The power promotor and the technology promotor overcome the barriers of unwillingness and of ignorance and they added a process promotor who will need to overcome the barriers of non-responsibility and non-communication between the organisational units and acts as navigator of the process (Hauschildt and Gemünden, 1999, Hauschildt and Kirchmann, 2001). Gemünden and Walter added the relationship promotor to the promotor model (Gemünden und Walter, 1995). This relationship promotor acts as the network connecting all areas both internal and external. The promotor model can be seen in figure 15.

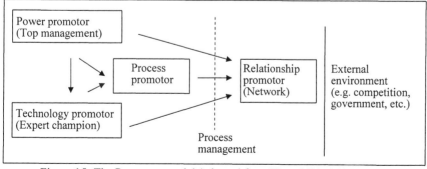

Figure 15: The Promotor model (adapted from Hauschildt, 2004, 215)

According to Hauschildt and Kirchmann the level of success of an innovation depends on the existence of a 'troika' of promotors (Hauschildt and Kirchmann, 2001). The division of labour thus becomes a critical success factor for achieving a fundamental change or creating an innovation. This is also the case for the implementation and acceptance of a gender balanced scorecard. Kaplan and Norton (1996, 287) identified three critical roles that must be played in building and embedding the balanced scorecard as a strategic management system:

1) Architect
2) Change agent
3) Communicator

These roles also apply to building the gender balanced scorecard and they can be compared to the promotors (identified in figure 15) which are important to make a change process happen. This comparison is made in table 10, which shows the complete gender balanced scorecard team and their role in the change process. The three roles Kaplan & Norton identified for the general balanced scorecard should be expanded with the fourth role, namely the power promotor, for the implementation and acceptance of the gender balanced scorecard.

The *power promotor* is the leader of the organisation and as also was mentioned earlier the process of change should always start at the top in order to be successful. The *architect/specialist promotor* is responsible for the process that builds the initial gender balanced scorecard and that introduces the scorecard to the management system. This person must be capable of educating the executive team and guiding the translation of the gender mainstreaming strategy into specific objectives and measures in ways that are non-threatening and do not trigger defensive reactions (Kaplan & Norton, 1996). The *change agent* will embed the scorecard into ongoing management processes and should have a direct reporting relationship to the CEO. The change agent helps managers redefine their roles, as required by the new system (Kaplan & Norton, 1996). The change agent for the gender balanced scorecard must possess a basic level of expertise regarding gender initiatives and should be an objective person. Another option would be to have a small team of change agents. Especially in larger firms this might be a good option. The *communicator/relationship promotor* is responsible for gaining the understanding, buy-in, and support of all organisational members, from the most senior levels down to teams and employees on the front lines and in the back offices (Kaplan & Norton, 1996). The relationship promotor should develop and manage the strategic communication campaign to reach and motivate all employees. This is a network role as the relationship promotor should possess (or gain) relationships that allow coverage of communication to all levels in the organisation.

Promotors for creating an innovation (Hauschildt & Gemünden)	Critical roles for building the balanced scorecard (Kaplan & Norton)	Roles needed for building and implementation of the gender balanced scorecard	Characteristics of roles for building and implementing a gender balanced scorecard:
Power promotor	-	Power promotor	**Top management/CEO:** ✓ takes the initiative, ✓ develops the mission/vision/strategy, ✓ reviews strategic fit of initiative, ✓ makes resources available (budget), ✓ overcomes barriers of unwillingness
Technology promotor	Architect	Specialist promotor	**Specialist in gender equality issues:** ✓ educates top management, reviews all alternative initiatives available, ✓ finds the actual solution for the problem, ✓ realises the project by translating the strategy into the required perspectives, the specific objectives/indicators and measures for the scorecard, ✓ identifies critical success factors under the perspectives, ✓ overcomes barriers of ignorance
Process promotor	Change agent	Change agent or team of change agents	**Middle management:** ✓ reports directly to CEO/top management, ✓ should be educated by the specialist promoter to a good level of expertise about the initiative, ✓ implements the scorecard into ongoing management processes, ✓ is an objective person, ✓ sets the dates for reviews, ✓ compiles reports and presentations about the initiatives, ✓ identifies problems and conflicts, ✓ motivates, informs and educates employees about the initiative
Relationship promotor	Communicator	Relationship/ network promotor	**Communication specialist:** ✓ communicates the initiative to all employees, ✓ achieves support and motivation from employees at all levels in the organisation for the initiative, ✓ develops the communication campaign to motivate all employees using technology such as: brochures, newsletter, bulletin boards, education programmes, company intranet and internet, etc.

Table 10: Promotors needed to achieve the change process for acceptance of the gender balanced scorecard

112

In figure 16 the specific promotor model which can assist with the building, implementation and acceptance of the gender balanced scorecard can be seen.

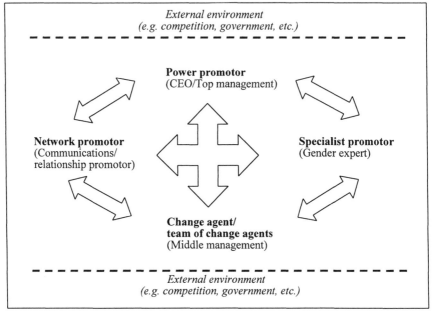

Figure 16: The gender balanced scorecard team; a promotor model for building, implementing and achieving acceptance of the gender balanced scorecard

Kaplan and Norton (2001, 213) also distinguish three processes that can further help to align the employees with the strategy:

1) Communication and education. Communication plans could include a mix of the following measures: meetings at certain time intervals, brochures, monthly newsletters, bulletin boards, education programmes, company intranet, and websites.

2) Developing personal and team objectives. On a personal level an organisation can develop a personal balanced scorecard for each individual employee. This would ensure that each employee has their personal objectives and measures accessible on a daily basis.

3) Incentive and reward system: the 'balanced pay check'. There have been many cases in which companies have successfully linked the balanced scorecard measures to reward systems.

To achieve the gender mainstreaming objectives it is very important that the overall benefits of such a strategy are clearly communicated to all employees.

The level of maturity of all employees towards gender equality has to be raised. Training and education can be critical success factors for this matter.

About the role of compensation, i.e. 'the balanced pay check', linked to the gender balanced scorecard Kaplan & Norton (2001) found out that all of the companies they studied made, or were planning to make, explicit linkages between the balanced scorecard and incentive pay. Most executives opted for a team-based, rather than an individual-based, system for rewarding performance. They used the business unit and division scorecard as the basis for rewards, an approach that stressed the importance of teamwork in executing strategy. Some companies cascaded the high-level corporate and business unit scorecards to lower levels of the organisation and in some cases personal scorecards were used to set personal objectives (Kaplan & Norton, 2001). However, especially with rewards on the individual level it is important to be cautious that the employees do not perform in such a way that they achieve the incentive measure in the wrong ways just to get the rewards. This risk is especially great for employees operating at a lower level and for the individual level rewards.

The linkage of compensation to the scorecard result is also critical for the gender balanced scorecard. First of all, it is likely to increase the level of maturity from top management towards gender initiatives if this is linked to their bonuses or to other incentive schemes. Secondly, it would lead to high motivation of all employees if they are personally or as a team accountable for the success of the gender balanced scorecard.

The change in the organisational culture will eventually show whether the initiatives to align all employees to the strategic objectives were successful. But a fundamental change will never be accepted without certain resistance to the initiative.

5.7.2 Resistance to change

Hausschildt mentions: "there is no innovation without resistance and there are no promotors without opponents (translated from Hauschildt, 2004, 217)." Also figure 14 (page 104) showed that resistance is an obstacle in the process from input (gender balanced scorecard) to output (engendered organisational culture). Resistance to change is a well-known barrier to innovation but also to fundamental changes in organisational culture. Kurt Lewin was one of the first authors who, in the 1940s, introduced the idea of managing and overcoming resistance to changes within an organisation. According to Lewin an issue is held in balance by the interaction of two opposing sets of forces – those seeking to promote change (driving forces) and those attempting to maintain the status quo (restraining forces) (Morgan, 1997).

The three-phase change model Lewin suggested involves: *unfreezing* an established equilibrium, then *drive the transition/change* and, finally, *refreeze* in a new equilibrium state (Morgan, 1997). Many following change initiatives are built on this idea but are expanded. For example John Kotter developed eight steps to guide organisations through change processes which will help to overcome eight reasons for failure of change initiatives. According to Kotter (1996) there are eight main reasons why change initiatives fail, which are: allowing too much complexity, failing to build a substantial coalition, failing to understand the need for a clear vision, failing to clearly communicate the vision, permitting roadblocks against the vision, not planning and getting short-term wins, declaring victory too soon and not anchoring changes in corporate culture. To prevent organisations from making these mistakes John Kotter (1996) created the following eight-stage change process:

1. Establishing a sense of urgency
2. Creating the guiding coalition
3. Developing a vision and strategy
4. Communicating the change vision
5. Empowering employees for broad-based action (and to clear obstacles)
6. Generating short-term wins
7. Consolidating gains and producing more change
8. Anchoring new approaches in the culture

According to Kotter (1996) it is crucial that the eight stages are followed in the above exact sequence. Step five of these eight stages is the empowerment of employees and the clearing of obstacles. Many authors agree that a very important aspect, and very often also the main obstacle in the change process, is the involvement of the employees and the emotional reactions of the employees to the change initiative (Piderit, 2000; Kotter, 2002; Cook, 2004; Holbeche, 2005). Especially, when the change is to implement a gender initiative to achieve gender equality/mainstreaming emotional reactions, and as a consequence resistance, is likely to occur.

According to Kaplan and Norton strategy focussed organisations are concluding that open reporting is better (Kaplan, Norton, 2001). But, because power is generally held at the top of corporations, information is also restricted to the top. Empowering employees means giving them information to make them powerful (Bill Catucci in Kaplan and Norton, 2001). This is a very difficult process of change which will have to lead to a new division of power, as information sharing is power sharing.

There are some additional types of resistance to change. According to Kotter and Schlesinger (1979) there are four reasons why certain people are resisting change:

1. Parochial self-interest (some people are concerned with the implications of the change for themselves and how it may effect their own interests rather than considering the effects for the success of the business)
2. Misunderstanding (communication problems, lack of information)
3. Low tolerance for change (certain people are very keen on security and stability in their work)
4. Different assessment of the situation (some employees may disagree on the reasons for the change and on the advantages and disadvantages of the change process)

De Jager writes that most people are reluctant to leave the familiar behind. We are all suspicious about the unfamiliar; we are naturally concerned about how we will get from the old to the new, especially if it involves learning something new and risking failure (de Jager, 2001). For a gender initiative this is also definitely a factor of resistance. The majority of employees, both male and female, will be used to the way things have always been done and the change away into a new situation is risky and will have personal consequences for all people involved. It is difficult for each individual to assess whether the change will have a positive impact for him or her or whether more negative things will occur. This low tolerance for change is a barrier of unwillingness as Hauschildt describes it. Hauschildt identifies barriers of unwillingness and barriers of ignorance which have to be overcome in order to achieve innovation (Hauschildt, 2004).

The barrier of unwillingness needs to be overcome by influence of the power promotor and the barrier of ignorance needs to be reduced through education and training provided by the specialist promotor together with the agents of change and the network promotor. That the 'promotors' cooperate together is a requirement for success. Hauschildt (2004) called this cooperation between the different promotors the 'troika' of promotoren. As many authors agree managing the change process should be a team effort and change leaders at every level in an organisation need to be able to understand the elements at work in any change process (for example: Hauschildt, 2004; Atkinson, 2005; Holbeche, 2005; Coghlan, et al., 2006). This cooperation between all parties involved is also important for the successful implementation of the gender balanced scorecard as a tool to change the organisational culture.

5.7.3 Dealing with resistance to the gender balanced scorecard

Kotter and Schlesinger (1979) have developed the following six change approaches to deal with resistance to change:

1. Education and communication – one of the best ways to overcome resistance is to educate people about the change beforehand. Up-front communication and education helps employees to see logic in the change effort.
2. Participation and involvement – when employees are involved in the change effort they are more likely to buy into the change rather than to resist it.
3. Facilitation and support – managers can head-off potential resistance by being supportive of employees during difficult times as this will help employees to deal with fear and anxiety during a change process.
4. Negotiation and agreement – Managers can combat resistance by offering incentives to employees not to resist change.
5. Manipulation and co-option – An effective manipulation technique could be to co-opt with the resisters or to bring a leader of the resisters into a change management group for the sake of appearances rather than their substantive contribution. This approach could be tricky and could even backfire and lead to more resistance.
6. Explicit and implicit coercion – This is a last resort approach when time is running out and under this approach managers explicitly or implicitly force employees into accepting change by making clear that resistance can lead to losing jobs, firing, transferring or not promoting employees.

The change approaches mentioned above can help to overcome resistance and can therefore also be of assistance when the gender balanced scorecard is introduced. The first approach, i.e. to educate and communicate, is a critical success factor to overcome resistance when the gender balanced scorecard is put to work. The detailed marketing/communication plan can assist organisations with this approach before they put the gender balanced scorecard to work. The second approach, i.e. participation and involvement, is also very important for the success of the gender balanced scorecard. It should become clear for all employees and other stakeholders that the gender balanced scorecard will be useful for all employees (male and female) and that it will help the organisation with creating a competitive advantage and therefore, improve the business results. When this can be communicated clearly and is understood by all people involved then also the third approach, i.e. facilitation and support, will be easily achieved as more employees at all levels will automatically support the gender initiative. The negotiation and incentives offering to align all employees at the different levels to the new gender balanced scorecard could be necessary in certain organisations. However, good communication and awareness raising for the initiative should help to avoid this step. The last two approaches are risky and could backfire. Therefore, these two approaches should really be avoided if possible.

Resistance should also not always be seen as negative as it could also play a useful role in organisational change. As Hubbard mentions, employee resistance to change is natural and common, and, in fact, some resistance is healthy for the organisation as it allows the organisation to challenge itself regarding the need for change by answering employee questions and responses (Hubberd, 2004). According to de Jager (2001) resistance is a very effective, very powerful, very useful survival mechanism. But, it is very difficult to understand the reasons for resistance as these are very often personal and unique to the individual employees of the organisation. For this reason it is critical that the levels of awareness to the gender initiative are raised and that the advantages of the gender initiative for all individual employees (male and female employees) become very clear. According to Thomas, diversity-maturity requires both an individual and organisational set of behaviours that drive success (Thomas, 1999). Diversity-mature individuals see themselves as responsible for addressing diversity effectively and they are aware that tension will occur as a result of accepting and implementing diversity in the organisational culture. It is very important though that this tension turns into positive outcomes and does not immobilize employees. According to Hubbard: "tension does not need to become conflict and can be avoided when it is clear for all individuals that the tension is part of the diversity process and is nothing personal. It is important that the diversity-maturity individuals become strategic business partners who comprehend what factors are needed to drive successful strategy implementation in their organisation (Hubbard, 2004, 22)."

When there are enough gender mature employees at different levels in the organisation they can act as change agents and help to facilitate the change process and address resistance of individual employees. Thus, in order to implement an effective gender mainstreaming process, the organisation would need to take extra steps to ensure that gender mainstreaming is fully integrated into the organisation's skill sets, culture, and that it is treated as a strategic capability issue. "The organisation has to foster a climate and culture that values differences and maximizes the potential of their employees and to achieve this, the organisation and the individuals within it should operate in a mature fashion (Hubbard, 2004, 21)." When the resistance at an individual level is addressed successfully, the maturity level of the employees is increasing and when, as a consequence the change effort starts to happen, the organisational culture of the organisation will start to change as an automatic result.

In chapter four the theoretical background on changing organisational culture was discussed in detail. It became clear that organisations that want to implement a gender balanced scorecard should attempt to create a more open culture to facilitate gender mainstreaming.

Large organisations can gain advantage from their scale by identifying and sharing their large information base of knowledge and experiences, but for this to occur they must promote a culture of information sharing (Kaplan & Norton, 2001). Open reporting on the balanced scorecard helps facilitate this cultural change. Open reporting breaks down the barriers of selfishness, and incentive compensation systems based on team scorecard performance further reduce these barriers (Kaplan & Norton, 2001).

The balanced scorecard is therefore a good tool to overcome resistance to change, especially when linked to incentives and other pay or bonus schemes. Furthermore, by giving employees continual access to the balanced scorecard, the organisation greatly amplifies its problem-identification, problem-solving, opportunity-creating, and knowledge sharing capabilities (Kaplan & Norton, 2001). It enlists the hearts and minds of all its employees, not just the chosen few at the top (Kaplan & Norton, 2001). This shows that the implementation of the gender balanced scorecard (like the holding balanced scorecard) will lead to a new organisational climate. When resistance is dealt with effectively through extensive communication and education, the way people think can be changed and an organisational culture which embraces gender mainstreaming can occur. It does become clear that effective communication can make or break the gender balanced scorecard initiative.

5.8 The gender balanced scorecard as a controlling tool – feedback & learning

From the seven steps involved with building the gender balanced scorecard (see also figure 13, page 98) there is now only one last step left, namely step seven: *feedback & learning*. According to Krell (2004) equality in organisations can be assessed by looking at the circle as seen in figure 17.

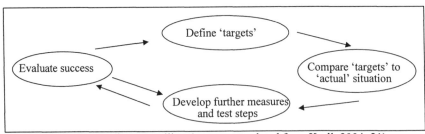

Figure 17: Equality controlling (source: translated from Krell, 2004, 21)

The basic idea behind this assessment is very similar to the balanced scorecard as controlling tool as both look at the target situation and then at the actual situation. However, the main difference is that the balanced scorecard would include the evaluation from the different perspectives and therefore is helpful, especially, as it also reveals the results as a card, i.e. on paper and therefore transparent and clear to everybody involved. According to Stiegler, gender controlling for the purpose of gender mainstreaming should also involve checking the access women have to programmes and financial resources and improving these. Prerequisite is that separate gender differentiated statistics are developed and analysed (translated from Stiegler, 1998). Separate statistics for male and female employees are also analysed under the different balanced scorecard perspectives.

5.8.1 Reporting on the gender balanced scorecard

When the targets are compared to the actual situation it will be necessary to analyse the data that are collected on the gender balanced scorecard. The data collected do not show any results but when relationships and trends are analysed it may become possible to see results and patterns. Also when the data collected are compared to results from previous periods it becomes possible to see trends. Examples of trends are: a decrease in the gap in pay differentials over time between men and women or which business unit has achieved its development plan in the best way over the last three year period.

When the data are analysed in this way it becomes possible to make extensive reports with graphical representation of the results which are interesting to all stakeholders of the organisation including the employees. These reports will also serve as the basis for feedback to all stakeholders and they will assist with learning from the gender balanced scorecard. Also the action plan and recommendations for the next steps should come from the report.

Key questions at this stage could include the following (Hubbard, 2004, 166):
1. What actionable recommendations were proposed based on the data presented?
2. Is the organisation following the proposed plan?
3. Did the actions taken make a difference toward building a more inclusive organisation? What results have you obtained from surveys, interviews, and the like?
4. What has changed in the measured data?
5. What worked and what did not work?
6. What successes or failures did similar business units have?

The feedback should also focus on analysing how the measures of the gender balanced scorecard have assisted women in their careers and whether it has improved their position within the organisation. But, also improvements of the work-life/family-life balance should be included in the feedback as this will have impact on the success and productivity of the employees

One of the methods available to assess gender specific results origins from Sweden and is called the 5-R method (www.gesir.at, 2005). This assessment is based on the following 5-Rs:

1. Representation – i.e. the participation of women
2. Resources – distinguished by gender, who has what resources of time, money, political and economic power, physical space, know-how, education and access to education, access to networks, but also new technologies, health care, living and housing, means of transportation?
3. Rights – do women and men have the same rights and can they make use of it in the same extend?
4. Realities (individual perception) – norms & values, that influence the sex roles – distribution of work by gender, attitude, behaviour and esteem and appreciation
5. Results – the value of gender mainstreaming needs to be measured and translated into results to show success.

The 5-R method could assist in providing top management and other stakeholders with an easy overview of the development and success of the gender balanced scorecard. The information fitting to the 5-Rs should be readily available on the gender balanced scorecard and thus it could be another effective way of showing the same results to the stakeholders.

As with the holding balanced scorecard the gender balanced scorecard will need to be reviewed and evaluated on a regular basis and when changes in the environment (external or internal) occur, adaptations should be made. This is an evaluation process which involves the complete gender balanced scorecard team, i.e. the power promotor (i.e. top management) the specialist promotor, the change agents and the network promotor, i.e. the communicator. These reviews have to happen on a regular basis and can also be used to inform other stakeholders about the results of the gender balanced scorecard process.

Another part of the evaluation will come from reviewing the organisational culture. This will show whether it has changed in such a way that it became an engendered culture. However, to review the organisational climate is a difficult task. Employee questionnaires or interviews could help to achieve this challenge.

As the gender balanced scorecard needs to be reviewed and adapted on a regular basis also the learning of the organisation needs to be a continuous process. The change of the organisation into an organisation with a gender sensitive culture is a continuous learning process and for this purpose regular feedback and analysis serve as the basis.

5.8.2 Issues and problems with the gender balanced scorecard

This evaluation of corporate culture also immediately is one of the difficulties with the gender balanced scorecard. Other areas of problems and issues with the gender balanced scorecard include the following:

- Difficult to measure and put a money value to the benefits of an intangible asset like gender mainstreaming, i.e. it is extremely difficult to create a tangible result from an intangible asset!
- The gender balanced scorecard needs total commitment from top management
- The need for incentives to get total commitment at all levels. This could lead to resistance at different levels in the organisation
- The need for open reporting and therefore a redistribution of power, as information sharing is power sharing
- Difficult to decide which gender metrics and measures are the right ones to include on the scorecard
- Difficult to decide how many gender measures should be included
- Designing a gender balanced scorecard is a complex issue
- The gender balanced scorecard is time consuming to design and introduce and it requires regular evaluation after introduction
- Difficult to evaluate changes in the organisational culture
- Difficult to evaluate indirect results from the gender initiatives, such as improved family relations, female employee satisfaction increase, etc.

5.9 Conclusion

The combination of the balanced scorecard and gender mainstreaming is a logical one since both require change. The balanced scorecard achieves change in organisational culture by communicating and aligning all employees to the overall organisational vision and strategy. To achieve gender mainstreaming in an organisation such a change in organisational culture is also a critical success factor. A detailed marketing plan for the gender initiative can help the organisation to provide the actual focus for the initiative and to market the gender balanced scorecard within the organisation. This chapter described all steps involved in the development of a gender balanced scorecard, which are:

Step one: Define the vision
Step two: Develop strategies for the perspectives to achieve this vision
Step three: Define indicators under the perspectives to be able to measure the results of the actions
Step four: Collect the data for the indicators and convert the contributions to money/tangible value
Step five: Identify the critical success factors
Step six: Develop the message-scorecard/action plan
Step seven: Feedback & learning

There are several options to design a gender specific balanced scorecard however, the combination of the traditional four balanced scorecard perspectives with one or more new perspectives seems to offer the most advantages for all organisations (with or without prior balanced scorecard experiences). The additional perspective would be the organisational culture perspective and optional perspectives could include community, leadership commitment or workforce profile. Gender specific strategies would then need to be identified for each of these perspectives. Following this, the next step is to decide on the metrics and measures for achieving the objectives and strategies.

For successful implementation and acceptance of the gender balanced scorecard the top management (i.e. the power promotor) needs to be fully committed to the project. They then need to align and motivate the other employees with help of the rest of the gender balanced scorecard team consisting of: a specialist promotor, the change agents and the communicator/network promotor. Incentives and bonus schemes could be a requirement to get full commitment from the top managers but also from other level employees. This could also help to overcome resistance.

Resistance is actually the main obstacle to the successful implementation of the gender balanced scorecard. There are barriers of ignorance but also barriers of unwillingness. Both types of resistance have to be dealt with. Especially, the individual employee might resist the new initiative when he or she does not understand the impact of the change process. Therefore, communication and education are critical success factors when resistance has to be dealt with. The feedback and evaluation will take place by analysing the data and regularly reviewing the overall gender balanced scorecard and making adaptations when necessary. Secondly, a review of the organisational culture can help to evaluate the success of the gender balanced scorecard.

With the completion of this chapter the three foundations (i.e. the general balanced scorecard, gender mainstreaming and organisational culture) that formed the theoretical base for the gender balanced scorecard are translated into the actual development of a gender balanced scorecard. In the next part the methodology and the empirical research will be discussed.

Part III: Methodology and Empirical Research

6 Methodology

6.1 Introduction

The purpose of this research is to offer solutions to organisations that want to implement gender mainstreaming in their organisational culture. A deductive approach is used and the way the project is built up can be seen in figure 18.

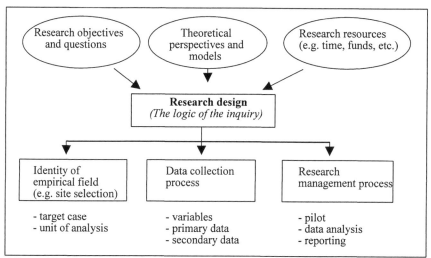

Figure 18: All aspects involved in designing and developing research (source: Yin, 1993, 110)

Table 11 shows where all the information for the steps involved in case study research (see figure 18) can be found.

Steps involved in research design:	Location:
Set the *objectives and questions*	Chapter 1
Theoretical perspectives and models	This was the subject of chapters: 2, 3, 4, 5
The *resources available*	Will be discussed in the limitations (see page 134)
Identity of the empirical field	According to Yin it is essential in case studies to have a *target* which makes it likely that you will complete your case study and you hope that your defined target is critical to the substantive field of interest (Yin, 1993, 110). The target of this work is to contribute new knowledge to the field of gender mainstreaming by researching a sample of organisations and combine this with theory/models.
The data collection process	Chapter 6 (in the detailed explanation of the methodology).
The research management process	The *data analysis and the report* about the collected data can be found in chapter 7

Table 11: Overview of all steps involved in this research design

6.2 Research design

Case studies are used extensively in social science research, including the traditional disciplines as well as practice-oriented fields such as public policy, social work and education (Yin, 1996). This empirical research will be done through case study research. The reason for this choice can be explained by the following definition of case study by Yin: "A case study is an empirical inquiry that investigates a contemporary phenomenon within its real-life context when the boundaries between phenomenon and context are not clearly evident and in which multiple sources of evidence can be used (Yin, 1996, 1)."

Because of the fact that gender mainstreaming is a relatively new expression in business it might be necessary to give additional background to the organisations being researched. Secondly, also the balanced scorecard is not a business model which is known to all businesses and their employees. For these reasons empirical research needs to be done in such a manner that explanations and background can be provided to the organisations which are selected as sample for this research. Furthermore, Yin (1996) states that case studies are the preferred strategy when 'how' or 'why' questions are being posed, when the investigator has little control over events and when the focus is on a contemporary phenomenon within some real-life context. For this particular case study the question is how organisations can change their organisational culture to include gender mainstreaming. And, secondly, how can the gender balanced scorecard instrument assist organisations in achieving this cultural change?

Table 12 shows that the use of a case study is appropriate for this project as the form of research question is 'how', the extent of control the investigator has over actual behavioural events is non existent and it focuses on a contemporary event instead of an historical event. The case study will be based on secondary research and primary research.

Strategy	Form of research question	Requires control over behavioural events?	Focuses on contemporary events?
Experiment	how, why	Yes	yes
Survey	who, what, where, how many, how much	No	yes
Archival analysis	who, what, where, how many, how much	No	yes/no
History	how, why	No	no
Case study	how, why	No	yes

Table 12: Relevant situations for different research strategies (source: Yin, 1996, 6)

6.2.1 Research options

Within the case study research several tools can be used (at the same time). Available research options include the survey research method of questionnaires or qualitative/non-survey research methods such as observation, protocols, projective techniques or interviews (Douglas and Craig, 1999, 154). However, according to Yin (1996, 78), the evidence for case studies may come from six sources: documents, archival records, interviews, direct observation, participants-observation, and physical artefacts. He already excludes the survey methods of questionnaires. Other reasons why questionnaires are not the right method for this dissertation will be described next.

Questionnaires

Questionnaires can be very effective to reach a large sample. However, response can be low, it may take a long time before the response is returned and it is not possible to gather any information besides the questions included in the questionnaire. This is possible in, for example, the case of interviewing. For the respondent group selected questionnaires are not the most effective method as it is difficult to gather all the information needed to solve this problem from a questionnaire. Besides, as Yin (1996) stated, it is not an appropriate data gathering tool for the case study method as research method.

Non-survey methods; information sources for case study research

Observation is not a relevant research method for this problem but could be effective if consumers buying behaviour would need to be observed in for example retail stores. It could give important information e.g. buying decision making processes of end consumers but it can not give all necessary information for this primary research objective as here there is no specific action that can be observed. Gender equality is a process and it is not observable.

The physical trace method (e.g. look at fingerprints on newspapers to estimate readership) and *the entrapment measures* (research the respondents reply when the purpose of the investigation is hidden from the respondent), which are also non-survey research methods (Douglas and Craig, 1999) can also be excluded from the discussion here as these methods cannot provide the needed information to solve this problem.

A *protocol* is a record of a respondent's verbalised thought processes while performing a decision task or while problem solving (Douglas and Craig, 1999, 162). This research method allows the respondent to respond freely and could be relevant if the end-consumers buying decision-making process would be the subject of research. For the respondents of this research this method is not appropriate.

The archival measures (research documents, mass media, sales records, etc.) could be used in addition to the interviews in order to gather relevant data for analysing the past experiences and performance of the sample organisation in achieving equality or in implementing the balanced scorecard. This could be useful information to assist in the interviews.

6.2.2 In-depth interviews

In-depth interviews is the last category of qualitative research and this method can include *individual in-depth interviews, focus groups and EPSYs* (i.e. Etude Projective Synapse used to stimulate group discussion) (Douglas and Craig, 1999). Because the respondents are not likely to discuss this sort of company information (i.e. personnel- and strategic management) in a group the focus group and the ESPY option are not appropriate. But, *individual in-depth interviews* are a very relevant research technique to achieve the objective of this dissertation. Therefore, in-depth interviewing has been chosen as the tool to gather the primary information.

In-depth interviewing is a good tool for the purpose of this research because it makes it possible to collect all the information needed (which would not have been possible in the case of questionnaires) during the conversation, i.e. during the interviews. The general purpose of individual in-depth interviews is to obtain attitudes and feelings about a product or service that would not surface in a structured interview (Sudman and Blair, 1998, 196). Besides this the in-depth interview is also the appropriate method to approach the target respondents of the research. In the last section it became clear that most of the other research methods would be more appropriate in the case of end-consumers being the target respondent group.

The interviews can be described as *focused interviews* because, even though the interviews are open-ended, a certain set of questions will be followed (Yin, 1996, 85). The risk of cultural bias or language problems will be low as the relevant languages are spoken by the interviewer.

Now that it has been decided to conduct a case study the next step will be to collect the evidence. Two types of research have been conducted to find the necessary information, namely secondary research and primary research.

6.2.3 Secondary research

The secondary desk research phase can be seen as the preliminary research phase. Only after gathering the relevant secondary information the primary research could be started. The secondary research was completed by making use of relevant literature, articles, annual reports and the Internet.

Three theoretical foundations have been identified and researched, namely: gender mainstreaming, the balanced scorecard and organisational culture. The strategic information gathered in the secondary research phase serves as the basis for the primary research.

6.2.4 Primary research

The objective of the primary research was to assess the current situation in the sample organisations and to examine how the organisations deal with the gender mainstreaming issue. Secondly, the objective would be to review how the sample organisations think about the use of the gender balanced scorecard as management tool to achieve gender mainstreaming in their organisational culture. The primary research focussed on:

1. Assessment of current situation in the sample organisation with respect to gender measures, i.e. which gender measures are implemented in the organisation, does the organisation deal with gender equality, etc.
2. Questions about the gender balanced scorecard as management instrument to achieve gender mainstreaming in organisational culture
3. Analysis of which perspectives and indicators would be important for the organisation on a gender balanced scorecard
4. Relatively small section about organisational culture, structure and other background about the organisation

The interview was broken down in two parts. The first part included questions about gender measures and the majority of the questions about the development of a gender balanced scorecard. The second part included the gender balanced scorecard perspectives and indicators (ABC questions) and some general background information about the organisation. This part was mostly filled out by the respondent before or after the interview date (four times without the interviewer being present). Both parts of the interview were sent to the respondents in advance in order that they could review the questions and prepare for the interview. The interview guidelines can be found in appendix two. The interviews had an approximate duration between 60 and 90 minutes and took place in the first four months of 2006. The primary research results will be dealt with in detail in the next chapter, i.e. chapter seven.

6.3 The scope of the research

The scope of the empirical research includes a sample of organisations from the Netherlands and Germany. Various studies have documented how gender interacts with national culture and also how national culture influences organisations. Therefore, in this section the national cultures of Germany and the Netherlands and its influences will be briefly analysed. This will be followed by a brief analysis of the two countries with respect to gender mainstreaming attitudes and actions and also a review of the research sample will be done.

6.3.1 Why select a sample from Germany and the Netherlands?
First of all, Germany and the Netherlands are two leading countries in terms of economic performance. Nevertheless, these two countries have traditionally used very different business ideas to achieve their positions world-wide. Globalisation is believed to be a powerful force that could reduce the diversity in employment relations among nations competing on global markets. However, the traditional models for employment in Germany and the Netherlands are still very different. In the Netherlands employment conditions have been subject to substantial change especially since the Dutch government feels the need to adapt to new market demands. In Germany these changes are much slower and because of the large difference in national cultures between these two countries there will most likely always be differences in employment conditions.

The Dutch answer to intensified international competition has been growing flexibility of employment conditions (Bolweg and Kluytmans, 1989, SER 1991, Albeda and Dercksen, 1994, CBS, 1996, Visser and Hemerijck, 1997; from Pauwe, 2004, 160). This shift to more flexibility is reflected in the increased number of flexible labour contracts (Haan, de Vos and de Jong, 1994, Remery, van Doorne-Huiskens and Schippers, 2002; from Pauwe, 2004, 160), the emphasis on the employability of the employee (Gaspersz and Ott, 1996; From Pauwe, 2004, 160), and the closer match between employment conditions and individual preferences or employee performance (Goslinga and Klandermans, 1996; From Pauwe, 2004, 161). This change in the Dutch employment conditions also fits to the structural changes organisations have gone through. The Netherlands has seen an increase in the number of flatter organisational structures which reduces hierarchy. As was argued before (see chapter 3.4.1) these new employment conditions and flatter structures, i.e. changes in the workplace, would suit female workers better than male employees as women are more used to dealing with flexible working hours and conditions. Therefore, the Netherlands is a very interesting market place to include in this research. With the employment characteristics mentioned above gender mainstreaming initiatives, like the gender balanced scorecard, could be very suitable for Dutch organisations to further improve employment conditions for female workers.

On the other hand in Germany the employment conditions have seen slower changes and many of the traditional employment values still prevail. However, as Schmid recognises the Europeanisation and globalisation of national economies, demographic and technological change and changes in women's labour market behaviour are posing new challenges for national labour markets (Schmid, 2005).

The gradual removal of the social and cultural barriers to women's participation in paid work, the de facto or statutory raising of the retirement age and the completion and extension of the European internal market have all contributed to the blurring of the social, spatial and political boundaries of national labour markets and increased the competition for jobs (Schmid, 2005). National labour market policy institutions involved in wage-setting, vocational qualifications and further training, the structuring of employment contracts (dismissal protection, working time regulation) and social protection are coming under pressure to adapt and labour market risks are increasingly being shifted on to individuals and firms in the form of flexibilisation, irregular earnings and enforced regional mobility (Schmid, 2005). Oschmiansky looked into the atypical employment forms that have gained significance in relation to the traditional 'regular employment relationship'. Atypical employment forms include agency work, marginal part-time work and temporary work (in Germany also the so called 'mini-jobs' and 'Ich-AG') and Oschmiansky recognises that the expansion of atypical employment forms in Germany have led to a rise in women's labour market participation (Oschmiansky and Oschmiansky, 2003). This is a similar development as was found in the Netherlands were many women work part-time and in other atypical employment forms, however, Germany is not as far down the road of change as the Netherlands already is.

A high number of the organisational structures in Germany are still very hierarchical as they have traditionally always been. Power is at the top of the organisation and the ways of conducting business are still very formal as also Hofstede identified. According to Hofstede the influence of the national culture on the organisational culture cannot be ignored. Hofstede defines national culture as: "the collective programming of the mind which distinguishes the members of one group or category of peoples from others" (Hofstede, 2001, 1). He actually identified four dimensions of cultural difference (Hofstede, 2001, 24):
1. Power distance
2. Individualism - collectivism
3. Uncertainty avoidance
4. Masculine - feminine

In his research he then connects a number of countries to the characteristics of these four different dimensions. The Netherlands are considered to possess a feminine culture whereas Hofstede places Germany into a masculine culture box. The differences in characteristics between these two cultures can be found in table 13.

Feminine National Culture	Masculine National Culture
• Work in order to live • Managers/leaders use intuition and strive for consensus • Stress on equality, solidarity and quality of work life • Expectation to be consulted • Resolution of conflict by compromise and negotiation	• Live in order to work • Managers expected to be decisive and assertive • Stress on inequality, competition among colleagues, and performance • Resolution of conflict by 'fighting'
Examples of countries with these characteristics: *Sweden, Norway, Denmark, The Netherlands*	Examples of countries with these characteristics: *Japan, Austria, Germany, Switzerland*

Table 13: The feminine – masculine dimension of national cultures compared
(source: Hofstede, 2001, 284)

In societies with clear rules supporting hierarchy, masculine culture organisations tend to be paternalistic and usually the power is centred at the top (Hofstede, 2001). This also explains why in Germany more organisations tend to favour hierarchical structures. On the other hand, in a society that emphasises egalitarianism organisations tend to pursue participation and democratic decentralisation of power (Hofstede, 2001). In these cultures flatter organisational structures tend to be implemented where employees are empowered in the decision-making process.

It can be stated that both Germany and the Netherlands are highly developed industrial countries and each country has achieved this in their own way. Human Resource Management is a highly valued and developed discipline in organisations in each country and therefore research in this area could be beneficial for organisations in both countries. Gender equality and gender mainstreaming will be issues that most organisations in both nations are familiar with whether they act upon it or not as shall be discussed in the next part. This will be beneficial for this research as it will allow the primary research to be done without first having to educate the sample organisations about gender mainstreaming. The same applies to management tools like the balanced scorecard. In both nations many organisations are familiar with this management tool and a large number of organisations are successfully using it already.

6.3.2 Gender mainstreaming in Germany and the Netherlands
Gender mainstreaming in Germany
The total population of Germany was 82.5 million in 2004. 59 percent of women (between 15-64 years old) participated in the labour market in 2003 which is the 8th place in the European Union (Statistisches Bundesamt, 2004). Part-time work was done by 38 percent of women which is the 4th place in the European Union (Statistisches Bundesamt, 2004).

The percentage of working mothers amounted to 61 percent in 2002 compared to 86 percent working fathers (Statistische Bundesamt, 2004). In an article published in 'Spiegel' Achleiter, who is a female professor in Munich, states that Germany has maintained the belief that mothers need to stay at home with their children and Germans have even coined the specific and highly derogatory term *'Rabenmutter'* to describe women who spend too little time with their children (Biehl, 2005). Women spend on average 12 hours per week on paid work compared to 22.5 hours for men (Statistisches Bundesamt, 2004). Unpaid work done by women amounts to 31 hours a week compared to 19.5 hours for men (Statistisches Bundesamt, 2004). Especially, the age of the children is important for childcare purposes. For couples with children under 6 years old childcare amounts to one third of the total unpaid working hours (Statistische Bundesamt, 2004).

In the same article the author also mentions a number of obstacles women face in Germany to achieve business success including the following: "scarcity of career assistance, childcare problems, lack of tax benefits and retirement insurance for married women (Biehl, 2005)." Childcare is a great obstacle because there are only very few pre-school places for children under three and secondly, because the primary school students also end their day before lunch, leaving little chance for mothers to work (Biehl, 2005). The tax problem is that, in many cases, much of the extra income a German woman earns by working gets taxed away, leaving her family with little more money than if she didn't work at all (Biehl, 2005). Thirdly, the retirement insurance for women in Germany allows, in many cases, that a widow receives 80 percent of her late husband's pension (Biehl, 2005). The article also mentioned that for career-oriented German women having a child simply isn't an option or when it does become possible, they are already too old to reproduce (Biehl, 2005). The average age women have their first child in 2001 was 28.4 compared to 26.6 in 1990. The average number of children has gone down to 1.3 per woman in 2003.

Women are still noticeably absent in the top tiers of German business and almost no other nation has such a low percentage of upper-level female managers according to a 2002 Wall Street Journal European career survey (Biehl, 2005). Women only hold 9.2 percent of jobs in Germany's upper and middle management positions, according to 2002 figures from the Hoppenstedt business databank compared to 8.2 percent in 1995 (not a very encouraging increase) (Biehl, 2005). Also the salary gap is still present in Germany as women earned around 25 percent less than men in 2001 (Statistische Bundesamt, 2004). These figures show that there is a long way to go before gender equality is achieved in Germany and thus before gender becomes mainstream.

However, let's review which actions the German government has implemented to facilitate this process of change. Because of the fact that gender mainstreaming has been given more and more attention as a key orientation at the European Union level also in Germany this issue has received greater political attention. Equality of opportunity for women and men is defined as a part of employment policy both at the level of political objectives in the annual 'National Action Plan for Employment' (NAP) and at the level of legal provisions in the Social Code III, and it is additionally supported by the interdepartmental government programme of 'women and occupation' (Müller and Kurtz, 2003). For active labour market policy, four substantial guidelines are relevant for the practical implementation of gender mainstreaming, which originate from EU guidelines and have been included in the Social Code III (Müller and Kurtz, 2003):

- The inclusion of women in measures of active labour market policy in proportion to their share of the unemployed, which was proposed by the EU
- Maintaining special programmes and concepts aimed at supporting women, which are intended to improve their occupational situation and eliminate existing disadvantages on the labour market
- Taking better into account the needs of women and special groups such as women returning to employment. This means that the benefits and schemes of active employment promotion should be arranged in such a way with regards to time, content and organisation that they take into account women's family circumstances
- And, the guideline regarding gender specific documentation and reporting of the results. This is done in integration balances, which are open to the public and have to be drawn up at the end of each financial year

At governmental programme level the incorporation of gender mainstreaming in national labour market policy is relatively advanced in Germany compared to the rest of Europe (Rubery, 2002, in: Müller & Kürtz, 2003). However, the implementation and the binding and permanent establishment of detailed concepts for gender mainstreaming is still in its infancy so far (Müller & Kürtz, 2003).

Firms also see themselves faced with the challenges of the changing workforce. Atypical employment forms are increasingly important including agency work, marginal part-time work and temporary work. Oschmiansky recognises that the expansion of atypical employment forms in Germany have led to a rise in the women labour market participation (Oschmiansky and Oschmiansky, 2003). Also Engelbrech and Jungkunst found that if part-time work continues to grow until 2010 as it has done in the past, there will be more employment opportunities for women than for men (Engelbrech, Jungkunst, 2000).

If the economic structure and the full-time/part-time ratio continue to develop, the female share of the labour force will continue to grow and firms will employ more women than before (Engelbrech, Jungkunst, 2000). In this way firms will be confronted increasingly with problems associated with the compatibility of family and occupation and personnel policy will have to be adapted accordingly (Engelbrech, Jungkunst, 2000). They continue to say that only if firms revise their way of thinking about female employees, can they safeguard qualified staff and thus maintain competitiveness.

With flexibilisation and atypical employment forms on the rise organisations will need to adapt their traditional male-oriented cultures and structures (hierarchies) in order to adequately handle these changes and stay competitive. However, also in this aspect the German firms are still very different from the Dutch firms of which many have already implemented flatter structures to deal with atypical employment forms.

Gender mainstreaming in the Netherlands
Currently, the Netherlands has seen a weak economic development which has also had its negative influence on the emancipation process. However, also before the recession there were some factors already negatively influencing emancipation especially from the side of the government.

The total population in the Netherlands was 16.3 million in 2004. In 2003 66 percent of women (between 15-64 years old) participated in the labour market which is the 3rd place in the European Union (Central Bureau of Statistics, 2004). 74 percent of women were working part-time which is the 1st place in the European Union (European Community, 2004). In 2003 a third of women worked for 35 hours a week or more compared to 50 percent in 1990. The ideal remains the 'one-and-a-half-earners' model, in which the man works around twice as many hours outside the home as the woman (Emancipation Monitor, 2004).

It is becoming more and more common to use childcare services as the majority of men and women believe that the mother-child relationship does not suffer if the mother goes out to work (Emancipation Monitor, 2004). When the Emancipation Monitor reviewed income levels they found out that pay differentials are narrowing. In 1995 women's hourly pay was 76 percent of that of men, but, by 2001 it had increased to 81 percent. The share of women in management posts has risen to 26 percent, however, in 2003 the senior management of the 100 biggest companies in the Netherlands contained only 5 percent women.

The main aim of the Dutch government's emancipation policy since 1985 is to achieve a society where everybody, irrespective of gender, has the possibility to lead an independent life and where women and men have the same rights, chances, freedom and (social) responsibilities (TK, 2000/2001). Independent life means economic independence through labour participation. This is a very important aspect of the government policy especially since it is a necessity that more women participate in the labour force because there will be shortages of labour in the future due to the ageing population. And, to maintain a good social system as many people as possible should be working. This makes paid labour the critical issue in the government emancipation policy for the long term. This emancipation policy was developed under the government of Mr Kok and has been taken over completely by the first and second government of Mr Balkenende. However, the current government has made some adaptations which were not always positive for the emancipation of women.

One of the reasons for the slower progress of emancipation according to the Emancipation Monitor appears to be the less forceful emancipation policy on the part of the government. The new life-course savings scheme, the work and care act and the child care act, introduced in order to make it easier for people to combine work and care tasks, are so unambitious in their design that they are likely to contribute little to making this combination easier. Secondly, the plans to increase the length of the working week will probably mean a step back in the emancipation process (Emancipation Monitor, 2004). The difference in working hours between men and women will thus widen again, and the opportunities for women to progress up the career ladder will consequently reduce.

The government has implemented several initiatives to support their emancipation policy. Examples are the ambassador network and a benchmark for organisations. The ambassador network is a network of people acting as ambassadors for women in the ambassador's own organisation or helping them access other organisations in the ambassador's network. The benchmark of the government offers organisations the possibility to check and compare for example the number of women in their organisation to other organisations in their industry. The government also implemented a nationwide campaign which should inform and stimulate men to take over more household tasks of women. However, according to the Emancipation Monitor 2004, no information is available with regards to the effects of these government initiatives.

Tijdens who researched women in management in the Netherlands states that over the last 10 to 20 years the participation rate of women has increased rapidly (Tijdens, in Davidson, et al., 2004). Furthermore, she comments that other striking findings include the decrease of homemaker careers among young women, the acceptance and increase of part-time employment and the rising share of women in managerial and entrepreneurial positions. However, the increase in participation of women has not been spread proportionally over all organisations, as male-dominated organisations seem to remain male-dominated, and female-dominated organisations seem to feminise. Both, self-selection by potential employees and selection by the organisation play a role in continuation of a masculine organisation culture (Tijdens, in Davidson, et al., 2004). With regards to future developments Tijdens mentions that the increased participation of women in the labour force and women's increasing purchasing power will force male-dominated organisational levels with predominantly masculine organisational culture to adopt feminine values. In the near future it is more likely that this hierarchical gender balance will be changed in female-dominated organisations than in male-dominated organisations which may lead to better career possibilities for women (Tijdens, in Davidson, et al., 2004).

According to the Emancipation Monitor (2004) employers in the Netherlands are more conservative in their views about emancipation than the Dutch population as a whole. In particular they have negative views on part-time working, which according to half the employers creates coordination and management problems. The leadership qualities of women are rated just as highly as those of men, but most employers regard combining management posts with part-time working hours as a problem: four out of ten believe that a management function cannot be combined with having the main responsibility for a family. Where employers have this negative view the proportion of women at all levels in their organisation is smaller. Employers who support a structural and forceful careers policy for women have a higher proportion of women at all levels of their organisation. Female employers have a more positive view of emancipation, and the proportion of women in all strata of their organisations is greater than among male employers.

Many companies employ all kinds of measures in a bid to increase the number of women progressing to more senior positions, however, little is known about the effectiveness of this policy; 'before' and 'after' measurements are rarely carried out (Emancipation Monitor, 2004). As far as statements can be made on the basis of the small number of studies that have looked at the effects of policy on the proportion of women in senior management positions, it would seem that a combination of measures is the most effective (Emancipation Monitor, 2004). There is some support that the following measures positively influenced promotion of women: part-time work in higher positions, job rotation, the so-called 'women-for-women' rule (i.e. for each woman leaving a new woman is hired), reducing the principle that the employee who works in the organisation the longest has the most rights, guarantees for return and child care solutions.

Also education, training, management development projects, mentoring and networking seem to positively support the promotion of women (Emancipation Monitor, 2004). Whether improving terms of employment has any impact on the proportion of women in senior posts is unknown. The Emancipation Monitor does suggest that incentive measures do appear to be effective, as do training programmes and mentoring. Nothing is known about the effects of cultural change on the proportion of women in senior positions (Emancipation Monitor, 2004). There is a need for more research into the effectiveness of the various measures according to the Emancipation Monitor 2004.

That there is a need for further research is clear and will also be describes in chapter 6.4 when the limitations to the research are identified. Germany seems to be only at the beginning of the road to achieving gender mainstreaming in all levels of the society, especially, due to traditional thinking and attitudes that still prevail in this traditional masculine culture. However, the government does recognise what needs to be done and attempts, at least in theory, to implement changes which will make it easier for women to combine family and work life.

It seems that the Netherlands is further along the same road that leads to gender equality in all areas of society but they also still have many obstacles in the way before gender mainstreaming is achieved. The fact that the Netherlands is a more feminine culture will have helped with the implementation of flexible working relationships and the acceptance of women in the workplace.

6.3.3 The sample
The six case study sample organisations selected from the Netherlands and Germany include two organisations which have prior experiences with the balanced scorecard as management tool but also four organisations with no prior experiences. The contact persons included human resource managers and middle management and both male and female respondents.

The organisations and interviewees are left anonymous. This is done on the request of three of the participating organisations and therefore also followed through for the remaining three participants. This does not impact the research as the objective of this research is *to test* whether the gender balanced scorecard would be accepted by organisations as instrument to include gender mainstreaming in organisational culture and not to actually implement this tool at this stage. This phase of research focuses on testing the opinions of management and personnel experts about such an instrument.

In table 14 an overview of the characteristics of the participating organisations for the case studies can be found.

	Case 1	Case 2	Case 3	Case 4	Case 5	Case 6
Country	NL	NL	NL (& G)	G (& NL)	G	G
Size of organisation	Medium	Large	Multi-national	Medium	Large	Multi-national
Type of industry	Tech-nology	Recruit-ment	Technology Electronics	Food	Energy	Telecom-munications
Prior use of balanced scorecard	No	No	Yes	No	No	Yes
Structure of organisation	Flat & Matrix	Flat	Matrix	Bureaucratic Hierarchical	Flat	Matrix
Approx. number of employees worldwide	600	13,000	160,000	3,800	1,000	49,000
Approx. turnover in 2004	> $ 500 million	> € 5 billion	> € 30 billion	> € 950 million	> 5 billion	> € 30 billion

Table 14: Overview of the characteristics of the participating organisations for the case studies

6.4 Limitations to the research

There are a number of limitations that had to be dealt with. First of all there is a **time and resource limitation** which restricts the research. However, by keeping the research question narrow enough it is no problem to stay within the boundaries of this limitation. This research aims to test the effectiveness and practicality of the gender balanced scorecard as new management instrument and does not attempt to implement such an instrument in practice. Follow-up research would be needed to further develop this instrument.

Secondly, also the sample size is a limitation. The **sample size** exists of six in-depth interviews but it is difficult to make generalisations about the outcome of these interviews. However, due to the resource limitation the sample size could not be extended.

Another limitation can be found in the fact that the concept of gender mainstreaming is not yet widely known, researched and accepted which **reduces the amount of relevant research and literature** for secondary research.

The **lack of acceptation of gender mainstreaming** and gender equality is also apparent from the amount of **resistance** to new instruments and gender measures from the side of organisations.

6.5 Conclusion

It can be concluded that the starting point of the empirical research was to design and develop the research. This was done according to the model developed by Yin (see figure 18), which shows all the aspects involved in designing and developing research.

The research method that was decided for this project is the case study method and the data collecting was done by means of in-depth interviews. The scope of the research included sample organisations from Germany and the Netherlands as these countries are both highly developed industrial countries with well-developed human resource strategies and where gender mainstreaming is at least a strategic aim of the respective governments which will make it easier to complete the research in these countries.

In the next chapter the empirical study, i.e. the primary research results, will be introduced and analysed.

7 Empirical Study; primary research results

7.1 Introduction

In chapter six it was explained why Germany and the Netherlands are interesting countries to select for this primary research. Both countries are well-developed in the area of personnel/human resource management and in these countries it is not a necessity to explain gender equality in detail because most people are familiar with this issue. In this chapter the outcomes of the primary research, i.e. the six in-depth interviews (three in the Netherlands and three in Germany) will be presented and analysed.

7.2 The results

The results of the primary research can be partly shown in graphical representation but the majority of the analysis is done in writing. The interview did not focus solely on the gender balanced scorecard but also on gender measures and organisational culture/structure because this surrounding information is important as this is information about the environment where the gender balanced scorecard should be implemented. This information gives further background about the maturity of the organisations towards gender issues. The analysis of the results will be divided into the following four parts:

1. Assessment of current situation regarding gender mainstreaming and gender measures
2. The gender balanced scorecard
3. Analysis of perspectives and indicators for a gender balanced scorecard
4. Organisational culture and structure

7.2.1 Gender measures & gender mainstreaming; current situation

Use of gender measures

With regards to gender measures one of the respondents in the Netherlands stated not to have special gender measures besides a small part (1/6th) of day-care costs for children that would be provided by the organisation. Two other respondents (one from the Netherlands and one from Germany) also stated that their organisation only implemented gender measures according to the legal requirement for childcare. The large German organisation did offer more gender measures in the form of mentoring, flexible hours and home office possibilities. The two multinational organisations offered the most complete package of gender measures including almost all measures available. The German multinational did mention however, that it depends on the hierarchical level of the employee and that the employee has to ask for participation as it does not apply automatically. In figure 19 the gender measures that were used by the different organisations included in the research can be found.

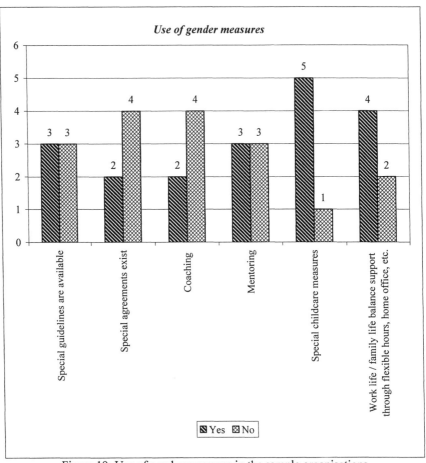

Figure 19: Use of gender measures in the sample organisations

Evaluation of gender measures
The majority of the respondents did the evaluation of the effectiveness of these gender measures via satisfaction questionnaires for the employees. One of the respondents did not use satisfaction questionnaires but uses the performance reviews that take place once a year to evaluate measures. Besides satisfaction questionnaires also interviews/performance reviews, an internal cultural survey or a general survey were used. One of the multinational organisations uses satisfaction questionnaires and besides this they also developed statistical reviews and an inclusion index.

Perceived importance of advantages of gender mainstreaming
How important the respondents believed the advantages of gender main-streaming are for their organisations can be seen in figure 20.

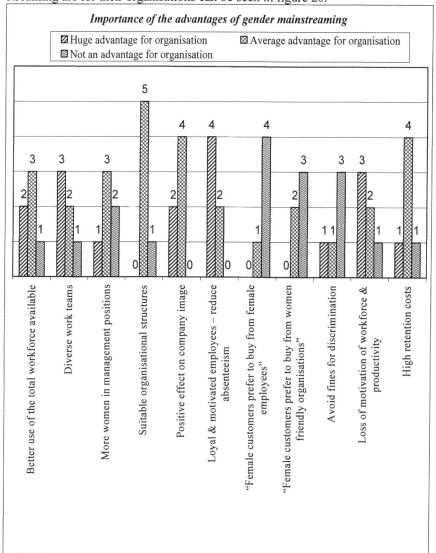

Figure 20: Perceived importance of advantages of gender mainstreaming for the sample organisations

The figure shows that the majority (four respondents) selected *'loyal & motivated employees – reduce absenteeism'* as the most important advantage of gender mainstreaming. This was followed by *'diverse work teams'* and *'loss of motivation of workforce & productivity'* which were selected by three respondents. In table 15 the reasons when an advantage of gender mainstreaming was seen as 'not important' can be found.

Advantage of gender mainstreaming	Reasons when 'not important'	
Better use of the total workforce available	"We have no problems with finding good employees."	
Diverse work teams	Work teams at low level consist for the majority of women.	
More women in management positions	Only few women in the company. "More women in management positions is not a business goal."	
"Female customers prefer to buy from female employees"	"Does not apply to this industry." Majority of staff at communication positions with external flex-workers are female. Sales not to people directly. Company is a 'white label' company therefore no influence of customer.	*Note:* 1 respondent selected *'not applicable'* as the majority of their customers is male
"Female customers prefer to buy from women-friendly organisations"	"Maybe in the future?" Sales not to people directly. Company is a 'white label' company therefore no influence of customer.	*Note:* 1 respondent selected *'not applicable'* as the majority of their customers is male
Avoid fines for discrimination	Maybe relevant in the USA (according to 3 respondents).	*Note:* 1 respondent selected *'not applicable'*
Loss of motivation of workforce & productivity	"Female in management positions in production could have negative influence (foreign culture problems)."	

Table 15: Reasons when advantage of gender mainstreaming was perceived 'not important' for the sample organisations

Main problems with achieving gender mainstreaming
One of the respondents mentioned that **lack of variety in the workforce** was a big part of the problem to achieving gender mainstreaming. In this organisation the workforce does not include many employees with children which has led to an organisational climate where everybody needs to work long hours and which in turn makes it almost impossible for female employees with young children to stay and work. According to two respondents **practical issues** like child support are an obstacle to achieving gender mainstreaming. Also the **'old boys' network'** was mentioned as an obstacle to achieving gender mainstreaming.

In figure 21 a graphical overview of the main problems with achieving gender mainstreaming can be found.

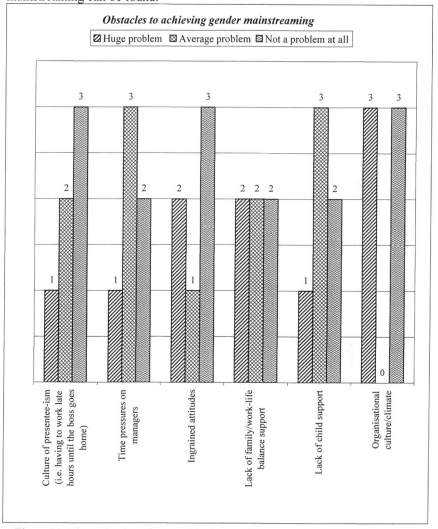

Figure 21: The main obstacles to achieving gender mainstreaming/equality for the sample organisations

7.3.2 The gender balanced scorecard

The second part of the interview dealt with the questions about the development of a gender balanced scorecard.

Prior use / experience with the traditional balanced scorecard
The two multinational organisations implemented, and currently use, the traditional balanced scorecard. The four other participating organisations did not implement the balanced scorecard. However, all respondents were familiar with the management concept of the balanced scorecard. One of the Dutch respondents has implemented an alternative management system called **VOICE**, which stands for the following **V**alue quality, **O**perational excellence, **I**ntegrity, **C**ustomers and partners and **E**mployees and should communicate the values and mission of the organisation to the employees.

Responsibility for the design and implementation of a gender balanced scorecard
Five respondents believe that the responsibility for the design and implementtation of a gender balanced scorecard should lie with the HRM/personnel department. Table 16 shows which combinations of responsibility were selected. For example three of the respondents believe that the HRM/personnel department should be responsible in cooperation with the CEO and top management team.

Responsible for design & implementation of gender BSC	Case 1	Case 2	Case 3	Case 4	Case 5	Case 6
CEO & top management team	Yes	Yes	Yes	Yes		
Personnel department / HRM department	Yes	Yes		Yes	Yes	Yes
One diversity/gender specialist (internal employee)					Yes	
A diversity team			Yes			
An external consultant						
Project teams or departments	Yes					
Assistance of gender experts						Yes

Table 16: Joint responsibility for the design and implementation of the gender balanced scorecard

This table shows that all the respondents believe that it should be a joint effort from two or more people/departments to design and implement a gender balanced scorecard. Figure 22 shows graphically who should carry the responsebility in the organisation for the design and implementation of the gender balanced scorecard according to the interviewees.

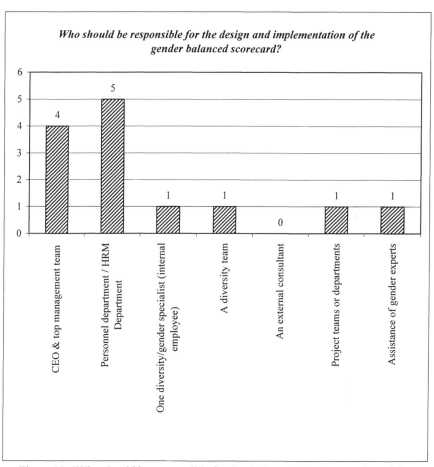

Figure 22: 'Who should be responsible for the design and implementation of the gender balanced scorecard?' according to the sample organisations

How to get commitment from top management
All respondents agreed that *eventually* the gender balanced scorecard instrument should be connected to bonuses/incentives for top management or in one case to the top management of the human resources department. Three respondents stated that first **awareness and acceptance levels** for such an instrument should be raised before this connection to bonuses should be put in place. In table 17 the responses of the interviewees to this question can be found.

	Responses to the question: should the results of a gender balanced scorecard be connected to incentives for top management in order to get commitment?
Case 1	Yes, a gender balanced scorecard should be connected to incentives/bonus schemes for the top management as this would force certain behaviours, creates good visibility on progress and achieves executive attention.
Case 2	Yes, currently the organisation is already working with bonuses connected to the overall company performance for the majority of staff. The bonuses for top management are already related to results and for such a gender initiative this should be extended as well. Especially, since the majority of top management is male but the majority of middle management and the rest of the workforce is female a bonus for top managers would give an extra push to the initiative.
Case 3	Yes, this should happen eventually but not in the beginning as this would lead to further resistance instead of to acceptance. After awareness and maturity towards the subject are raised further then it should definitely be done.
Case 4	No, as the decisions would then be made with focus on money and not on the target. However, after such an instrument would be introduced and has achieved acceptance then eventually this connection could be made.
Case 5	No, the gender balanced scorecard should not be connected to bonus schemes for the top management because the positive impact alone should be enough. Besides, top management needs to support every scorecard or initiative that they decide to implement without connecting it to monetary bonuses. First of all, the awareness of top management should be raised towards the issue of gender mainstreaming/equality before bonus connections can be put in place.
Case 6	Yes, the implementation and execution of a gender balanced scorecard may be connected to bonus schemes of HR-top management (not CEO-level), but with regard to the neutrality of career opportunities in respect of gender, religion, etc. Consequently, the existence of instruments serving as a frame should be assessed and related to bonus schemes, not the obligation to achieve certain quotas (to make sure that only qualification decides on staffing).

Table 17: Responses to the question: should the results of a gender balanced scorecard be connected to incentives/bonuses for top management in order to get commitment?

To the question whether the respondents could think of other ways to get commitment from top management for the implementation of a gender balanced scorecard only the two respondents from the multinational organisations had ideas. One respondent answered that a ½-day awareness session should help which is a measure that they already put in place. This session is especially about inclusion, not so much about diversity. The other respondent stated that the implementation of principles helping to achieve gender equality in company guidelines could be another way (besides bonuses) to get the commitment from the top management for the implementation of a gender balanced scorecard.

Resistance to the gender balanced scorecard
In table 18 the responses to the question whether the introduction of the gender balanced scorecard would lead to resistance can be found.

	Responses to the question: Would the introduction of a gender balanced scorecard lead to resistance?
Case 1	Yes, the Dutch part of the organisation traditionally has been a quite macho culture/organisation. The products used to be very male customer-oriented technological products and maybe partly as a result of this many of the employees in the Dutch office were male. The IT/technological industry has always been quite a male industry (e.g. it is a fact that not many women study an IT subject) and therefore issues like gender equality have not really been stressed as important in the European organisation. Therefore, it is very likely, that there would be resistance to the implementation of such a tool as many employees wouldn't recognise the importance of it for the organisation.
Case 2	The respondent does not think that there would be a lot of resistance in the organisation towards new gender initiatives, as the majority of the employees are currently female. The HR-consultants which form the majority of the workforce are all well educated (minimum is either higher education degree or university degree) and very often female (probably 85%) which makes the workforce of this organisation quite unique.
Case 3	Yes, this would lead to high resistance in the organisation. The respondent believes that resistance would be a bigger issue with regards to gender measures than towards the general diversity/cultural issues. As she stated: "Sometimes I go into ridiculous discussions and afterwards I conclude that it was resistance toward the new diversity measures and ideas. We try to increase awareness of the subject and we found that we can only introduce one or two indicators at a time which are easy to understand and therefore easier to accept. Step by step we continue but we start only with indicators which make total business sense and are very outcome-related (e.g. return on investment for initiatives)."
Case 4	Yes, specific gender initiatives would be difficult to implement and would encounter high resistance. An important reason according to the interviewee is that the organisation is a factory and the majority of employees on the factory floor (mostly low skilled labour) are from different cultures and religions. The interviewee remarked: *"I believe that to successfully manage our multicultural work environment is challenging enough for us."* He continued: *"under the diversity management that we do undertake in this area - i.e. cultural and religious conflict managing/avoiding - a small part of gender management is included as well, even, if this is not actively managed but only passively acted upon."* Furthermore, the interviewee believes that gender should not influence the decision-making process about which candidate gets the job. He believes that this is another issue that would lead to high resistance in the organisation.
Case 5	Resistance to such initiatives are likely to occur. This may happen at all levels in the organisation not only from the top managers (who like to do things in the 'old ways'). The interviewee also has the opinion that the best person should get the job independent of gender.
Case 6	Resistance to a gender balanced scorecard would occur when certain committed quotas have to be achieved. If it would be designed as an instrument that only serves to achieve gender equality then the resistance should be limited.

Table 18: Responses to the question: Would the introduction of a gender balanced scorecard provoke resistance?

In most of the organisations it is likely that resistance to the introduction of a gender balanced scorecard would occur. The only exception is the second case study where the majority of the employees are highly educated females and for this reason such initiatives are more likely to be accepted by the vast majority.

Acceptance and possible implementation of the gender balanced scorecard as instrument to change organisational culture and include gender mainstreaming
In Germany one respondent mentioned that gender initiatives are more likely to be implemented in positive economic circumstances. This organisation is currently not hiring new employees and do not plan to change this in the near future.

As the respondent explained: *"Until the economic situation improves and the company improves its business results the focus of the personnel department is not on structural changes, policies and improvements but on daily management of the personnel issues. Hopefully in the future when the economy booms again this can change and there will also be a focus on different managerial issues or new instruments that could improve the private life of the employees."* He added that he believes that all employees in Germany are currently just happy to have their job and that he does not hear many complaints from employees about their situation at all.

The respondent from the Dutch multinational organisation thinks that a gender balanced scorecard as a strategic instrument to achieve gender equality would be difficult to introduce and maybe it is taking it a step too far and too specific. She prefers the diversity issue as a complete concept (were gender is only one special part). Especially, since it is her belief that the resistance would be higher to a gender specific instrument whereas the diversity/inclusion concept is easier to accept (as it is a management trend). Besides this she also thinks that you would have too many different scorecards, i.e. a special gender scorecard, a special cultural scorecard, etc. this would get too complicated and difficult to manage. In table 19 the responses to this question can be found.

	Responses to the question: *"Do you think that a gender balanced scorecard could be a tool that could help to change the organisational culture of your organisation?"*
1	*"I do believe this because it helps to get all employees involved in the business and it motivates them to believe in a certain mission. Furthermore, it would increase their understanding of the reasons behind certain business decisions. Thirdly, a specific gender balanced scorecard would really achieve a focus on the problem. However, for our European organisation it would not be relevant but in the USA more interest may exist. Especially, since in the USA the costs of litigation against an employer for unequal treatment could be considerable. For our Dutch offices the relevance of such a tool is currently lacking and until the profitability situation has improved gender equality measures will not be part of our strategy."*
2	*"What I noticed is that the organisation has gotten harder and more demanding because the market conditions are getting harder. At bad economic times, when demand is lower than the supply of labour, the organisational climate is harder and more commercial. In other periods when demand is higher than the supply of labour then it is softer. In such periods new HR-initiatives could be introduced in the organisation. However, currently the situation is not all that favourable and therefore, it is unlikely that such a scorecard would be introduced to the strategic aims of the organisation. Besides this, gender is not a real urgent problem and no complaint has arrived at the top so why would active measures be undertaken? It is more likely that our HR consultants would introduce the concept to potential clients who are interested in human resource solution packages."*
3	*"In our organisation we have set the target already to move to 10% women in top management positions around the 2008 mark which is progress but not really break-through progress. We have put people in place in the corporate headquarters that focus solely on diversity and inclusion issues. Measuring is maybe not as extensive as you are proposing with a gender balanced scorecard but we do get an overview of were we are, what the trends are, what the competitors do. This is already a step forward. We, at HR, can measure anything that can really help us to underpin a business case and with such information you could go to the top managers and they would listen and seriously consider steps forwards. Indicators which are not directly measurable (soft indicators) would be very hard to convince the right people to take it forward. Therefore, the key performance indicators have to be credible and robust."*
4	*"As a manufacturing organisation we encounter a multi-cultural environment where merely the different religions and cultures are leading to tension between people. If we would try to aim at 'balancing' male and female employees we would - without a doubt - encounter a lot of resistance at all levels in the organisation but mainly at the factory floor."* The interviewee does not think that such an instrument would be accepted currently in the German offices. Maybe when the economic situation improves people in the organisation are more open to such initiatives. In the Dutch offices such an initiative could find support from a small majority.
5	*"I believe that we don't need a specific gender balanced scorecard, because our culture is open to everybody who is qualified."* The interviewee continued that gender equality is not a strategic aim and that management is not aware of a situation that would demand such initiatives.
6	*"A gender balanced scorecard could only be a good instrument if it was designed to monitor issues with regards to gender equality. However, if it would be used as an instrument to steer quotas for the sake of quotas then it would not be a very useful instrument and it would actually be received with high resistance in the organisation. This organisation has already developed extensive measures and initiatives in the area of gender equality also by using statistical analysis. Some of these statistics could maybe be used on the official balanced scorecard to achieve a focus on them. However, a special gender balanced scorecard sounds too difficult to achieve and would also be very complex to implement in this organisation."*

Table 19: Responses to the question: "Do you think that a gender balanced scorecard
could be a tool that could help to change the organisational culture?"

7.3.3 The perspectives and gender indicators
This part of the interview was given to the respondents in order that they could fill this out before or after the interview. First of all, the four traditional perspectives were analysed and the respondents could decide whether the indicators under this perspective would be 'important', 'of average importance' or 'not important' for their organisations. Then four optional additional perspectives were analysed in the same way.

Traditional four perspectives
1. Financial perspective
In table 20 the perceived importance of the indicators under the financial perspective can be found.

Financial perspective	Really important	Average importance	Not important	Not applicable
Turnover per employee, differentiating between men and women	4	0	2	
Amount of money saved as a result of gender initiatives	1	4	1	
Benefits costs as a percentage of payroll or revenue	0	6	0	
Return on investment for the gender initiatives	4	2	0	
Gender initiative expenses per employee	5	0	1	
Gender initiative budget as a percentage of sales	0	3	3	
Reduced litigation costs	0	1	2	3

Table 20: Perceived importance of the indicators under the financial perspective

The most important indicator is the 'gender initiative expenses per employee' selected by five respondents as really important. This is followed by 'return on investment for the gender initiatives' and 'turnover per employee differentiating between men and women' which four of the six respondents stated to be really important. However of the two respondents that found the indicator: 'turnover per employee differentiating between men and women' not important one stated as remark that the majority of employees are female which would make this indicator not relevant. The reduced litigation costs were not applicable in Europe according to three respondents. They believe that this could be relevant in, for example, the USA.

2. Customer perspective

In table 21 the perceived importance of the indicators under the customer perspective can be found.

Customer perspective	Really important	Average importance	Not important	Not applicable
Market share division between female and male customers and the representation in the workforce of male and female employees	3	0	1	2
Percentage diverse customer satisfaction	3	0	1	2
Number of new customers attracted by male and female employees	1	2	3	
Percentage customer retention by male and female employees	2	2	2	
Number of solutions offered per client by male and female employees	0	2	4	
Percentage on-time delivery rating by male and female employees	0	1	5	
Profitability by male and female customers	0	3	1	2
Number of customer complaints successfully dealt with by male and female employees	0	3	2	1
Number of customer awards received	2	2	1	1

Table 21: Perceived importance of the indicators under the customer perspective

Under the customer perspective no indicators were selected to be really important by a majority of respondents. One issue was that two respondents are working in organisations that do not directly deal with customers. The third respondent noted that the majority of their customer base is male. For these three respondents several indicators were not applicable or important for these reasons.

3. Internal business processes perspective

In table 22 the perceived importance of the indicators under the internal business processes perspective can be found. Under this perspective two indicators are really important for all six interviewees, namely: 'employee satisfaction and female employee satisfaction (to be assessed with questionnaires)' and 'social audit results'. With regards to 'throughput time per business action for male and female employees' two respondents remarked that this would be too difficult to measure for an individual employee as this is teamwork. According to one respondent this also applies for 'new product introduction' as this is also a team effort.

Internal Business processes perspective	Really important	Average importance	Not important
Throughput time per business action for male and female employees	0	4	2
New product introduction and design (male versus female employees)	0	4	2
Number of awards received for equality/diversity initiatives	1	3	2
Employee satisfaction and female employee satisfaction (to be assessed with questionnaires)	6	0	0
Social audit results	6	0	0

Table 22: Perceived importance of the indicators under the internal business processes perspective

4. Learning and growth perspective

In table 23 the perceived importance of the indicators under the learning and growth perspective can be found.

Learning and growth perspective	Really important	Average importance	Not important	Not applicable
Number of female employees	4	2	0	
Number of female managers / leaders	3	3	0	
Number and percentage of gender-competent/trained employees	2	0	4	
Comparison of educational budget spent on women and men	1	2	3	
Motivation index	6	0	0	
Productivity (male vs. female employees)	3	3	0	
Cross functional assignments (male vs. female employees)	0	4	1	1
Personal goal achievement (male vs. female employees)	0	4	2	
Ethic violations	5	0	1	
Percentage of employees with advanced degrees for male and female employees	0	4	2	
Number of innovations initiated by male vs. female employees	0	3	2	1
Empowerment index (i.e. the number of female employees vs. male employees that have received a certain level of power or authority to make higher level decisions)	3	2	1	

Table 23: Perceived importance of the indicators under the learning and growth perspective

The 'motivation index' was an indicator that all six respondents selected as really important. This was followed by 'ethic violations' which five interviewees found really important. One of the respondents who found the 'percentage of employees with an advanced degree' not important mentioned that in their organisation approximately 95 percent of the employees have an advanced degree.

Additional Perspectives
The results to the question: *'which of the following (optional) additional perspectives would be relevant perspectives for your organisation to add on to the gender balanced scorecard?'* can be found in figure 23.

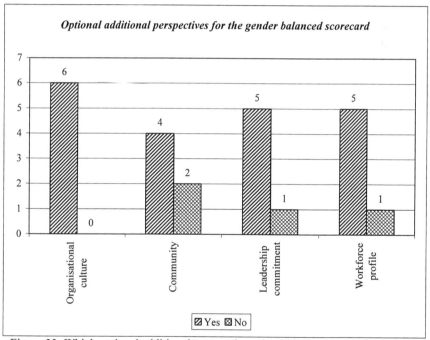

Figure 23: Which optional additional perspectives should be included on the gender balanced scorecard according to the sample organisations

It shows that all respondents agreed that the **organisational culture** perspective should be included on the gender balanced scorecard. One of the respondents commented that the organisation is aiming to develop a culture of inclusion and to do this it is critical to continue with awareness raising and to increase the support of management.

According to two respondents the **community** perspective was not very relevant to their business. On the contrary, one other respondent stated here that **the community perspective** should definitely be on their scorecard as this organisation wants to be involved in the society and be a responsible organisation that adds positively to the community. Another respondent who mentioned that **community** should also be a different perspective explained that this would help to focus on cultural differences in the world and communities.

One respondent had some doubt with regards to the **leadership commitment perspective** whether it should be separate or not. She commented that this perspective might fit under the organisational culture perspective as well but in the end decided to leave it as a separate perspective. Two other respondents did decide that **leadership commitment** should be included under the **organisational culture perspective** and should not be a separate perspective. One of them remarked that the indicators under leadership commitment would fit very well under the cultural perspective and should not be treated separately. Only one respondent did not select leadership commitment as a separate perspective.

The respondent who doubted whether leadership commitment should be treated separately (or under organisational culture) also had doubts about the **workforce profile perspective**. She mentioned that the indicators under this perspective might also be divided over the traditional four perspectives. However, in the end also here she decided to leave it as a separate perspective. One other respondent had the same comment about **workforce profile** and did not select it as a separate perspective but said that he would separate the indicators mentioned and divide them over the four traditional perspectives.

1. Organisational culture
In table 24 the perceived importance of the indicators under the organisational culture perspective can be found.

Three indicators were selected as really important by five of the six respondents, namely: 'absence rate/percentage absenteeism', 'percentage favourable ratings on climate/culture surveys for male and female employees' and 'organisation's 'openness' ratings'.

Organisational culture	Really important	Average importance	Not important	Not applicable
Percentage favourable ratings on cultural audit	1	4	0	1
'Employer of choice' ratings versus top 5 to 10 competitors	3	1	1	1
Perception of consistent and equitable treatment of all employees	4	2	0	
Gender equity tied to management compensation	1	3	2	
Absence rate / percentage absenteeism	5	1	0	
Retention rate of critical human capital	2	2	2	
Percentage gender initiatives fully implemented	1	4	1	
Percentage favourable ratings on climate/culture surveys for male and female employees	5	1	0	
Average time for dispute resolution	0	5	1	
Employee referral rate by male and female employees	0	4	2	
Percentage gender-based pay differentials	2	4	0	
Percentage work-life balance benefits utilised	3	1	1	1
Workplace flexibility index ratings	0	5	1	
Organisation's 'openness' ratings	5	1	0	

Table 24: Perceived importance of the indicators under the organisational culture perspective

2. Community

The community perspective was selected by four of the six respondents. Two respondents think that this should not be a separate perspective on the gender balanced scorecard. In table 25 the perceived importance of the indicators under the community perspective can be found.

'Company image' was selected as most important indicator by three of the four respondents. It has to be noted that all respondents agreed that 'percentage subcontracting euros to women-owned businesses' was not an important indicator.

Community	Really important	Average importance	Not important
Percentage subcontracting euros to women-owned businesses	0	0	4
Money given to the community	1	1	2
Awards received from the community	2	2	0
Company image (e.g. being an 'employer of choice' for potential female employees)	3	1	0

Table 25: Perceived importance of the indicators under the community perspective

3. Leadership commitment
Leadership commitment was selected by five out of the six respondents. One respondent choose not to include this perspective as a separate perspective. In table 26 the perceived importance of the indicators under the leadership commitment perspective can be found.

Leadership commitment	Really important	Average importance	Not important
Leadership participation in designing the vision and strategies for achieving gender mainstreaming	4	1	0
The number of female employees in formal mentoring programmes with the leader	2	3	0
The number of female employees personally selected by the leader for special assignments	0	3	2
The percentage of gender objectives that are tied to key strategic business objectives connected to the bonus and compensation of the leader	1	2	2
The representation mix on the organisation's board of directors	3	2	0
Leadership representation on the gender steering committee and advisory boards	2	2	1
The degree of personal participation in creating an inclusive climate/culture	2	3	0
The ability of the leader to overcome tension when it arises in the change process	3	1	1
Money and other resources allocated by the leader to the gender mainstreaming initiative	4	1	0
The number of executives and managers that are competent due to training in dealing with gender mainstreaming issues	1	2	2
Leadership behaviour towards work–life balance issues (such as flexible working hours, glass-ceiling issues and family leave policies)	4	1	0

Table 26: Perceived importance of the indicators under the leadership commitment perspective

The following indicators were selected by four of five respondents as really important: 'leadership participation in designing the vision and strategies for achieving gender mainstreaming', 'money and other resources allocated by the leader to the gender mainstreaming initiative' and 'leadership behaviour towards work–life balance issues (such as flexible working hours, glass-ceiling issues and family leave policies)'.

4. Workforce profile
Also the workforce profile perspective was selected by five of the six respondents. In table 27 the perceived importance of the indicators under the workforce profile perspective can be found.

Workforce profile	Really important	Average importance	Not important	Not applicable
Percentage female new hires	0	4	1	
Percentage female managers and officials	2	3	0	
Percentage female survival and loss rate	4	1	0	
Percentage turnover by length of service	1	3	1	
Percentage absenteeism for male and female employees	3	1	1	
Percentage voluntary turnover: exempt and non-exempt	1	4	0	
Percentage involuntary turnover: exempt and non-exempt	1	4	0	
Number of offers to female interviewees	0	4	1	
Cost per hire	0	1	4	
Number returning from leave for male and female employees	1	2	1	1

Table 27: Perceived importance of the indicators under the workforce profile perspective

Only one indicator was selected as really important by four of the five respondents namely 'percentage female survival and loss rate'. On the contrary, the 'cost per hire' was selected by four respondents as not important.

7.3.4 Organisational structure & culture

Organisational structure
Table 28 shows the different structures the sample organisations in the different countries have adopted.

	Structure of organisation	Size of organisation	Country
Case 1	Flat & Matrix	Medium	NL
Case 2	Flat	Large	NL
Case 3	Matrix	Multinational	NL (& G)
Case 4	Bureaucratic/hierarchical	Medium	G (& NL)
Case 5	Flat	Large	G
Case 6	Matrix	Multinational	G

Table 28: Structures of sample organisations

Prior attempts to change organisational culture
Five of the six respondents are not aware of active attempts to change the organisational culture of the organisation. In one of the Dutch sample organisations an internal cultural audit is done regularly to review whether the culture fits the aims and goals of the organisation.

In one of the multinational organisations active attempts to change the organisational culture of the organisation have been undertaken. This was done based on the outcomes of research among high potential talents which left the organisation. They were questioned about their experiences with the organisational culture and they where invited to join round-table discussions about key issues. From these interviews and discussions it was found that the organisational culture had four main issues with regards to leadership. These issues were handled and addressed. The senior managers are now fulfilling a 360-degree feedback evaluation where the employees under this leader also can give their feedback. One of the questions was: "what do we actually expect from our leaders?" Based on the outcome one of the aims became to achieve behavioural changes in the leaders. Leadership issues have actually been the only reason for the organisation to try and change its culture (by changing leadership behaviour). Diversity is not a key issue at this point. For this reason cultural changes are not initiated but there are people in place with diversity as their special focus and the diversity challenge is being addressed in the organisation at all levels.

Comparison between German and Dutch organisational cultures
It is very difficult to describe the organisational culture of an organisation, especially, since the feeling about the climate/culture is quite subjective. However, some of the interviewees described the organisational culture of their organisation according to their perception.

A Dutch respondent describes the organisational culture as: *"very open and informal (quite Dutch probably) and everybody calls the CEO and other top managers by their first names"*. The structure of this organisation in the Netherlands can be called flat, however, there are clear layers to the top but there are very few layers.

One of the German respondents mentioned that the German business has had an old and pretty conservative culture, which is currently undergoing change. As he mentioned: *"today it seems not to be any longer important what gender it is in the organisation. The international focus has taken over and the changes in the economies and environment have led to adaptations in the culture of the organisation."* This organisation has also adopted a flat structure and as the respondent mentioned the company is first of all an international organisation and secondly a German company.

There were two respondents who had worked in both the Dutch and German offices and because of this they were able to make a comparison between these two organisational cultures in both countries.

First of all, the interviewee from one of the two multinational organisations was able to compare the organisational cultures of the German organisation to the Dutch organisation. She concluded that the openness of the Dutch organisation is much bigger. The traditional German hierarchical structures still prevail and the top down approach is widespread. In the Netherlands it tends to be a flatter line of command and the individual is allowed to act more upon own initiatives (less bureaucracy and formal rules). Maybe, this can also be explained by the national culture, as the Germans are more familiar with following rules and regulations in the formal way. They are not familiar with laissez-faire management styles and might not really feel comfortable if this would be demanded from them. However, the 'old boys' network' is in place in both organisations. This still is the main obstacle to the upwards promotion of highly talented female employees.

Gender measures are good in both cultures. In Germany the governmental regulations (e.g. the female employee who takes parental leave has the right to return to her old job for the duration of three years) are very good. In the Netherlands the concepts of job-sharing and part-time work are widespread and accepted which allows more women to combine family-life with work-life. Even in higher positions part-time work starts to be accepted for female employees in the Netherlands which is a good step forward to achieving more equality.

One other respondent was able to offer a comparison between the organisational cultures of the Dutch office/factory to the German factory and stated the German offices are definitely more official, bureaucratic and hierarchical. As he stated: *"In Holland it is easier for employees to come into the personnel department and discuss their personal situation. In Germany this doesn't happen very often. Partly because the Germans are currently afraid to loose their jobs as the economic situation is bad but also because of the culture of the people. In Holland everything is less formal and an example here is that people address each other by their first names."*

7.6 Conclusion

The primary research results have been the subject of this chapter. The analysis of the interviews could be divided in four parts. First of all the current situation in the participating organisations with regards to gender measures was analysed. The second part of the interview dealt with the gender balanced scorecard development. Thirdly the perspectives and indicators of a gender balanced scorecard were analysed. The last part was about the organisational structure and culture. In the next chapter the conclusions will be drawn about these results connected to the theoretical knowledge gathered in chapters 2, 3, 4 and 5.

Part IV: Conclusions and Recommendations

8 Conclusions

In this chapter the theoretical background will be combined with the results of the empirical research which together will serve as the basis for the conclusions.

Reasons for gender mainstreaming
It can be concluded that due to the economic, legal and demographic changes (for example the aging population) in Germany and the Netherlands, and the changes in the markets and the nature of work in these countries, the interest to include more female employees in the workplace is increasing (see Ch. 1, p 22). It can create a competitive advantage for organisations to have a balanced workforce of both female employees and male employees (see Ch. 3.4, p 44). The advantages of gender mainstreaming can be identified in three different business areas: the human resource advantage, the marketing advantage and the cost element (see table 2, p 46). The primary research showed that the majority of the respondents (four out of six respondents) found 'loyal & motivated employees – reduce absenteeism' to be the most important advantage of gender mainstreaming This was followed by 'loss of motivation of workforce & productivity' and 'diverse work teams' which three of the respondents selected as really important advantage of gender mainstreaming (see figure 20, p 138).

One of the main dilemmas many female employees face (at a certain time in their career) is how to combine work-life with family-life. Solutions for organisations when they want to assist with this issue are offered at a wider scale nowadays but they often focus on short term practical solutions (i.e. the general gender measures). Solutions to change the organisational culture of the organisation to embrace gender mainstreaming are not researched very often (see Ch. 3.6, p 57).

However, according to three respondents of the primary research the organisational culture is an obstacle to gender mainstreaming and if this would change the work-life/family-life balance would improve. Other important obstacles are ingrained attitudes ('old boys' network') and lack of family-life/work-life balance support according to two of the respondents (see figure 21, p 140). When the organisational culture would change also changes in organisational structure will usually occur (see Ch. 4.2.1, p 64). The organisational structure has to fit to the culture and the strategy of the organisation.

Organisational structure and culture
For this reason many organisations have adopted flatter structures in order to deal with the new challenges that surround them. Also in Germany flatter structures are becoming more popular. From the complete research sample only one German organisation still uses a hierarchical structure and according to the respondent this organisation is also quite negative towards gender measures and issues and the culture is very closed and hierarchical (closed system with tight control, Hofstede, 2001, see also Ch. 4.2, p 61). On the other hand, one other German respondent mentioned that his organisation has actually started to change (not actively managed) away from this traditional hierarchy and in this organisation flat structures are introduced and the culture starts to change into a more international culture where not many typical German characteristics are left (for example shorter lines of command and first names are used leading to an open system with loose control according to Hofstede, 2001) (see Ch. 4.2, p 61 and Ch. 7.3.4, p 155).

It is very difficult to change corporate cultures and many cultures are still too often imbued with 'male values' of dominance, aggression, competition and 'transmitting' rather than 'receiving' (Davidson, et al., 2004, see Ch. 4.3.2, p 69). This was also recognised by one of the Dutch respondents who noticed that there where few women are at high positions who have a private life with children. The respondent stated that the culture is a macho culture and the employees are very ambitious (working long hours) which leaves no space for work-life/family-life balance even though the structure is a flat/matrix combination. Most respondents were not aware of active attempts of the organisation to change the culture/climate. Only the Dutch multinational had undertaken active attempts to change the culture with regards to leadership issues they identified. None of the respondents are aware of active changes to achieve gender mainstreaming/equality in the organisational culture (see Ch. 7.3.4, p 155). Changing corporate culture is a very complex process which involves support from all levels in the organisation but, as most experts agree, it should be initiated at the top (see Ch. 4.3.2, p 69).

The amount of available gender measures and the effectiveness and use of these gender measures will of course have a huge impact on the organisational culture of the organisations. When more people (also male employees) would make use of these measures it would become normal for the total workforce and will have impact on the organisational climate. Some conclusions can be drawn from the assessment of the current situation with regards to gender measures in the sample organisations (see Ch. 7.2.1, p 136). Special childcare measures are used most by five of the six sample organisations followed by work-life/family-life balance support through flexible hours, home office, etc. Mentoring and special guidelines are used by three organisations and coaching and special agreements are put in place in two organisations in the sample. The most complete packages are offered by the multinational organisations in both the Netherlands and Germany. Three respondents mentioned that gender measures are only offered to comply with the legal requirements of the government. The three other respondents offered all measures required by the government but on top a complete package of additional measures. The evaluation of the effectiveness of gender measures is done by the majority of the respondents via satisfaction questionnaires or during the yearly performance reviews (see Ch. 7.2.1, p 136).

Gender balanced scorecard
The gender balanced scorecard could offer a good alternative way to review the performance of the organisation with regards to gender measures. The traditional balanced scorecard is a set of measures that gives top management a fast but comprehensive view of the business from four perspectives (Kaplan & Norton, 1992, see also Ch. 2.2.1, p 27). The balanced scorecard is a tool to achieve change which is exactly what also the gender balanced scorecard aims to achieve, namely a change in organisational culture to include gender mainstreaming (see also Ch. 5.3.3, p 80). With regards to the development of a specific gender balanced scorecard it can be concluded that first of all general awareness and the levels of acceptance should be raised towards the issue of gender equality and gender mainstreaming (see also Ch. 3.5.1, p 53). To find out what the level of maturity of top management is in the organisation a number of criteria can be analysed which can be taken from social audits or from total equality management initiatives (see Ch. 3.5.2, p 54). When this is analysed a marketing/communications plan can help to raise the awareness and maturity of the employees towards a gender initiative like the gender balanced scorecard (see Ch. 5.4, p 82). Then, the organisation could start to design the gender balanced scorecard, which should be a combination of the traditional balanced scorecard perspectives plus any relevant additional perspectives (see Ch. 5.5.1, p 86). There are seven steps organisations would go through when they develop a gender balanced scorecard: define the vision, develop strategies for the perspectives to achieve this vision, define indicators under the perspectives to be able to measure the results of the actions, collect the data for the indicators and convert the contributions to money/tangible value, identify the critical success factors, develop the message-scorecard/action plan and feedback and learning (see Ch. 5.5.1, p 86).

However, the research shows that at the moment the implementation of a complete gender balanced scorecard is not very likely to take place in the sample organisations (see Ch. 7.3.2, p 141). Even the organisations that are the furthest ahead with gender measures and awareness are doubtful that this instrument could be implemented at this stage. There are a number of obstacles to the successful implementation of the gender balanced scorecard including complexity of design and instrument, bad economic situation, how to measures intangible assets, the name of the initiative and resistance to the initiative. That it is a complex management tool to design is clear and therefore high commitment would be needed towards the implementation of the gender balanced scorecard.

A second issue that led to doubt (for at least two respondents) about the implementation of such an instrument is the current bad financial situation of the organisation (see Ch. 7.3.2, p 141). Organisations that have achieved negative business results are more likely to ignore personnel issues. Their main focus is to improve the business results, i.e. the profits, and therefore, there is no time or budget to work on specific HRM issues. One German organisation also stated that the economic performance of the country has an impact on the focus of the organisation. Owing to the fact that Germany is currently in recession the outlook for the organisation in the direct future is negative and therefore the personnel department should only focus on daily business not on strategic issues for improvement. Because two organisations from both countries mentioned that first the business results should improve before strategic issues can become a business aim it can be concluded that this is not country-specific but applies to organisation across the borders.

How can an intangible asset like gender mainstreaming create tangible results? Any initiative an organisation decides to implement should be able to demonstrate payback in a certain period of time and the results should be tangible (see also Ch. 5.5.3, p 94). For this reason it is important that the management of the organisation is able to convert soft data into money value that can show tangible results for the initiative. The special gender indicators under the different perspectives of the gender balanced scorecard can actually be a great help to show the tangible results of the gender initiative.

What's in a name? Another negative aspect of the gender balanced scorecard that could lead to resistance is the name of the management tool. Several of the interview partners mentioned that a general diversity initiative is a more popular term and is likely to be accepted by management at all levels both male and female (see Ch. 7.3.2, p 141). They usually place the gender initiatives under the name diversity initiatives or inclusion initiatives to overcome (mainly male) resistance. Popular terms to use currently are *'diversity'*, *'inclusive climate/ culture'* and *'inclusion'*. These terms are used in popular management literature and therefore acceptance for specific gender initiatives under such an overall name is easier. Therefore, it can be concluded that it is important to give gender measures and initiatives a name that can easily be accepted by middle and higher management (which is still very often male dominated).

Resistance
Resistance is probably the biggest obstacle to the implementation of the gender balanced scorecard. One Dutch respondent of the primary research was very much in favour of the gender balanced scorecard idea because it would get the employees focussed on the issue but rejected it for their European business due to the fact that the importance of the problem would not be recognised by the majority of the employees and it would lead to resistance (see Ch. 7.3.2, p 141). She could imagine that it would be introduced in the USA as litigation costs might be high there in gender legal cases. All other respondents also mentioned that the biggest concern they had with such an instrument would be the high amount of resistance that would occur. The only exception in the research was a Dutch organisation where the majority of the employees are highly educated females. Some part of the resistance would come from organisations having a macho/male culture and another part because the awareness is lacking for the importance of this issue. Two interviewees were very reluctant to the idea and commented that this would be another way of setting quotas (i.e. so many female employees have to be in place) instead of focussing on the best person for the job.

Hauschildt identified barriers of unwillingness and barriers of ignorance which have to be overcome to achieve innovation and these two barriers also apply to the gender balanced scorecard (see also Ch. 5.7.2, p 108). There are six change approaches that can help to deal with resistance to change (Kotter and Schlesinger, 1979, see Ch.5.7.3, p 111): education and communication, partici- pation and involvement, facilitation and support, negotiation and agreement, manipulation and co-option and explicit and implicit coercion. The open reporting of the gender balanced scorecard together with extensive education and communication could be an effective way to lower these barriers of ignorance and unwillingness. This is especially important because it is essential that the resistance to a gender balanced scorecard is solved and that the levels of awareness and acceptance are increased before the gender balanced scorecard could be introduced successfully.

Here the promotor model could also be used which could assist with aligning all employees with the new strategy (see Ch. 5.7.1, p 103). The promotor model can be used to manage the process of change that would lead to the acceptance of an engendered organisational culture. In table 10 (p 106) the characteristics of the roles of the promotoren for building and implementing a gender balanced scorecard can be found. This table shows the need for a technology promotor with specialist knowledge about gender issues, a process promotor in the form of middle management, a relationship promotor, i.e. a communication specialist and a power promotor in the form of support by the top management team and the CEO. Also the respondents in the primary research all agreed that it should be a joint effort of two or more departments and/or gender specialists to design and implement a gender balanced scorecard (see Ch. 7.3.2, p 141). If a gender balanced scorecard would be developed and introduced the majority of the respondents (five of six) had the opinion that this should be done by the personnel/HRM department of the organisation. The other party that should be involved according to four respondents is the CEO and the top management team. Three respondents would give responsibility to both parties, i.e. the CEO/top management team in cooperation with the personnel/HRM department. It can therefore be said that such an initiative should be introduced by at least the CEO/top management team (power promotor) in combination with the personnel/HRM department (technology promotor) and when needed additional assistance from gender experts can be put in place.

How to get commitment from the CEO and top management (the power promotor)? It can be concluded from the primary research that the only way to get commitment from top management will be to combine the results of the gender balanced scorecard to incentives/bonuses for top management (see Ch. 7.3.2, p 141). All respondents agreed that this eventually will have to happen but they do not agree on when this should be done. Some respondents think that first awareness/acceptance should be raised before such a connection could be put in place otherwise resistance could occur. However, to get the commitment of the leader is a critical success factor in the gender balanced scorecard project and without it the project is doomed to fail.

The gender balanced scorecard perspectives and indicators
An important step in the development of a gender balanced scorecard is identifying the critical success factors (see also Ch. 5.6.1, p 99). When they are identified they should be compared to the vision, mission and strategy to review to which extend it is a relevant factor to analyse and include on the gender balanced scorecard. Furthermore, for the actual design of a gender balanced scorecard the perspectives and gender indicators which should be on the gender balanced scorecard need to be selected (see Ch. 7.3.3, p 147).

It can be concluded that under the *financial perspective* three indicators were identified as being really important to the majority of the respondents: gender initiative expenses per employee (five respondents), return on investment for the gender initiative (four respondents) and turnover per employee differentiating between men and women (four respondents).

Under the *customer perspective* there were no really important indicators that were selected by a clear majority. The main reason for this is that two respondents do not have direct customer contact and one respondent has a very male customer base. For the other respondents market share division between female and male customers and the representation in the workforce of male and female employees (three respondents) was really important and also the percentage diverse customer satisfaction (three respondents).

About the *internal business processes perspective* it can be concluded that two indicators were really important, namely employee satisfaction and female employee satisfaction (to be assessed with questionnaires) and social audit results as these were selected by all respondents to be really important.

Under the *learning and growth perspective* also one indicator was selected by all respondents to be really important namely the motivation index. This was followed by ethic violations (five respondents) and number of female employees (four respondents).

From the four traditional perspectives it can be concluded that – even though each gender balanced scorecard is unique and would be specially designed for the organisation – three gender indicators were selected by all respondents to be really important:
- Employee satisfaction and female employee satisfaction (to be assessed with questionnaires)
- Social audit results
- The motivation index

With regard to additional perspectives that could be added to the gender balanced scorecard all respondents agreed that the organisational culture perspective should be definitely included (see Ch. 7.3.3, p 147). It can be said that the community perspective really depends on the line of business of the organisation whether this should get a place on the scorecard or not. However, more and more organisations wish to become 'employer of choice' and to achieve this they try to go beyond just complying with the regulations. For such organisations the community perspective could be a good way to analyse their effort in this area. The leadership commitment perspective was selected by five out of the six respondents. Two respondents doubted whether the indicators under this perspective should be included on the organisational culture perspective. The same applies to the workforce profile perspective. These indicators could also be divided over the different other perspectives. However, five out of the six respondents did select it as a separate perspective.

It can be said that under the *organisational culture perspective* three indicators were selected as really important by five respondents, namely: 'absence rate/percentage absenteeism', 'percentage favourable ratings on climate/culture surveys for male and female employees' and 'organisation's 'openness' ratings'.

Under the *community perspective* 'company image' was selected as most important indicator by three of the four respondents.

The following indicators were selected by four of five respondents as really important on the *leadership commitment perspective*: 'leadership participation in designing the vision and strategies for achieving gender mainstreaming', 'money and other resources allocated by the leader to the gender mainstreaming initiative' and 'leadership behaviour towards work-life balance issues (such as flexible working hours, glass-ceiling issues and family leave policies)'.

Under the *workforce profile perspective* only one indicator was selected as really important by the majority of the respondents (five respondents) namely 'percentage female survival and loss rate'.

Feedback and learning: the gender balanced scorecard as controlling tool
The last step in the development process of a gender balanced scorecard is feedback and learning (see Ch. 5.8, p 113). Open and regular reporting about the gender balanced scorecard are essential ingredients for the success of the project as this will allow for the organisation to track progress and to learn from the gender balanced scorecard instrument. The feedback will show how the measures of the gender balanced scorecard have assisted women to improve their position in the organisation as well as to help them to improve their family-life/work-life balance. The evaluation will also show how the organisational culture has changed after the implementation of the gender balanced scorecard instrument.

On the overall, it can be concluded that a gender balanced scorecard could be designed, developed and implemented successfully (even if this would be a complex issue) when it would be initiated, receives backup and support from all four promotors involved including the power promotor (CEO/Top management). This is also the main problem with the instrument as **resistance** is the biggest obstacle to its development in the first place. Another problem with gender mainstreaming is the difficulty to create tangible results from intangible assets. However, many of the indicators could be analysed without this problem. Therefore, if the level of maturity towards- and awareness of gender issues increases then the gender balanced scorecard could be an instrument that could assist organisations with their performance review to see whether their organisational culture is a culture that includes gender mainstreaming and, secondly, in the long term it could be an instrument that could assist organisations with the actual change process when they aim to become an organisation that includes gender mainstreaming in their organisational culture. One very important success factor to remember for this process is: *for organisational culture to change in a gender sensitive culture it is critical that the way people think is changed!*

9 Recommendations

The gender balanced scorecard instrument could serve as a base to achieve change in organisational culture which could lead to an organisation which embraces gender mainstreaming. In this chapter recommendations for organisations who want to achieve this aim will be given. Secondly, this chapter will identify recommendations for future research areas. Finally, also problems and limitations to the research will be identified.

The first recommendation for organisations that are dealing with gender issues is to review the level of maturity and acceptance in the organisation. As resistance is the biggest obstacle to gender initiatives it is important to start from this point and then see how awareness can be raised at all levels in the organisation. However, the starting point for the gender initiative should be at top management level. They should establish how ready they are and how ready their organisation is for the implementation of a gender initiative. When the level of awareness and level of maturity is analysed this will automatically show the amount of resistance that can be expected with the introduction of new gender measures or indicators. Improvements in this area can be analysed using employee questionnaires or other gender indicators. Also social audits and total equality management initiatives can be very helpful here.

It could positively influence the participants in the change process if the gender initiative is given a name that is easily acceptable for all people involved. Therefore it might be recommendable that gender initiatives are placed under an overall diversity initiative or inclusion initiative header. Especially, for top management which is still often male dominated this could help to increase support for the initiatives. When the levels of awareness and acceptance towards the gender initiative are raised successfully, the next phase of the design and development of a gender balanced scorecard can be initiated.

Because each balanced scorecard is uniquely developed for the organisation that decides to use it, the design of such a scorecard will look different for each situation and organisation. Besides using the four traditional perspectives, i.e. financial, customer, internal business processes and learning and growth, each organisation should review which additional perspectives should be added. It can be recommended to include the organisational culture perspective on every gender balanced scorecard as this is very relevant to the aim and was also selected by all respondents as very important. The community perspective could be interesting for organisations that want to become 'employer of choice' or have strong relationships and involvement in the community. Indicators under the leadership perspective could be separated and placed under the organisational culture perspective depending on the individual situation of the organisation and its leader. The same applies to the workforce profile which includes many statistical analysis indicators which could fit to other perspectives as well.

From the primary research results several gender indicators can be isolated that were really important to the majority of the respondents. The top three that were selected by all respondents as really important were:

1. Employee satisfaction and female employee satisfaction (to be assessed with questionnaires) (six respondents)
2. Social audit results (six respondents)
3. Motivation index (six respondents)

Other indicators that were selected by the majority of respondents as really important include the following:

- Gender initiative expenses per employee (five of six respondents)
- Ethic violations (five of six respondents)
- Absence rate/percentage absenteeism (five of six respondents)
- Percentage favourable ratings on climate/culture surveys for male and female employees (five of six respondents)
- Organisation's 'openness' ratings (five of six respondents)
- Leadership participation in designing the vision and strategies for achieving gender mainstreaming (four of five respondents)
- Money and other resources allocated by the leader to the gender mainstreaming initiative (four of five respondents)
- Leadership behaviour towards work–life balance issues (such as flexible working hours, glass-ceiling issues and family leave policies) (four of five respondents)
- Percentage female survival and loss rate (four of five respondents)
- Company image (three of four respondents)
- Return on investment for the gender initiative (four of six respondents)
- Turnover per employee differentiating between men and women (four of six respondents)
- Number of female employees (four of six respondents)
- Market share division between female and male customers (three of six respondents)
- Representation in the workforce of male and female employees (three of six respondents)
- Percentage diverse customer satisfaction (three of six respondents)

If organisations believe that they are not ready to develop and implement the complete gender balanced scorecard instrument it can be recommended that they start by placing some of these really important indicators that are relevant to their business on their traditional balanced scorecard (if they use this) or analyse them within their own performance measurement systems. The results of this analysis might lead to an increase in awareness and level of acceptance towards the issue in the organisation and then in its turn to an extension of the gender initiative.

Another recommendation can be made in the area of changing the organisational culture. The primary research has shown that not many organisations (except the Dutch multinational) are actively monitoring their organisational culture. When organisational culture should be changed it can be recommended to first analyse the current situation (i.e. draw the cultural map from Hofstede but then specifically comparing female and male aspects). Only after this is done the gaps and inequalities can be recognised and changes can be planned. Organisations should put change agents in place and the promotor model could be of good assistance here to help them get the right team of change agents.

As Jung and Küpper (2001) mentioned the actual implementation of gender mainstreaming by using measurement instruments, such as checklists, has to be developed and tested in practice. That is also one of the most important recommendations here. The gender balanced scorecard should be tested in practice in sample organisations. To do this, further research should be done including a practical test of this instrument in an organisation to review the effectiveness in practice and over a long time span.

It is important to understand that there may not be one best way to approach the measurement and management of business performance (in this case in the measurement of gender equality) for this is a very complex concept and the existing frameworks can only partially address it, essentially, they provide valuable point solutions (Neely, Adams & Kennerley, 2002).

This describes the limitation to this research as well. However, hopefully a valuable point solution is offered by this work. Even if only certain aspects of the research would be put into practice by organisations and this would help to improve the work-life/family-life balance situation of female employees the work could be called successful.

As a final recommendation it should be stated that for gender to become 'mainstream' it is very important that all indicators are analysed for both female and male employees. An example could be to review how many men make use of the option to work part-time. If the outcome is that this has increased in an organisation the gender mainstreaming measures could be successful. Gender should become 'mainstream' and for this reason it can be recommended that analysis should include both men and women. If men are no longer judged for working fewer hours (i.e. part-time) or top managers can easily state that they support gender equality without receiving 'funny' looks then gender mainstreaming initiatives have changed the way people think which is the prerequisite for the successful implementation of gender mainstreaming in organisational culture.

> *"The world we have created is a product of our way of thinking.*
> *It cannot be changed without changing the way that we think."*
> -Albert Einstein-

Bibliography

Literature

Aaker, D.A., Kumar, V., Day, G.S. – Marketing Research, John Wiley & Sons, Inc., USA, Eighth Edition, 2004

Ackermann, K.F. – Balanced Scorecard für Personalmanagement und Personalführung: Praxisansaetze und Diskussion, 1. Aufl., Gabler Wiesbaden, 2000

Ashkanasy, N.M., Härtel, C.E.J., Zerbe, W.J. – Emotions in the workplace; Research, theory and practice, Quorum Books, Westport, USA, 2000

Assig, D., Beck, A. – Frauen revolutionieren die Arbeitswelt. Das Handbuch zur Chancengerechtigkeit, München Verlag: Vahlen, 1996

Atkinson, P. – How to become a change master: real-world strategies for managing change, Spiro, 2005

Albrecht, M.H. – International HRM: Managing diversity in the workplace, Blackwell Publishers Ltd., Oxford, England, 2001

Autenrieth, C., Chemnitzer, K, Domsch, M.E. – Personalauswahl und – Entwicklung von weiblichen Führungskräften, Campus-Verlag, 1993

Becker, B.E., Huselid, M.A., Ulrich, D. – The HR Scorecard – Linking People, Strategy and Performance, Harvard Business School, Boston, Massachusetts, USA, 2001

Beckhard, R., Harris, R.T. – Organizational transitions: managing complex change, 2nd edition, AddisonWesley, 1987

Beckhard, R., Prichard, W. – Changing the essence, San Francisco, Jossey Bass, 1992

Behning, U. – Gender mainstreaming in the European employment strategy, European Trade Union Institute (ETUI), Brussel, 2001

Bendl, R. – Chancengleichheit am Arbeitsplatz für Frauen – Integration in die strategische Unternehmensführung, München/Mering, Rainer Hampp Verlag, 1997

Bendl, R. – Interdisziplinäres Gender- und Diversitätsmanagement: Einführung in Theorien und Praxis, Linde Verlag, Wien, Österreich, 2004

Blom, H., Meier, H. – Interkulturelles Management: interkulturelle Kommunikation, internationales Personalmanagement, Diversity-Ansätze im Unternehmen, Verlag neue Wirtschafts-briefe, 2. Auflage, 2004

Blyton, P., Blunsdon, B., Reed, K., Dastmalchian, A. – Work-life integration: international perspectives on the balancing of multiple roles, Palgrave Macmillan, 2006

Bradburn, N.M., Sudman, S., Wansink, B. – Asking questions: the definitive guide to questionnaire design – for market research, political polls, and social and health questionnaires, Jossey-Bass, San Francisco, USA, 2004

Bronwen, R. – Construction of management: competence and gender issues at work, Edward Elgar, Cheltenham, England, 2003

Cameron, E. – Making sense of change management: a complete guide to the models, tools and techniques of organisational change, Kogan Press, 2004

Catalyst (Wellington, S.) – Advancing women in business – The Catalyst Guide, Jossey-Bass Publishers, San Francisco, 1998

Cohen, D.S. – Heart of change field guide: tools and tactics for leading change in your organization, Harvard Business School Press, 2005

Clutterbuck, D. – Managing work-life balance: a guide for HR in achieving organisational and individual change, London, UK, Chartered Institute of Personnel and Development, 2003

Coghlan, D, Rashford – Organizational change and strategy: an interlevel dynamics approach, Routledge, 2006

Cokins, G. – Performance management: finding the missing pieces (to close the intelligence gap), John Wiley & Sons Inc., New Jersey, USA, 2004

Cook, S., Macaulay, S., Coldicott, H. – Change management excellence: using the four intelligences for successful organizational change, Kogan Page, 2004

Cox, T, Jr. – Creating the multicultural organization, Jossey-Bass, San Francisco, USA, 2001

Davidson, M.J., Burke, R.J. – Women in management worldwide: facts, figures and analysis, Ashgate Publishing, Ltd., Hants, England, 2004

Davidson, M.J., Burke, R.J. – Women in management: current research issues, Volume II, Sage Publications Ltd., London, England, 2000

Domsch, M.E., Ladwig, D.H., Tenten, E. – Gender equality in Central and Eastern European countries, Lang, 2003

Domsch, M.E., Hadler, A, Krüger, D. – Personalmanagement & Chancengleichheit: betriebliche Massnahmen zur Verbesserung beruflicher Chancen von Frauen in Hamburg, Rainer Hampp Verlag, 1994

Domsch, M.E., Ladwig, D.H. – Handbuch Mitarbeiterbefragung – Springer, 2006

Domsch, M.E., Macke, H., Schöne, K. – Weibliche Angestellte im Deutschen Transformationsprozeß, Rainer Hampp Verlag, 1996

Domsch, M.E., Regnet, E. – Weibliche Fach- und Führungskräfte – Wege zur Chancengleichheit, Schäffer Verlag, 1990

Domsch, M.E., Regnet, E., Rosenstiehl, L. von – Führung von Mitarbeitern: Fallstudien zum Personalmanagement, 2. Auflage, Schaeffer-Poeschel, 2001

Douglas, S.P., Craig, C.S. - International Marketing Research, John Wiley & Sons, 2nd Edition, 1999

Fitz-enz, J. – The ROI of Human Capital, Amacom, New York, USA, 2000

Fombrun, H., Van Giel, C. – Fame and fortune: How successful companies build winning reputations, Pearson Professional Education, 2003

Friedag, H.R., Schmidt, W. – My Balanced Scorecard: Das Praxishandbuch für Ihre individuelle Lösung; Fallstudien, Checklisten, Präsentationsvorlagen, 1. Aufl., 2000

182

Friedag, H.R., Schmidt, W. – Balanced Scorecard: Mehr als ein Kennzahlensystem, Freiburg, 2. Aufl. 2000

Friedag, H.R., Schmidt, W. – Balanced Scorecard, Freiburg, 2002

Friedag, H.R., Schmidt, W. – Balanced Scorecard at work: strategisch – taktisch – operative, Freiburg, 1. Aufl. 2003

Frost, B. – Measuring Performance, Measurement International, Dallas, USA, 2000

Gehringer, J., Walter, M.J. – Mitarbeiter erfolgreich machen: Personal gezielt auswählen und fördern mit dem Balanced-Scorecard-Ansatz, Metropolitan-Verlag, Regensburg/Berlin, 2003

Gemünden, H.G., Walter, A. – Beziehungspromotoren – Schlüsselpersonen für zwischenbetriebliche Innovationsprozesse, 1995; in: Hauschildt, J., Gemünden, H.G. – Promotoren – champions der Innovation, 2. Aufl., Gabler, Wiesbaden, 1999

Goffee, R., Jones, G. – The character of a corporation: How your company's culture can make or break your business, HarperCollins Business, London, England, 2000

Groetzinger, M., Uepping, H. – Balanced Scorecard im Human Resources Management: Strategie, Einsatzmoeglichkeiten, Praxisbeispiele, Luchterhand, Neuwied, 2001

Hadler, A. – Frauen & Führungspositionen – Prognosen bis zum Jahr 2000, Peter Lang, 1995

Harrison, M.I. – Diagnosing organizations: methods, models and processes, Sage Publications, Inc., London, England, 3rd Edition, 2005

Harvard Business Review – On measuring corporate performance, Harvard Business School Press, USA, 1998

Harvard Business Review – On culture and change, Harvard Business School Press, USA, 2002

Hauschildt, J. – Promotoren – Antriebskräfte der Innovation, Reihe BWL aktuell, Nr. 1, Universität Klagenfurt, 1998

183

Hauschildt, J., Gemünden, H.G. – Promotoren – Champions der Innovation, Gabler, Wiesbaden, 2. Aufl., 1999

Hauschildt, J. – Innovationsmanagement, Verlag Vahlen München, 3. Aufl., 2004

Hofstede, G., Hofstede, G.J. – Cultures and Organizations: software of the mind, McGraw-Hill, New York, 2nd edition, 2005

Hofstede, G. – Culture's consequences: comparing values, behaviours, institutions and organizations across nations, Sage Publications Ltd., London, England, 2001

Hofstede, G. – Cultures and Organizations, HarperCollins Publishers, 1994

Hofstede, G.J., Pedersen, P.B., Hofstede, G. – Exploring culture: exercises, stories and synthetic cultures, Intercultural Press, Inc., Maine, USA, 2002

Holbeche, L. – Understanding change: theory, implementation and success, Elsevier Butterworth-Heinemann, 2005

Hollinshead, G., Leat, M. – International Human Resource Management, FT Prentice Hall, England, 2004

Horvath & Partner – Balanced Scorecard umsetzen, Schaeffer-Poeschel, Stuttgart, 2000

Hubbard, E.E. – Diversity Scorecard: evaluating the impact of diversity on organizational performance, Elsevier Science/Butterworth-Heinemann, Oxford, England, 2004

Ilsley, R. – Best Practice: what it is and how to implement it, Management Books 2000 Ltd., Gloucestershire, England, 2004

Jacobs, J.A., Gerson, K. – Time divide: work, family and gender inequality, Harvard University Press, London, England, 2004

Jung, D., Küpper, G. – Gender Mainstreaming und betriebliche Veränderungsprozesse, Kleine Verlag, Bielefeld, 2001

184

Kaplan, R.S., Norton, D.P. – Strategy Maps: Converting intangible assets into tangible outcomes, Harvard Business School Press, Boston, Massachusetts, USA, 2004

Kaplan, R.S., Norton, D.P. – The strategy-focused organization: how balanced scorecard companies thrive in the new business environment – Boston, 2001

Kaplan, R.S., Norton, D.P. – The Balanced Scorecard: Translating strategy into action, Harvard Business School Press, Boston, USA, 1996

Katz, P., Katz, M. – The feminist dollar, New York, Plenum, 1997

Klenke, K. – Women and Leadership: a contextual perspective, Springer New York, USA, 1996

Kodz, J. – Work-life balance: beyond the rhetoric, Institute for Employment Studies, 2002

Kotter, J.P. – Leading Change, Harvard Business School Press, Boston, USA, 1996

Kotter, J.P., Cohen, D.S. – Heart of change: real-life stories of how people change their organizations, Harvard Business School Press, 2002

Krell, G. – Chancengleichheit durch Personalpolitik: Gleichstellung von Frauen und Männern in Unternehmen und Verwaltungen; rechtliche Regelungen – Problemanalysen – Lösungen, Wiesbaden, Gabler, 4. Aufl., 2004

Kunz, G. – Die Balanced Scorecard im Personalmanagement: ein Leitfaden für Aufbau und Einführung, Campus Verlag, Frankfurt/Main, 2001

Land, K., Mönig-Raane, M., Pettersson, G., Sommer, M. – Die kleine große Revolution Gender Mainstreaming; Erfahrungen, Beispiele, Strategien aus Schweden und Deutschland, VSA-Verlag, Hamburg, 2004

Leary-Joyce, J. – Becoming an employer of choice: make your organisation a place where people want to do great work, Chartered Institute of Personnel and Development, 2004

MacDonald, M., Sprenger, E, Dubel, I. – Gender and organisational change, Royal Tropical Institute, Amsterdam, the Netherlands, 1997

185

Maier, M. – On the gendered substructure of organization: Dimensions and dilemmas of corporate masculinity. In G.N. Powell (Ed.), Handbook of gender and work. Sage, Thousand Oaks, 1999

Maisel, L.S. – Performance Measurements Survey, American Institute of Certified Public Accountants, 2001

Meyer, M.W. – Rethinking performance measurement, Cambridge University Press, Cambridge, England, 2003

Mintzberg, H., Ahlstrand, B, Lampel, J. – Strategy Safari, New York, Free Press, 1998

Morgan, G. – Images of organization, Thousand Oaks, Sage Publications, Inc., 2nd Edition, 1997

Neely, A., Adams, C, Kennerley, M. – The performance prism: the scorecard for measuring and managing business success, Prentice Hall / Pearson Education Ltd., London, England, 2002

Niven, P.R. – Balanced Scorecard, New York, John Wiley & Sons, 2002

Olve, N.-G., Roy, J., Wetter, M. – Performance Drivers: a practical guide to using the balanced scorecard, John wiley & Sons, West Sussex, England, 2000

Paton, R. – Managing and Measuring Social Enterprises, Sage Publications Ltd., London, England, 2003

Pauwe, J. – HRM and performance: achieving long term viability, Oxford University Press, Oxford, England, 2004

Peters, S., Bensel, N. – Frauen und Männer im Management: Diversity in Diskurs und Praxis, Gabler Verlag, Wiesbaden, 2002

Peters, T.J., Waterman, R.H. – In search of excellence, Warner Books, Inc., New York, 1982

Phillips, J.J., Stone, R.D., Phillips, P.P. – The Human Resources Scorecard, Butterworth-Heinemann, Boston, USA, 2001

Powell, G.N., Graves, L.M. – Women and men in management, Sage Publications Inc., London, England, Third Edition, 2003

Powell, G.N. – Gender & Work, Sage Publications, 1999

Rajan, A., Martin, B., Latham, J. – Harnessing workforce diversity to raise the bottom line, Create, London, England, 2003

Rosenstiehl, L. von, Regnet, E., Domsch, M.E. – Führung von Mitarbeitern. Handbuch für erfolgreiches Personalmanagement, Schaeffer-Poeschel, Stuttgart, 5. Aufl., 2003

Schein, E. – The corporate culture survival guide: Sense and nonsense about culture change, Jossey-Bass, San Francisco, USA, 1999

Schein, E.- Organizational Culture and Leadership, 1993; in: classics of Organizational Theory, Shafritz, J. and Ott, J.S., eds., Harcourt College Publishers, Fort Worth, USA, 2001

Schein, E.- Organizational Culture and Leadership, Jossey-Bass, San Francisco, USA, 2004

Schmidt, V. – Gender Mainstreaming – an innovation in Europe? Budrich, Opladen, 2005

Stiegler, B. – Frauen im Mainstreaming: politische Strategien und Theorien zur Geschlechterfrage, Friedrich Ebert Stiftung, Bonn, 1998

Sudman, S., Blair, E. - Marketing Research - A problem solving approach, McGraw-Hill, 1998

Tannen, D. – You just don't understand, HarperCollins Publishers, New York, 2001

Thomas, R.R., Woodruff, M.I., Thomas, R.R. Jr. – Building a House for Diversity, Amacom, New York, 1999

Torrington, D., Hall, L., Taylor, S. – Human Resource Management, Pearson Education Ltd., Essex, England, Sixth Edition, 2005

Trompenaars, F., Hampden-Turner, C. – Managing people across cultures, Capstone, Chichester, 2004

Trompenaars, F., Hampden-Turner, C. – Riding the waves of culture: understanding cultural diversity in business, 2nd edition, London, Brealey, 2005

Trompenaars, F., Wooliams, P. – Business across cultures, Capstone Publishing Ltd., West Sussex, England, 2003

Verheul, I. – Is there a (fe)male approach? Understanding gender differences in entrepreneurship, Erasmus Research institute of management, Rotterdam, 2005

Welpe, I., Schmeck, M. – Kompaktwissen Gender in Organisationen, Peter Lang Verlag, Frankfurt, 2005

Witte, E. – Das Promotoren-Modell, 1973, (S. 9-42) in: Hauschildt, J., Gemünden, H.G., Promotoren – Champions der Innovation, 2. Aufl., Gabler, Wiesbaden, 1999

Wunderer, R., Dick, P. – Frauen im Management, Luchterhand, 1997

Yin, R.K. Applications of Case Study Research. Sage Publications, 1993

Yin, R.K. Case Study Research: Design and Methods. Sage Publications, 2nd Edition, 1996

Articles, Internet Sites & Miscellaneous Sources

Alber, J., Delhey, J., Keck, W., Nauenburg, R., Social Science Research Centre (WZB), Berlin – First European Quality of Life Survey 2003, European Foundation for the Improvement of Living and Working Conditions, Luxembourg: Office for Official Publications of the European Communities, 2004

Audit berufundfamilie gGmbH – Audit berufundfamilie, Chancen für Ihren Unternehmenserfolg, Berufundfamilie gGmbH, Frankfurt/M., Januar, 2006 (www.beruf-und-familie.de)

Bajdo, L.M. – Perceptions of organizational culture and women's advancement in organizations: A cross cultural examination, www.findarticles.com, Gale Group, 2002

188

Biehl, J.K. – Berlin may get a female chancellor, but it's still a man's world, Spiegel, September 2005

Bundesministerium für Familie, Senioren, Frauen und Jugend – Bilanz 2003 der Vereinbarung zwischen der Bundesregierung und den Spitzenverbänden der Deutschen Wirtschaft zur Förderung der Chancengleichheit von Frauen und Männern in der Privatwirtschaft, Berlin, 2003

Bundesministerium für Familie, Senioren, Frauen und Jugend – Nationale Strategien zur Umsetzung der Aktionsplattform der 4. Weltfrauenkonferenz, 1997

Catalyst – The Bottom line: connecting corporate performance and gender diversity, www.catalystwomen.org, 2004

COM 2001 – Commission of the European Communities; Proposal for a council decision on guidelines for member states' employment policies for the year 2002, COM (2001) 511 final, 2001/0208 (CNS), September 2001

Commonwealth Secretariat, Leo-Rhynie, E. – A Quick Guide to Gender Mainstreaming in Education – London, 1999

Commonwealth Secretariat – The 1995 Commonwealth Plan of Action on Gender and Development: A commonwealth Vision Agreed in Principle – London 1995

De Jager, P. – Resistance to change: a new view of an old problem, The Futurist, May/June, pp 24-27, 2001

Deutscher Gewerkschaftbund – ISA Informationen zur Sozial- und Arbeitsmarktpolitik, Ausgabe 7/2001

Dreas, S., Klenk, T. – Wie kommt Gender Mainstreaming in die Organisation; Implementationsbedingunen für Gender Mainstreaming in unterschiedlichen Organisationstypen, Sozialwissenschaften und Berufspraxis, H. 3, Jg. 27, 2004

Emancipation Monitor 2004 – SCP (Sociaal en Cultureel Planbureau) and CBS (Centraal Bureau voor de Statistiek) – Dutch Emancipation Report November 2004

Engelbrech, G., Jungkunst, M. – Future of Labour – Future of Women? IAB Labour Market Research Topics 41, 2000

EP-First – HR Index benchmarks 2003/2004

European Community – Gender equality in development co-operation: from policy to practise – the role of the European Commission – Office for official publications of the European Communities, Luxembourg

European Commission - A guide to gender impact assessment (Website: www. Europa.eu.int/comm./employment_social)

Folkerts, L., Hauschildt, J. – Personelle Dynamik in Innovationsprozessen, Die Betriebswirtschaft, Vol. 62, pp1-17, 2002

Hauschildt, J. – Promotoren – Erfolgsfaktoren für das Management von Innovationen, ZFO, Vol. 70, pp. 332-337, 2001

Hauschildt, J., Kirchmann, E. – Teamwork for innovation – the „troika" of promotors, R&D Management, Vol. 31, pp. 41-49, 2001

Hubbard, E.E. – Building a Diversity Measurement Scorecard, Hubbard Diversity Measurement & Productivity Newsletter, June 2002

Kaplan, R.S., Norton, D.P. – The Balanced Scorecard: Measures that drive performance, Harvard Business Review (January – February 1992)

Kaplan, R.S., Norton, D.P. – Putting the Balanced Scorecard to work, Harvard Business Review (September – October 1993)

Kaplan, R.S., Norton, D.P. – Using the Balanced Scorecard as a strategic management system, Harvard Business Review (January – February 1996)

Kotter, J.P., Schlesinger, L.A. – Choosing strategies for change, Harvard Business Review, pp 106-114, 1979

Krell, G. – Managing Diversity und Gender Mainstreaming: ein Konzeptvergleich, Sozialwissenschaften und Berufspraxis, H. 4, Jg. 27, 2004

Lyness, K.S., Thompson, D.E. – Climbing the corporate ladder: Do female and male executives follow the same route? Journal of applied psychology, 85 (1), p86-101, 2000

Marshall, J. – Organisational cultures and women managers: Exploring the dynamics of resilience, Applied Psychology: an international review, Nr 42 (4), p313-322, 1993

Müller, P., Kurtz, B. – Active labour market policy and gender mainstreaming in Germany, Institut für Arbeitsmarkt- und Berufsforschung der Bundesanstalt für Arbeit, Nr. 50, 2003

Piderit, S.K. – Rethinking resistance and recognizing ambivalence: a multidimensional view of attitudes toward an organizational change, Academy of management, 794, October, 2000

Research Institute for Social Development – Gender Equality: Striving for justice in an unequal world, www.unrisd.or, Geneva, 2005

Solomon, C.M. – Cracks in the Glass Ceiling – dealing with sex discrimination in corporate culture, www.findarticles.com, Workforce magazine, Gale Group, 2001

Statistisches Bundesamt – Frauen in Deutschland – Im Blickpunkt, Wiesbaden, 2004

TK (2001/2002) – Long-term planning regarding Emancipation – from the Dutch government – i.e.: Meerjarenbeleidsplan emancipatie, Handelingen tweede kamer, vergaderjaar 2000/2001, nr. 3.

Total E-Quality Deutschland e.V. – Award information and Newsletters – www.total-e-quality.de, 2005

United Nations – Beijing Declaration of the Fourth World Conference on Women – 1995

Waterman, R.H., Peters, T.J., Phillips, J.R. – Structure is not organisation, Business Horizons (June1980, pp 14-26)

Woodward, A.E. – Gender mainstreaming in European policy: innovation or deception? – Discussion paper, Vrije Universiteit Brussel, October 2001

www.economist.com/countries/Germany - Country Briefings: Germany, From the Economist Intelligence Unit, May 2004

www.efqm.org – European Foundation for Quality Management

www.europa.eu.int – European Union Site including information about employment, equal opportunities and gender mainstreaming

www.genderdax.de – List of top organisations for career oriented women (Top Unternehmen für karriereorientierte Frauen)

www.gesir.at – website from GESIR in Austria showing instruments which can assist in gender mainstreaming in regional development

www.sas.com – website from SAS showing software packages for balanced scorecard design

www.un.org/womenwatch/ - website from the United Nations Inter-Agency Network on Women and Gender Equality

www.un.org/womenwatch/ - website from the United Nations Inter-Agency Network on Women and Gender Equality - Women and the Economy, Fact Sheet No. 6, June 2000

www.wz-berlin.de – Prof. Dr. Schmid, G.– Labor Market Policy and Employment, WZB, printed: 08-11-2005

www.wz-berlin.de – Oschmiansky, H, Oschmiansky, F. – Labor Market Policy and Employment, Discussion Paper SPI 2003-106, WZB, printed: 08-11-2005

Appendix One: Case Studies

A total of six case studies are compiled from the in-depth interviews. Three case studies refer to Dutch organisations and three are about German organisations. Two case study organisations are located in both the Netherlands and Germany and the interviewee could make comparisons between the two locations based on personal experiences and knowledge about the two places.

Overview of case studies:

Characteristics	Case 1	Case 2	Case 3	Case 4	Case 5	Case 6
Country	NL	NL	NL (& G)	G (& NL)	G	G
Interviewee(s)	Female & Male	Female	Female	Male & Female	Male	Male
Position of main interviewee	Senior communications and PR Manager (& HR-Manager)	HR-Consultant	International HR-Project Manager	HR-officer (& Product Manager)	Head of department	Head of department
Size of organisation	Medium	Large	Multi-national	Medium	Large	Multi-national
Type of industry	Technology	Recruit-ment	Technology Electronics	Food	Energy	Tele-com-muni-cations
Prior use of bal. scorecard	No	No	Yes	No	No	Yes
Structure of organisation	Flat & Matrix	Flat	Matrix	Bureau-cratic / Hier-archical	Flat	Matrix
Approx. nr of employees worldwide	600	13,000	160,000	3,800	1,000	49,000
Approx. turnover in 2004	> $ 500 million	> € 5 billion	> € 30 billion	> € 950 million	> 5 billion	€ 30 billion

Case Study One
- **Medium sized organisation**
- **Type of business: Technology**
- **The Netherlands**

This organisation belongs to an American corporation (quoted on the NASDAQ) operating in the technology market. They are operating world-wide and their head office for Europe is situated in the Netherlands. The organisations in other European countries serve as regional sales offices. The turnover in Europe has been static with a tendency to decline and therefore the European part of the organisation has recently been under increased pressure to cut costs.

The organisation does **not** use the traditional balanced scorecard. The business structure that fits to the organisation is a **combination of a flat structure and a matrix structure**. The interviewee is currently working as Senior Communications and PR Manager in the Dutch office. She has been working for this organisation for 8 years in different positions. She discussed certain issues/questions with the HRM manager during/after the interview and gave final additional feedback at a later stage per telephone to complete the questions.

Part I: General background about the organisation

	World-wide	Europe	The Netherlands
Industry	Technology		
Turnover in 2004	+/-$500 Ml	Not available	Not available
Number of employees in 2004	600	100	70
Number of female employees in 2004	250	40	35
Number of female employees working part-time	Not available	1	1
How many women are employed in middle and top management level?	50	9	8
How has the number of female employees changed in your organisation over the past three years? + /- ..... % (up / down/ static)	Static	Static	Static

Part II: Gender Measures

The organisation merely developed the gender measures as they are required by the government. This means that 1/6 part of day-care costs for **child care** are paid by the organisation. There are some possibilities for **work life / family life** balance through **home office** working however, this is not officially specified. The interviewee beliefs that more gender measures would be available in the US office as the governmental regulations might require more actions from organisations in this area.

Due to the fact that a written policy for equal opportunities is not readily available the **effectiveness is also not measured**. However, the interviewee believes that the **satisfaction questionnaires** (every second year) and **interviews** (i.e. performance reviews) they do with the employees would show if there would be issues in this area.

The following two **advantages of gender mainstreaming** were the **most important** for the organisation: diverse work teams and the positive effect on company image. More women in management positions, loyal & motivated employees – reduce absenteeism, loss of motivation of workforce & productivity and high retention costs were advantages of gender mainstreaming which were of **average importance**. **Not important** were better use of the total workforce available and as the interviewee stated the organisation has no problem with finding good employees. Secondly, the statements "female customers prefer to buy from female employees" and "female customers prefer to buy from women friendly organisations" do not really apply as the customer base includes mainly male customers. "Avoid fines for discrimination" might be applicable in the USA but currently not in the Dutch / European offices and, finally, suitable organisational structures is not important according to the interviewee.

The **main problems with achieving gender equality** in the organisation include: culture of presentee-ism and as the interviewee notes team pressure and the attitude of the majority of the workforce demands long hours from each team member, i.e. each employee if they want to belong to the team. Also ingrained attitudes are a big part of this. The family/work life balance is not part of the organisational culture/climate as everybody in the team has to make the same long working hours. Furthermore, the interviewee added *lack of variety of the workforce* as a huge problem and as she explains: *"there are not many employees with young children; the problem is not really present in the organisation because the workforce mainly includes young, single & ambitious employees. Women with children often leave or return to lower positions and eventually decide to leave."* Time pressures on managers and lack of child support are **average problems** according to the interviewee. Child support is a practical issue and time pressure is subjective.

Part III: Development of a gender balanced scorecard
The organisation has not implemented the traditional balanced scorecard. However, the interviewee explained that the organisation uses a comparable management system called **VOICE**, which stands for the following:

- **Value Quality:** We incorporate quality in every aspect of our business including our products, services, processes, relationships with employees, customers and business partners.
- **Operational Excellence:** Is how we approach our work as well as our attitude in all we do and how we go about getting it done.
- **Integrity:** We approach our work and treat each other in an honest ethical, professional and respectful manner.
- **Customers and Partners:** Our relationships with our customers and partners are the foundation of our business and a key indicator of our success as an organisation.
- **Employees:** are our most valuable and valued asset.

The interviewee believes that a **specific gender balanced scorecard** as a management tool to achieve gender equality in the organisation could only work if the organisation would include the aim of gender equality in the organisational strategy. Currently, they would not consider **implementing** this strategic instrument for gender equality as it is not part of the strategic aims. The organisation's **first priorities** are to **return to profitability**. As the interviewee states: *"in times of profitability there are more initiatives on cultivating a right culture or work climate environment."*

With regards to the question whether there would be **resistance** if the organisation decided to implement a gender balanced scorecard the interviewee answered yes. She explained that the Dutch part of the organisation traditionally has been a quite macho culture/organisation. The products used to be very male customer oriented technological products and maybe partly as a result of this many of the employees in the Dutch office were male. The IT/technological industry has always been quite a male industry (e.g. it is a fact that not many women study an IT subject) and therefore issues like gender equality have not really been stressed as important in the European organisation. Therefore, it is very likely, that there would be resistance to the implementation of such a tool as many employees wouldn't recognise the importance of it for the organisation.

The results of a gender balanced scorecard could be **evaluated** by monitoring and evaluating certain statistical data for example employee turnover, statistical information available about women in general in the organisation or via the employee satisfaction surveys which is done every other year. However, the interviewee believes that this should be done over a number of years to be able to see progress for women (e.g. considerable increases in the level of satisfaction shown by the satisfaction surveys over five years). According to the interviewee the **HRM department** should probably be **responsible for the design** of a gender balanced scorecard as they have the relevant expertise. The **executive team-members** should take care of the **implementation/execution.** They are also responsible for the implementation of the **VOICE** system. The vice-presidents of the corporation all receive a small part of the voice tool for which they carry sole responsibility (for example the vice president of operations is responsible for operational excellence, etc.). They have to coach, monitor and report on executive level about the developments. The **implementation** is done by project teams or by departments.

There have been **no attempts to change the organisational culture** of this organisation that the interviewee is aware of.

A gender balanced scorecard should be **connected to incentives / bonus schemes for the top management** as this would force certain behaviours, creates good visibility on progress and achieves executive attention.

To the question: **"Do you think that a gender balanced scorecard could be a tool that could help to change the organisational culture of your organisation in order that gender mainstreaming / gender equality becomes part of the culture?"** the interviewee answered as follows: *"I believe that a gender balanced scorecard could be a tool that could help to change the organisational culture of the organisation in order that gender mainstreaming / gender equality becomes part of the culture because it helps to get all employees involved in the business and it motivates them to believe in a certain mission. Furthermore, it would increase their understanding of the reasons behind certain business decisions. Thirdly, a specific gender balanced scorecard would really achieve a special focus on the problem. However, for our European organisation it would not be relevant but in the USA more interest may exist in the HRM department for such a tool. Especially, since in the USA the costs of litigation against an employer for unequal treatment could be considerable. For our Dutch offices the relevance of such a tool is currently lacking and until the profitability situation has improved special gender equality measures will not be part of our strategy."*

Part IV: The gender balanced scorecard perspectives and indicators
Question 1: Looking at the *four traditional perspectives* on a gender balanced scorecard: how important would the following gender indicators be for your organisation? **A = really important, B = average, C = not important**

The financial perspective
Most important under the **financial perspective** were *turnover per employee* (differentiating between men and women) if you take other variables that are involved into account and *return on investment for the gender initiatives* as a long term measurement. Amount of money saved as a result of gender initiatives, benefits costs as a percentage of payroll or revenue, gender initiative expenses per employee and gender initiative budget as a percentage of sales

could be seen as **average important** indicators. Reduced litigation costs were **not important** according to the interviewee.

Customer perspective
For the customer perspective the following indicator was selected as **most important**: *percentage customer retention by male and female employees*. Of **average importance** were: number of new customers attracted by male and female employees, number of solutions offered per client by male and female employees, number of customer complaints successfully dealt with by male and female employees and number of customer awards received. Percentage on-time delivery rating by male and female employees was identified as being **not important**.

The interviewee noted that 'market share division between female and male customers and the representation in the workforce of male and female employees', secondly 'the percentage diverse customer satisfaction' and finally, 'profitability by male and female customers' were **not applicable** as the customer base exists of mainly male customers.

Internal Business processes perspective
The interviewee selected *employee satisfaction and female employee satisfaction* (to be assessed with questionnaires) together with *social audit results* as the two indicators that were seen to be **really important** indicators. The other indicators were seen as **average important** according to the interviewee and these were: throughput time per business action for male and female employees, new product introduction and design (male vs. female employees) and number of awards received for equality/diversity initiatives.

Learning and growth perspective
Under the learning and growth perspectives the interviewee identified five indicators as being **really important,** namely: *comparison of educational budget spend on women and men, motivation index, productivity (male vs. female employees), ethic violations* and the *empowerment index* (i.e. the number of female employees vs. male employees that have received a certain level of power or authority to make higher level decisions). Of **average importance** were: number of female employees, number of female managers / leaders, personal goal achievement (male vs. female employees), percentage of employees with advanced degrees for male and female employees and employee suggestions (male vs. female employees). Only one indicator was **not important** under this perspective, namely: number and percentage of gender-competent employees. The interviewee selected cross functional assignments (male vs. female employees) and number of innovations initiated by male vs. female employees as being not applicable.

Question 2: Which of the following (optional) additional perspectives would be relevant perspectives for your organisation to add on to the gender balanced scorecard?

The interviewee would include **organisational culture** as a separate perspective. **Leadership commitment** and **workforce profile** also make sense as separate perspectives. However, the **community** perspective was not very relevant according to the interviewee.

Question 3: Which indicators would be important for your organisation for the additional perspectives you selected in question two? **A = really important, B = average, C = not important.**

Organisational culture perspective
Under the organisational culture perspective the following seven indicators would be **really important:** *perception of consistent and equitable treatment of all employees, gender equity tied to management compensation, absence rate / percentage absenteeism, retention rate of critical human capital, percentage gender initiatives fully implemented, percentage favourable ratings on climate/culture surveys for male and female employees, percentage gender based pay differentials* and *organisation's "openness" ratings.*

The following two indicators would be **average important:** average time for dispute resolution and employee referral rate by male and female employees. Workplace flexibility index ratings were **not important.**

Three indicators were **not applicable** according to the interviewee namely: percentage favourable ratings on cultural audit, "employer of choice" ratings versus top 5 to 10 competitors which is only done in the USA and finally, percentage work-life balance benefits utilised as there are not many official agreements available in this area.

Community perspective
This perspective was not selected by the respondent.

Leadership commitment
Under the leadership commitment perspective most indicators were given **really high importance,** namely:

- *Leadership participation in designing the vision and strategies for achieving gender mainstreaming*
- *The number of female employees in formal mentoring programmes with the leader*
- *The percentage of gender objectives that are tied to key strategic business objectives connected to the bonus and compensation of the leader*
- *The representation mix on the organisation's board of directors*
- *Leadership representation on the gender steering committee and advisory boards*
- *The degree of personal participation in creating an inclusive climate / culture*
- *The ability of the leader to overcome tension when it arises in the change process*
- *Money and other resources allocated by the leader to the gender mainstreaming initiative*
- *The number of executives and managers that are competent due to training in dealing with gender mainstreaming issues*
- *Leadership behaviour towards work–life balance issues (such as flexible working hours, glass-ceiling issues and family leave policies).*

The only other indicator left which was given **average importance** was the number of female employees personally selected by the leader for special assignments.

Workforce profile
Percentage female survival and loss rate, percentage absenteeism for male and female employees, percentage voluntary turnover: exempt and non-exempt and *percentage involuntary turnover: exempt and non-exempt* were the indicators that were given **really high importance**. Of **average importance** were: percentage female new hires, percentage female managers and officials and number of offers to female interviewees. Percentage turnover by length of service and cost per hire were identified as **not important**. Number returning from leave for male and female employees was selected as **not applicable**.

Case Study Two
- **Large organisation**
- **Type of business: HR-services (recruitment)**
- **Country: The Netherlands**

This group of companies is one of the largest temporary and contract staffing organisations in the world. In the Netherlands -where it was founded- it is the market leader. The company's mission is to match demand and supply of labour and offer HR-services. The organisation has **not** implemented the **traditional balanced scorecard**. The structure of the organisation in the Netherlands can be called **flat**, however, there are clear layers to the top but there are very few layers. The interviewee (Dutch national) has been working as HR-consultant in this organisation for almost 10 years and has been situated at different locations within the Netherlands.

Part I: General background about the organisation

	World-wide	The Netherlands
Industry	HR-Services	HR-Services
Turnover in 2004	> € 5 bln	Not available
Number of employees	+/- 13,000	+/- 5,000
Number of female employees	Not available	Not available
Number of female employees working part-time	Not available	Not available
How many women are employed in middle and top management level (approx. percentage)?	Not available	Many in middle mgt / None in top mgt
How has the number of female employees changed in your organisation over the past three years? + /- ..... % (up / down/ static)	Up	Up

Part II: Gender measures
This organisation specialises in HR-solutions. One part of the group of companies is a HR consultancy. The main part of the organisation is recruitment of personnel. Therefore, one of the basic statements the organisation has with regards to gender measures is that: "**all the HR procedures we develop must promote equal opportunity and treatment**" for the personnel. There are some **special guidelines** available but these are not widely known to all employees according to the interviewee. With regards to **childcare measures** the organisation fulfils its obligations according to the legal requirements but there is a **gap in work life – private life support**. The possibility of part-time work is offered but the employee has to meet certain requirements and conditions. Flexible hours or home-office work is not possible mainly due to the fact that the employees have to be in the office during office hours to meet

with the potential flex-workers (the people placed in client organisations for project work). These options are not available at any level in the organisation.

The evaluation of the gender measures and other measures is done via **satisfaction questionnaires** for the employees. Furthermore, an **internal cultural survey** is done to review the organisational cultural fit to the strategic aims.

The following **advantages of gender mainstreaming for the organisation** were the **most important** for the organisation according to the interviewee: better use of the total workforce available, loyal & motivated employees – reduce absenteeism and loss of motivation of workforce & productivity.

Average importance was given to the following advantages of gender mainstreaming for the organisation: more women in management positions, suitable organisational structures, positive effect on company image, "female customers prefer to buy from women friendly organisations" and high retention costs.

According to the interviewee the following were **not important**: diverse work teams because the majority of the employees are female at lower level, "female customers prefer to buy from female employees" for the same reason that the majority of communication with flex workers and clients is done by female employees and thirdly, avoid fines for discrimination which is not applicable in the Netherlands yet according to the interviewee.

According to the interviewee the **main problems with achieving gender equality** in the organisation are the lack of family/work-life balance support and the lack of child support. The interviewee mentioned that the main issues are practical issues like child support and not attitude issues. Therefore, culture of presentee-ism, time pressures on managers, ingrained attitudes and the organisational culture/climate are all selected as **not a problem** to achieving gender equality.

Part III: Development of a gender balanced scorecard
The organisation has **not** implemented the **traditional balanced scorecard**. But, the organisation uses **benchmarking** (our 'copy & paste' concept as the interviewee calls it) and occasionally other tools to review the actual performance situation and compare against competitors. Learning from competition/market and improving their situation by doing this is important for the organisation.

Responsibility for the **design and implementation** of a gender balanced scorecard should be partly the **CEO and the top management team** but mostly the **HRM department**. External consultants are hardly ever used by this organisation.

With regards to **bonuses for top management** connected to the performance of a gender balanced scorecard the interviewee remarked the following: *"currently the organisation is already working with bonuses connected to the overall company performance for the majority of staff. The bonuses for top mgt are already related to results and for such a gender initiative this should be extended as well. Especially, since the majority of top mgt is male but the majority of middle mgt and the rest of the workforce is female a bonus for top managers* *would give an extra push to the initiative.*" The interviewee could not think of other effective ways to get the full commitment from top management.

The respondent does not think that there would be a lot of **resistance** in the organisation towards new gender initiatives, as the majority of the employees are currently female. The HR-consultants which form the majority of the workforce are all high educated (minimum is either higher education degree or university degree) and very often female (probably 85%) which makes the workforce of this organisation quite unique.

The respondent is not aware of **active attempts to change the organisational culture.** However, an internal cultural audit is done regularly to review whether the culture fits to the aims and goals of the organisation. With regards to the culture the respondent described it as very open and informal (quite Dutch probably) and everybody calls the CEO and other top managers with their first names, i.e. Ben and Leo. The company has put priority on the retention of quality personnel but there is quite a lot of change in the HR-consultant job (lowest possible level entry at high education degree level). This is a job often seen as a starter job. For the promotion of employees many training is offered and a special 'Blue Sky' programme is developed. This identifies potential managers at early stages.

Even though the culture focuses on delivering perfection to the customer it is sometimes difficult for the internal employees to get the perfect HR-solution. For example it is not possible to work flexible hours or to have home office working. Also child benefit and other support to achieve a better work / private life balance are often lacking. The interviewee e.g. had problems to arrange that she can be on time at the child day-care to pick up her children at six in the evenings. Also part-time work is not easy to arrange. She could work three days but it had to be three in a row and she had to be employed for the minimum of two years before this could be arranged. Therefore, the interviewee is a bit sceptical about the gender friendly HR solutions internally. According to the interviewee the main issue is that there is enough qualified labour available on the labour market currently and therefore the employees who have children do not complain about the situation. Another issue is that it is a nice organisation to work for because of the openness and the flat and informal structure. The groups of employees at the offices (majority are all female) are very often good friends. However, the top management is only male and this is where the direction and strategies are coming from mostly.

To the question: **"Do you think that a gender balanced scorecard could be a tool that could help to change the organisational culture of your organisation in order that gender mainstreaming / gender equality becomes part of the culture?"** the interviewee answered as follows: *"What I noticed is that the organisation has gotten harder and more demanding because the market conditions are getting harder. At bad economic times, when demand is lower than the supply of labour, the organisational climate is harder and more commercial. In other periods when demand is higher than the supply of labour then it is softer. In such periods new HR-initiatives could be introduced in the organisation. However, currently the situation is not all that favourable and therefore, it is unlikely that such a scorecard would be introduced to the strategic aims of the organisation. Besides this, gender is not a real urgent problem and no complaint has arrived at the top so why would active measures be undertaken? If there is no problem then we do not need to take action. It is more* *likely that our special department of HR consultants would introduce the concept to potential clients who are interested in Human Resource solution packages. "*

Part IV: The gender balanced scorecard perspectives and indicators
Question 1 Looking at the *four traditional perspectives* on a gender balanced scorecard: how important would the following **gender indicators** be for your organisation? (**A = really important, B = average, C = not important**)

The financial perspective
Under the financial perspective *return on investment for the gender initiatives* was the only indicator selected as **really important**. Amount of money saved as a result of gender initiatives, benefits costs as a percentage of payroll or revenue and gender initiative budget as a percentage of sales were of **average importance**. **Not important** were gender initiative expenses per employee and turnover per employee, differentiating between men and women as approximately 85% of the employees are female. Reduced litigation costs were **not applicable** according to the interviewee.

Customer perspective
Three indicators were seen as the **most important**, namely: *market share division between female and male customers and the representation in the workforce of male and female employees, percentage diverse customer satisfaction* and *number of customer awards received*. Percentage customer retention by male and female employees and profitability by male and female customers were of **average importance** to the respondent. Four indicators were seen as **not important**: number of new customers attracted by male and female employees, number of solutions offered per client by male and female employees, percentage on-time delivery rating by male and female employees and number of customer complaints successfully dealt with by male and female employees.

Internal Business processes perspective
Under the internal business processes perspective two indicators were seen as **important**: *employee satisfaction and female employee satisfaction (to be assessed with questionnaires)* and *social audit results*. The number of awards received for equality/diversity initiatives was seen as **average** important. **Not important** were new product introduction and design (male vs. female employees) and throughput time per business action for male and female employees as this is difficult to measure because of teamwork.

Learning and growth perspective
Under this perspective four indicators were selected as **very important**, namely: *number of female managers / leaders, the motivation index, ethic violations* and *the empowerment index (i.e. the number of female employees vs. male employees that have received a certain level of power or authority to make higher level decisions)*. **Average importance** was given to the number of female employees, productivity (male vs. female employees), cross functional assignments (male vs. female employees) and personal goal achievement (male vs. female employees). Number and percentage of gender-competent employees, comparison of educational budget spend on women and men and number of innovations initiated by male vs. female employees was seen as **not important**. Also the 'percentage of employees with advanced degrees for male and female employees' indicator was seen as **not important** as the majority of the employees have higher degrees.

Question 2: Which of the following (optional) **additional perspectives** would be relevant perspectives for your organisation to add on to the gender balanced scorecard?

The interviewee would include all additional perspectives on the gender balanced scorecard. With regards to **organisational culture** she had no doubt that it should be on the scorecard. The same was for the **community perspective** as the organisation wants to be involved in the society and be a responsible organisation that adds positively to the community. *Extra note from the interviewee:* In Belgium they have developed a special diversity department. This department and this initiative (which is also partly executed in the Netherlands) focused on helping long term unemployed and disabled people to get back into employment. This does not focus on gender equality but more on other minority groups but it shows the engagement of the organisation in the community. With regards to the **leadership commitment perspective** the respondent had some doubts whether it should be separate or not. She commented that this perspective might fit under the organisational culture perspective as well but in the end decided to leave it as a separate perspective. The same applies to the **workforce profile**. The indicators under this perspective might also be divided over the traditional four perspectives according to the respondent. However, in the end she also here decided to leave it as a separate perspective.

Question 3: Which **gender indicators** would be important for your organisation for the additional perspectives you selected in question two? (**A = really important, B = average, C = not important**)

Organisational culture perspective
Six indicators under the organisational culture perspective were seen to be **very important**, namely: *"employer of choice" ratings versus top 5 to 10 competitors, perception of consistent and equitable treatment of all employees, absence rate / percentage absenteeism, percentage favourable ratings on climate/culture surveys for male and female employees, percentage work-life balance benefits utilised* and *organisation's "openness" ratings*. **Less important** were: percentage favourable ratings on cultural audit, gender equity tied to management compensation, percentage gender initiatives fully implemented, average time for dispute resolution, employee referral rate by male and female employees, percentage gender based pay differentials and workplace flexibility index ratings. Under this perspective only one indicator was seen as **not important** namely the retention rate of critical human capital.

Community perspective
The community perspective was also important for this organisation according to the respondent. The following two indicators were seen as **very important**: *awards received from the community* and *company image (e.g. being an employer of choice for female potential employees)*. **Not important** were the percentage subcontracting euros to women-owned businesses and money given to the community

Leadership commitment
The following four indicators were **very important** for the respondent: *leadership participation in designing the vision and strategies for achieving gender mainstreaming, the representation mix on the organisation's board of directors, money and other resources allocated by the leader to the gender mainstreaming initiative* and *leadership behaviour towards work–life balance issues (such as flexible working hours, glass-ceiling issues and*

family leave policies). **Average importance** was given to: the number of female employees in formal mentoring programmes with the leader, the number of female employees personally selected by the leader for special assignments, the percentage of gender objectives that are tied to key strategic business objectives connected to the bonus and compensation of the leader, leadership representation on the gender steering committee and advisory boards and the degree of personal participation in creating an inclusive climate / culture. **Not important** were the ability of the leader to overcome tension when it arises in the change process and the number of executives and managers that are competent due to training in dealing with gender mainstreaming issues.

Workforce profile
Percentage female managers and officials was the only indicator selected as **very important** under this perspective. **Average importance** was put on: percentage female survival and loss rate, percentage turnover by length of service, percentage voluntary turnover: exempt and non-exempt, percentage involuntary turnover: exempt and non-exempt, number returning from leave for male and female employees. Percentage female new hires, percentage absenteeism for male and female employees, number of offers to female interviewees and cost per hire were **not important** according to the respondent. Especially, under this perspective the interviewee noted that it is difficult in the organisation to give validation to such indicators as the majority of the employees are female.

Case Study Three
- **Multinational organisation**
- **Type of business: Technology (electronics)**
- **Countries: The Netherlands & Germany**

This multinational is operating globally in the technology market. They produce and sell consumer electronics and domestic appliances among other things. The interview took place in the Dutch headquarters of the organisation. The organisation has been using the **traditional balanced scorecard** and also a specific HR-Scorecard. The structure of the organisation is a **matrix structure**. The interviewee is currently working as International HR-Project Manager in the Dutch Headquarters of the organisation. She has been working in the HRM departments of the Dutch office (headquarters) and in the German office (factory). Therefore, it was possible to get feedback about both offices and the organisational/cultural differences. The interviewee is German and has been working in the German offices for 3 years before being relocated to the Netherlands were she has been in the Dutch headquarters of the organisation for approx. 2.5 years.

Part I: General background about the organisation

	World-wide	The Netherlands	Germany
Industry	Technology	-	-
Turnover in 2004	> € 30 billion	-	-
Number of employees end of 2004	Approx. 160.000	>25.000	Not available (but +/-30.000 in rest of Western Europe excl. Netherlands)
Number of female employees end of 2004	38%	20%	30%
Number of female employees working part-time	Not available	Not available	Not available
How many women are employed (in middle and) top management level? (**Aim is to raise this to 10% in five years**)	5% top mgt.	N/A	N/A
How has the number of female employees changed in your organisation over the past three years? + /- ..... % (up / down/ static) (**Since 2002 active aim to raise the percentage of women in organisation**)	Up	Slightly up	Up

Part II: Gender Measures

The organisation has developed extensive policies for HRM purposes. Policies and measures are compared on a regular basis to measures of competitors in this area and benchmarking is being done. During the last two years even more is being done in the special area of diversity and as special part of this area also gender measures are extended. **Mentoring and coaching** are gender measures which are used around the world. Furthermore, specific gender **guidelines and agreements** are used in a number of countries (e.g. in the USA, the Netherlands and Germany). **Special childcare measures** are offered in both the Netherlands and Germany and these do fulfil the legal requirements set by the respective governments. In the Netherlands **part-time work** is an additional possibility which is widely accepted. This is not very common in Germany. **Work life / family life balance support** through flexible hours and home office possibilities are offered in the Dutch offices. In the German office this is not very common.

The **evaluation of these gender measures** is done via satisfaction surveys / questionnaires among employees. Also statistical reviews are used and an inclusion index has been developed by this multinational organisation.

The following **advantages of gender mainstreaming for the organisation** were the **most important** for the organisation according to the interviewee: diverse work teams, more women in management positions, loyal & motivated employees – reduce absenteeism, loss of motivation of workforce & productivity and high retention costs.

The following advantages of gender mainstreaming were of **average importance** for the organisation: better use of the total workforce available, suitable organisational structures and positive effect on company image

Not important were "female customers prefer to buy from female employees" because this does not apply in this specific technology industry. Secondly, "female customers prefer to buy from women friendly organisations" is not important yet but this might become more important in the future and may already apply in the USA. The third statement which is not an important advantage of gender mainstreaming is avoiding fines for discrimination. This could be applicable in the USA but not in Europe.

The interviewee selected the following **main problems with achieving gender equality** in the organisation: organisational culture/climate and ingrained attitudes. She explained this by saying that also in this organisation the 'old boys' network' is still a big obstacle to achieving gender equality. In the organisation the perfect candidate for promotion to the higher levels in management is still very often the '50year old Dutch male'. However, the senior management has put the aim in place to increase the level of women in top management positions to 10% in five years time and to achieve this they are focussing on finding and hiring top talent female employees. Also in the overall organisation the aim is to increase the amount of female employees. **Less important issues** with achieving gender equality are a culture of presentee-ism (not really applicable in the organisation) and time pressure on managers. The interviewee found a lack of family/work-life balance support and a lack of child support practical obstacles to achieving gender mainstreaming. She believes that practical obstacles are easier to overcome than the attitude and behavioural changes.

Part III: Development of a gender balanced scorecard
The organisation has implemented the **traditional balanced scorecard**. Furthermore, the organisation also has a specific **HRM scorecard** in place.

On the special HR-Scorecard also some **diversity and gender specific key indicators** are placed, for example an employee engagement index, an inclusive leadership index, the number of leadership top potential female employees, the number of women in senior management and an inclusion index. These indicators are placed under competences and growth.

Employee engagement is measured on a yearly basis and it is measured in addition to employee satisfaction because the organisation believes that to achieve organisational effectiveness employee engagement is more important (engagement being a combination of attitudes and priorities that has a consistent and predictable impact on behaviour). The engagement index is an average of three items – "Overall I am extremely satisfied with this organisation as a place to work", "I would gladly refer a good friend or family member to this organisation for employment" and "I rarely think about looking for a new job outside of this organisation." The index score for 2004 was 58% favourable / 3.51 mean score, on a scale from 1 to 5.

The inclusion index is an average of the responses to four items from the employee engagement questionnaire used throughout the company - "I feel that I am part of a team", "My ideas and opinions count", "This organisation values my contribution" and "This organisation is committed to providing equal opportunities to all employees". The inclusion index for this organisation in 2004 was 54% favourable / 3.41 mean, on a scale from 1 to 5.

Note: During the interview the interviewee had her personal balanced scorecard printout immediately at hand which shows that the balanced scorecard has been well integrated in the organisation. She was very familiar with the concept and could explain exactly how it works and which purposes it serves.

With regards to the specific **gender balanced scorecard** as an instrument to achieve gender equality in the organisation the interviewee believed that it would be too specific. She thinks that it is important to first raise the general awareness about diversity further in the organisation. Last year was already a big step forward with the implementation of the special **diversity and inclusion team** chaired by the president (team includes: a newly appointed Vice President of global diversity and inclusion + one specialist employee + 10 champions in different levels and areas of the organisation). The next step will be ½-day awareness training for the senior management team and the different departments.

The **diversity and inclusion team** has put a gender network and female executive network in place. First they start to raise the awareness and maturity towards the issues and then further steps will be taken. However, a gender balanced scorecard seems too specific and would probably lead to higher **resistance** toward the issue. Furthermore, there is no **sense of urgency** with regards to the issue of gender equality in the organisation. However, that same sense of urgency is applicable to solving the issue of diversity and inclusion. The interviewee also believes that this has to do with the fact that diversity and inclusion are new management ideas/buzz words which have recently received a lot of attention in management literature and in business magazine articles which are therefore easier to accept by management as a priority.

The interviewee is convinced about the fact that the implementation of a specific gender balanced scorecard would lead to high **resistance** in the organisation. She believes that resistance would be a bigger issue with regards to gender measures than towards the general diversity/cultural issues. *As she stated: "Sometimes I go into ridiculous discussions and afterwards I conclude that it was resistance toward the new diversity measures and ideas. We try to increase awareness for the subject and we found that we can only introduce one or two indicators at a time which are easy to understand and therefore easier to accept. Step by step we continue but we start only with indicators which make total business sense and are very outcome related (e.g. return on investment for initiatives)."*

Furthermore, she thinks that many senior managers do understand the issues but they do not link the issues to their own **behaviour**. They don't ask themselves the question: "why do I have only one woman in my department." They are not against women at all (definitely not conscious) but they are not aware that they need to change some of the "old ways of working" in order to become a women friendly leader/manager.

The interviewee believes that the diversity and inclusion team in cooperation with the president and senior managers should be **responsible for the design and the implementation** of a specific gender balanced scorecard.

With regards to **connecting a gender balanced scorecard to incentives / bonus schemes for the top management** she thinks that this should happen eventually but not in the beginning as this would lead to further resistance instead of to acceptance. After the awareness and maturity towards the subject are raised further then it should definitely be done. First people need to understand the urgency and the business sense behind the ideas for them to be able to accept it. Therefore, it is the plan to first raise the awareness of everybody for about two years and then connect it to bonuses. Certain other indicators of our balanced scorecards are currently connected to bonuses of senior managers and top leaders (for example employee engagement). If asked whether she could think of **other ways to get the commitment from top management** for the implementation of a gender balanced scorecard she answered that the ½-day awareness session should help. This session is especially about inclusion, not so much about diversity. The **review and evaluation of the results of a gender balanced scorecard** should be done via surveys and statistical analysis.

To the question: **"Do you think that a gender balanced scorecard could be a tool that could help to change the organisational culture of your organisation in order that gender mainstreaming / gender equality becomes part of the culture?"** the interviewee answered as follows: *"In our organisation we have set the target already to move to 10% women in top management positions around the 2008 mark which is progress but not really break-through progress. We have put people in place in the corporate headquarters that focus solely on diversity and inclusion issues. Measuring is maybe not as extensive as you are proposing with a gender balanced scorecard but we do get an overview of were we are, how are the trends, what do the competitors do. This is already a change and a step forward toward maturity and awareness. We, at HR, can measure anything that can really help us to underpin a business case and with such information you could go to the top managers and they would listen and seriously consider steps forwards. Indicators which are not directly measurable (soft indicators) would be very hard to communicate and to convince the right people to take it forward toward implementation. Therefore, the key performance indicators have to be credible and robust."*

There have been **attempts to change the organisational culture of the organisation** in the past. This was done because of the outcomes of a research among high potential talents which left the organisation. They were questioned about their experiences with the organisational culture and they where invited to join round table discussions about key issues. From these interviews and discussions it was found that the organisational culture had four main issues with regards to **leadership**. These issues were handled and addressed. The senior managers are now fulfilling a 360 degree feedback evaluation were the employees under this leader also can input their feedback. It was questioned: "what do we actually expect from our leaders?" Based on the outcome one of the aims became to achieve behavioural changes from the leaders. **Leadership issues** have actually been the only reason for the organisation to try and change its culture (by changing leadership behaviour). Diversity is not a key issue at this point. For this reason cultural changes are not initiated but there are people in place with diversity as their special focus of work and the diversity challenge is being addressed in the organisation at all levels.

The **personal opinion of the interviewee about the development of a gender balanced scorecard as a strategic instrument to achieve gender equality** is that it would be difficult to introduce and maybe it is taking it a step too far and too specific. She prefers the diversity issue as a complete concept (were gender is only one special part). Especially, since it is her belief that the **resistance** would be higher to a **gender specific instrument** whereas the **diversity/inclusion concept** is easier to accept (as it is a management trend). Besides this she also thinks that you would have too many different scorecards, i.e. a special gender scorecard, a special cultural scorecard, etc. This would get too **complicated and difficult to manage**.

When the interviewee compared the organisational **cultures of the German organisation to the Dutch organisation** she concluded that the **openness of the Dutch organisation** is much bigger. The traditional **German hierarchical structures** still prevail and the top down approach is widespread. In **the Netherlands** it tends to be a **flatter line** of command and the individual is allowed to act more upon **own initiatives** (less bureaucracy and formal rules). Maybe, this can also be explained by the national culture, as the Germans are more familiar with following rules and regulations in the formal way. They are not familiar with laissez-faire management styles and might not really feel comfortable if this would be demanded from them. However, the **'old boys' network'** is in place in both organisations. This still is the main obstacle to the upwards promotion of highly talented female employees. Gender measures are good in both cultures. In **Germany the governmental regulations** (e.g. the female employee who takes parental leave has the right to return to her old job for the duration of three years) are very good and in **the Netherlands the concept of job sharing and part-time working** are widespread and accepted which allows for more women to combine family-life with work-life. Even in **higher positions part-time work** starts to be accepted for female employees in the Netherlands which is a good step forward to achieving more equality.

Part IV: The gender balanced scorecard perspectives and indicators
Question 1: Looking at the *four traditional perspectives* on a gender balanced scorecard: how important would the following gender indicators be for your organisation? **A = really important / B = average / C = not important**

The financial perspective
Under the **financial perspective** *turnover per employee* (differentiating between men and women) and *return on investment for the gender initiatives* were identified as the **most important**. Benefits costs as a percentage of payroll or revenue were **really important to average important**. Gender initiative expenses per employee and gender initiative budget as a percentage of sales could be seen as **average important** indicators. Finally, the amount of money saved as a result of gender initiatives and reduced litigation costs were **not important** according to the interviewee.

Customer perspective
For the customer perspective the following two indicators were selected as **most important**: *market share division between female and male customers and the representation in the workforce of male and female employees* and secondly *the percentage diverse customer satisfaction*. Of **average importance** were: number of new customers attracted by male and female employees, percentage customer retention by male and female employees, profitability by male and female customers, number of customer complaints successfully dealt with by male and female employees and the number of customer awards received. Number of solutions offered per client by male and female employees and percentage on-time delivery rating by male and female employees were identified as being **not important**.

Internal Business processes perspective
Employee satisfaction and female employee satisfaction (to be assessed with questionnaires) together with *social audit results* were the two indicators that were seen to be **really important** indicators. The number of awards received for equality/diversity initiatives was of **average importance**. Finally, two indicators that were **not important** according to the interviewee were: throughput time per business action for male and female employees and new product introduction and design (male vs. female employees).

Learning and growth perspective
Under the learning and growth perspectives the interviewee identified five indicators as being **really important**, namely: *number of female employees, number of female managers / leaders, motivation index, ethic violations* and the *empowerment index* (i.e. the number of female employees vs. male employees that have received a certain level of power or authority to make higher level decisions). Of **average importance** were: comparison of educational budget spend on women and men, productivity (male vs. female employees), cross functional assignments (male vs. female employees), percentage of employees with advanced degrees for male and female employees, number of innovations initiated by male vs. female employees and Employee suggestions (male vs. female employees). Only two indicators were **not important** under this perspective, namely: number and percentage of gender-competent employees and personal goal achievement (male vs. female employees).

Note: The interviewee explained that she is convinced that only those indicators that make common business sense and are 'easily' measurable in figures (i.e. no 'soft' indicators) will be accepted by management as indicators with outcomes that should be taken seriously and should be dealt with.

Question 2: Which of the following (optional) additional perspectives would be relevant perspectives for your organisation to add on to the gender balanced scorecard?

The interviewee would definitely include **organisational culture** as a separate perspective. She commented that the organisation is aiming to develop a culture of inclusion and to do this it is critical to continue with awareness rising and to increase the support of management. **Community** should also be a different perspective as this would help to focus on cultural differences in the world and communities. **Workforce profile** also makes sense as a separate perspective as this would help to show also differences in industries. However, the **leadership commitment** perspective should be included under the **organisational culture perspective** and should not be a separate perspective.

Question 3: Which indicators would be important for your organisation for the additional perspectives you selected in question two? **A = really important, B = average, C = not important.**

Organisational culture perspective (with the leadership commitment included)
Under the organisational culture perspective (with the leadership commitment included) the following indicators would be **really important**:
- *Absence rate / percentage absenteeism*
- *Retention rate of critical human capital*

- *Percentage favourable ratings on climate/culture surveys for male and female employees*
- *Percentage gender based pay differentials*
- *Organisation's "openness" ratings*
- *The number of female employees in formal mentoring programmes with the leader*
- *The representation mix on the organisation's board of directors*
- *Leadership representation on the gender steering committee and advisory boards*
- *Money and other resources allocated by the leader to the gender mainstreaming initiative*

The following two indicators would be **really important to average important**: the degree of personal participation in creating an inclusive climate / culture and the ability of the leader to overcome tension when it arises in the change process. Of **average importance** are: percentage favourable ratings on cultural audit, "employer of choice" ratings versus top 5 to 10 competitors, perception of consistent and equitable treatment of all employees, gender equity tied to management compensation, percentage gender initiatives fully implemented, percentage work-life balance benefits utilised, workplace flexibility index ratings, leadership participation in designing the vision and strategies for achieving gender mainstreaming, the percentage of gender objectives that are tied to key strategic business objectives connected to the bonus and compensation of the leader and leadership behaviour towards work–life balance issues (such as flexible working hours, glass-ceiling issues and family leave policies). The interviewee found the following four indicators **not important**: average time for dispute resolution, employee referral rate by male and female employees, the number of female employees personally selected by the leader for special assignments and the number of executives and managers that are competent due to training in dealing with gender mainstreaming issues.

Community perspective
Under the community perspective there were *no indicators* seen as **really important**. The following two indicators were identified as **average important**: awards received from the community and company image (e.g. being an employer of choice for female potential employees). Percentage subcontracting euros to women-owned businesses and money given to the community were seen as **not important**.

Workforce profile
The percentage female managers and officials and *the percentage turnover by length of service* were the two indicators that were given **really importance**. **Really important to average important** was the percentage female survival and loss rate. Five indicators were of average importance: percentage female new hires, percentage absenteeism for male and female employees, percentage voluntary turnover: exempt and non-exempt, percentage involuntary turnover: exempt and non-exempt and the number of offers to female interviewees. Cost per hire and number returning from leave for male and female employees were identified as **not important**.

Case Study four
- **Type: Medium sized organisation**
- **Type of business: Food**
- **Country: Germany**

This organisation is a food manufacturers operating European-wide. The organisation is part of a group of companies operating in the (luxury) food industry. The overall organisation has been a medium sized family company for many years. The subsidiary (food specialist) were the interview took place has production plants in both Germany and the Netherlands. The organisation is a business to business ('B to B') organisation and does not sell directly to end consumers. The organisation does **not** use the traditional balanced scorecard. The business structure that fits to the organisation is a **bureaucratic / hierarchical structure**. The interviewee is working in the Human Resource Department of the German manufacturing plant. He is a Dutch national who has worked in both the Dutch offices and now in the German office. During the interview also a female product manager joined in order that she could talk about her personal experiences within the German organisation.

Part I: General background about the organisation

	World-wide	Germany
Industry	Food	Food
Turnover in 2004	> € 950 million	> € 300 million
Number of employees in 2004	+/- 3,800	+/-400
Number of female employees in 2004	Not available	+/- 70
Number of female employees working part-time	Not available	+/- 10
How many women are employed in middle and top management level (approx. percentage)?		+/ - 5%
How has the number of female employees changed in your organisation over the past three years? + /- ... % (up / down/ static)		Up

Part II: Gender Measures
According to the interviewee the organisation does not have an extensive written policy with regards to gender measures. They adhere to the **legal requirements** but other than that the measures are dealt with on a case to case basis by the HR department. Especially, since the Dutch and German organisation are manufacturing sites the main part of the labour force is low skilled labour and special measures are not normally requested by this part of the labour force. As the female product manager also stated: "usually, only the administrative employees and other office employees make use of specific personnel policies." If an employee has a personal issue (either private or professional) they can contact the HR department and solutions can be found for this specific issue. But the personnel policies are **not active only reactive** upon demand.

Due to the fact that the personnel policies for gender measures are only developed upon demand there is also **not a specific measurement tool** available for measuring effectiveness. The employees in the offices (not on the factory floor) have **performance reviews** on a yearly basis.

According to the interviewee there were **no advantages** of gender mainstreaming that could be rated as **very important**. However, the interviewee rated the following as being of **average importance**: better use of the total workforce available, diverse work teams, suitable organisational structures, positive effect on company image and loyal & motivated employees – reduce absenteeism. **Not important** were: more women in management positions, avoiding fines for discrimination, "female customers prefer to buy from female employees", "female customers prefer to buy from women friendly organisations", loss of motivation of workforce & productivity and high retention costs. The interviewee explained with regards to the choice of more women in management positions that this is not a business goal currently. And he continued to note that more women on management positions could have a negative impact on the performance of the factory due to the fact that many employees are of foreign nationalities and may not accept it that their boss is a woman. With regards to the customers being female the interviewee explained that this is of no direct influence as the organisation is a white label company which sells only to companies/intermediaries and not to the end consumer directly. Therefore, these advantages were not relevant for the organisation.

The interviewees both believed that the **organisational culture / climate** is the main obstacle to achieving gender equality. Female management would most likely lead to high **resistance** from the employees on the factory floor as these are mostly from different cultural and religious backgrounds. **Work/family balance** is not an issue as the office employees work only normal hours and usually not late hours.

Part III: Development of a gender balanced scorecard
The organisation has **not** used the traditional balanced scorecard but both interviewees are familiar with the balanced scorecard tool.

The interviewee does **not** think that a specific gender balanced scorecard could be an instrument that would be successful in their organisation. Especially, since **gender equality is not a business aim** at the moment. An important reason according to the interviewee is that the organisation is a factory and the majority of employees on the factory floor (mostly low skilled labour) are from different cultures and religions. Therefore, specific gender initiatives would be difficult to implement and would encounter high **resistance**. Furthermore, the interviewee believes that gender should not influence the decision making process about which candidate gets the job. He believes that this is another issue that would lead to high **resistance** in the organisation. The interviewee remarked: *"I believe that to successfully manage our multicultural work environment is challenging enough for us."* He continued: *"under the diversity management that we do undertake in this area – i.e. cultural and religious conflict managing/avoiding - a small part of gender management is included as well, even, if this is not actively managed but only passively acted upon."* He also mentioned that the organisation is currently not hiring new employees and are not planning to change this in the near future. Until the economic situation improves and the company improves its business results the focus of the personnel department is not on structural changes, policies and improvements but on daily management of the personnel issues. Hopefully in the future when the economy booms again this changes and there will also be a focus on different managerial issues or new instruments that could improve the private life of the employees. He added that he thinks that all employees in Germany are currently just happy to have their job and that he does not hear many complaints from employees about their situation at all.

Responsibility for the design and the implementation of a specific gender balanced scorecard should lie with the top management team and the CEO together with the personnel department / HRM team.

With regards to the question whether the gender balanced scorecard should be connected to **bonus schemes for the top management** the interviewee answered with **no** as the decisions would than be made with **focus on money and not on the target**. However, he added, that after such an instrument would be introduced and has achieved acceptance then he thinks eventually this connection could be made. The interviewee said that the owner should initiate the project and therefore be the **owner, i.e. champion**, of the project. This should help to achieve commitment from the top level.

In this organisation no attempts have been made so far to change the corporate culture. Therefore, the interviewee cannot remark about this. However, he compared the **culture** of the Dutch office/factory to the German factory and stated the German offices are definitely more **official, bureaucratic and hierarchical**. In Holland it is easier for employees to come into the personnel department and discuss their personal situation. In Germany this doesn't happen very often. Partly because the Germans are currently afraid to loose their jobs as the economic situation is bad but also because of the culture of the people. In Holland everything is **less formal** and an example here is that people address each other with their first names.

To the question: **"Do you think that a gender balanced scorecard could be a tool that could help to change the organisational culture of your organisation in order that gender mainstreaming / gender equality becomes part of the culture?"**
The interviewee stated as follows: *"as a manufacturing organisation we encounter a multi-cultural environment were merely the different religions and cultures are leading to tension between people. If we would try to aim at 'balancing' male and female employees we would – without a doubt - encounter a lot of resistance at all levels in the organisation but mainly at the factory floor."* The interviewee does not think that such an instrument would be accepted currently in the German offices. Maybe when the economic situation improves people in the organisation are more open to such initiatives. In the Dutch offices it is more likely that such an initiative could find support from a small majority of employees.

Part IV: The gender balanced scorecard perspectives and indicators
Question 1: Looking at the *four traditional perspectives* on a gender balanced scorecard: how important would the following **gender indicators** be for your organisation? A = **really important, B = average, C = not important**

The financial perspective
Turnover per employee, differentiating between men and women and *the amount of money saved as a result of gender initiatives* were the two indicators that were selected as being **really important**. The following three indicators were selected as **average important**: benefits costs as a percentage of payroll or revenue, return on investment for the gender initiatives and gender initiative expenses per employee. The gender initiative budget as a percentage of sales was seen as **not important**. Finally, reduced litigation costs were not applicable as the interviewee noted that this may be important in the USA but not in Europe at this point in time.

The customer perspective
The customer perspective was not important for this interviewee as he explained that the organisation only produces for intermediaries and therefore does not interact with the end customer. The intermediaries are their customers and these are always organisations not consumers. Therefore, he gave all indicators under the customer perspective a C-rating as being **not important**.

Internal Business processes perspective
Employee satisfaction and female employee satisfaction (to be assessed with questionnaires) and *social audit results* were the two indicators selected as **really important**. Of **average importance** for the interviewee were: throughput time per business action for male and female employees and new product introduction and design (male vs. female employees). And, thirdly, the interviewee found the number of awards received for equality/diversity initiatives **not important**.

Learning and growth perspective
Under this perspective the interviewee selected three indicators as being **really important**: *number of female managers / leaders, number and percentage of gender-competent employees* and *productivity (male vs. female employees)*.**Less important** (i.e. average importance) was personal goal achievement (male vs. female employees). The other indicators under this perspective were given the C-rating of **not important**: comparison of educational budget spend on women and men, cross functional assignments (male vs. female employees), ethic violations, percentage of employees with advanced degrees for male and female employees, number of innovations initiated by male vs. female employees and the Empowerment index (i.e. the number of female employees vs. male employees that have received a certain level of power or authority to make higher level decisions).

Question 2: Which of the following (optional) **additional perspectives** would be relevant perspectives for your organisation to add on to the gender balanced scorecard?

Organisational culture would definitely be included onto the scorecard. But, the interviewee would also include the **leadership commitment** perspective under the culture perspective. He thinks that those indicators fit very well under this cultural perspective and should not be treated separate. The **community perspective** was not applicable to this organisation. Finally, the **workforce profile** was also not selected as a separate perspective but the interviewee said that he would separate the indicators mentioned and divide them over the four traditional perspectives.

Question 3: Which **gender indicators** would be important for your organisation for the additional perspectives you selected in question two? **A = really important, B = average, C = not important**

Organisational culture perspective (combined with the leadership commitment perspective)
The interviewee selected the following indicators of the organisational perspective and the leadership perspective as being **very important**:
- *Percentage favourable ratings on cultural audit*
- *Absence rate / percentage absenteeism*

- *Organisation's "openness" ratings*
- *Leadership participation in designing the vision and strategies for achieving gender mainstreaming / equality*
- *The degree of personal participation in creating an inclusive culture*
- *The ability of the leader to overcome tension when it arises in the change process*
- *Leadership behaviour towards work–life balance issues (such as flexible working hours, glass-ceiling issues and family leave policies)*

The following indicators were found to be of **average importance**: perception of consistent and equitable treatment of all employees, percentage favourable ratings on climate/culture surveys for male and female employees, average time for dispute resolution, percentage gender based pay differentials, workplace flexibility index ratings, the number of female employees in formal mentoring programmes with the leader, the number of female employees personally selected by the leader for special assignments, the representation mix on the organisation's board of directors, money and other resources allocated by the leader to the gender mainstreaming initiative and the number of executives and managers that are competent due to training in dealing with gender mainstreaming issues.

Under the organisational culture perspective the following indicators were selected as **not important**: "employer of choice" ratings versus top 5 to 10 competitors, gender equity tied to management compensation, retention rate of critical human capital, percentage gender initiatives fully implemented, employee referral rate by male and female employees and the percentage work-life balance benefits utilised. There were no indicators under the leadership perspective which were selected as being **not important** at all.

Case Study five
- **Type: Large organisation**
- **Type of business: Energy industry**
- **Country: Germany**

This organisation operates worldwide in the energy industry. The organisation does not use the **traditional balanced scorecard** but the interviewee is familiar with the balanced scorecard as management tool. The structure of the organisation is a **flat structure**. The interviewee is a German national and head of a department in this organisation. He has been working for this organisation as expatriate in different countries but is currently located in Germany.

Part I: General background about the organisation

	World-wide	Germany
Industry	Energy	
Turnover in 2004	> € 5 billion	Not available
Number of employees (approx.)	1.000	Not available
Number of female employees	250	Not available
Number of female employees working part-time	50	Not available
How many women are employed in middle and top management level (approx. percentage)?	10%	Not available
How has the number of female employees changed in your organisation over the past three years? + /- ... % (up / down/ static)	+5-8%	Not available

Part II: Gender measures
The organisation fulfils the requirements set by the governments in the countries they operate in for **gender measures**. Therefore special agreements exist partly, namely were they are required. **Mentoring** is also part of the gender measures available. Furthermore, **special childcare measures** are in place and **work-life / family life balance support** is also available in the form of flexible hours and home office possibilities. Besides this the organisation participates in **'girl's day'** which is a special day when organisations open their doors to show young girls which jobs are available and what they entail in order that more girls choose career paths that are different from the 'normal' girl's choices. The **evaluation** of these gender measures is done with the use of **surveys**.

The following **advantages of gender mainstreaming** were **very important** for this organisation: diverse work teams, loyal & motivated employees – reduce absenteeism and to avoid fines for discrimination. Five advantages of gender mainstreaming were seen as average important, namely: better use of the total workforce available, suitable organisational structures, positive effect on company image, loss of motivation of workforce & productivity and high retention costs. Not important were more women in management positions, "female customers prefer to buy from female employees" and "female customers prefer to buy from women friendly organisations". These last two reasons were not applicable as this organisation does not sell directly to customers/people.

There were no really huge problems with achieving gender equality in the organisation but **average obstacles** are time pressure on managers, ingrained attitudes and lack of child support. Culture of presentee-ism, lack of family/work-life balance support and organisational culture/climate were no problems at all according to the interviewee. Because of the international character of the organisation and the flat structure the culture / climate in the organisation is very open. However, some of the old ways and conservative thinking are still part of it, especially at the top.

Part III Development of a gender balanced scorecard
The organisation has **not** implemented the **traditional balanced scorecard** but the respondent is familiar with the concept.

According to the interviewee the HRM department in combination with one gender specialist (internal employee) should be **responsible for the design and the implementation** of a specific gender balanced scorecard.

The interviewee does not believe that the gender balanced scorecard should be connected to **bonus schemes for the top management** because the positive impact alone should be enough. Besides, the top management needs to support every scorecard or initiative that they decide to implement without connecting it to monetary bonuses. He thinks that first of all the awareness of the top management should be raised towards the issue of gender mainstreaming/equality before bonus connections can be put in place. The whole subject of gender equality is a delicate issue to put on the strategy aims of the organisation. If too much stress would be put on it then chances are high that the management rejects the whole initiative. On the other hand, if the introduction is slow then the measures may be faster/easier accepted all around. **Resistance** to such initiatives are likely to occur. This may happen on all levels in the organisation not only from the top managers (who like to do things in the 'old ways'). The interviewee also has the opinion that **the best person should get the job independent of gender.**

The respondent is not aware of organised attempts to **change the organisational culture** of the organisation but the German business has had an old and pretty conservative culture, which is currently in a kind of change progress. Today it seems not to be any longer important what gender it is in the organisation. The international focus has taken over and the changes in the economies and environment have led to adaptations in the culture of the organisation.

To the final question: **"Do you think that a gender balanced scorecard could be a tool that could help to change the organisational culture of your organisation in order that gender mainstreaming / gender equality becomes part of the culture?"** The respondent answered: "I believe that we don't need a specific gender balanced scorecard, because our organisation and culture is open to everybody who is qualified (or knows the CEO best)." He continued to say that gender equality is not a strategic aim in the organisation and that management is also not aware of a difficult situation that would demand such initiatives at the moment.

Part IV: The gender balanced scorecard perspectives and initiatives
Question 1: Looking at the *four traditional perspectives* on a gender balanced scorecard: how important would the following **gender indicators** be for your organisation? **(A = really important, B = average, C = not important)**

Financial perspective
For the financial perspective two indicators were selected as being **really important**: *turnover per employee, differentiating between men and women* and *return on investment for the gender initiatives.* The following indicators were of **average** importance for the respondent: amount of money saved as a result of gender initiatives, benefits costs as a percentage of payroll or revenue and gender initiative expenses per employee. Gender initiative budget as a percentage of sales was seen as **not important** and reduced litigation costs were not applicable as this is not very likely in European countries.

Customer perspective
The customer perspective is for this organisation not very relevant as the organisation does **not deal with direct customers.** The organisation searches for natural resources around the world and then sells these to the organisations that sell further to the consumers. Therefore, under the customer perspective four indicators were selected as not important: number of new customers attracted by male and female employees, percentage customer retention by male and female employees, number of solutions offered per client by male and female employees and percentage on-time delivery rating by male and female employees. Five other indicators were selected as not applicable: market share division between female and male customers and the representation in the workforce of male and female employees, percentage diverse customer satisfaction, profitability by male and female customers, number of customer complaints successfully dealt with by male and female employees and number of customer awards received.

Internal Business processes perspective
Employee satisfaction and female employee satisfaction (to be assessed with questionnaires) and *social audit results* were the two indicators that were selected as being **most important**. Following this the throughput time per business action for male and female employees and new product introduction and design (male vs. female employees) were of **average importance** to this organisation according to the respondent. Finally, number of awards received for equality/diversity initiatives was not important.

Learning and growth perspective
Under this perspective the following indicators were seen as **really important**: *number of female employees, motivation index, productivity (male vs. female employees)* and *ethic violations*. Of average importance were the following indicators: number of female managers / leaders, cross functional assignments (male vs. female employees), percentage of employees with advanced degrees for male and female employees, number of innovations initiated by male vs. female employees and the empowerment index (i.e. the number of female employees vs. male employees that have received a certain level of power or authority to make higher level decisions). Three indicators were selected as not important: number and percentage of gender-competent employees, comparison of educational budget spend on women and men and personal goal achievement (male vs. female employees).

Question 2: Which of the following (optional) **additional perspectives** would be relevant perspectives for your organisation to add on to the gender balanced scorecard?
The respondent selected all four additional perspectives organisational culture, community, leadership commitment and workforce profile to be put on the gender balanced scorecard.

Question 3: Which **gender indicators** would be important for your organisation for the additional perspectives you selected in question two? (**A = really important, B = average, C = not important**)

Organisational culture perspective
Under the organisational culture perspective the following indicators were selected as being **very important**: *"employer of choice" ratings versus top 5 to 10 competitors, perception of consistent and equitable treatment of all employees, absence rate / percentage absenteeism, percentage favourable ratings on climate/culture surveys for male and female employees, percentage work-life balance benefits utilised* and *organisation's "openness" ratings*. Average important were: percentage favourable ratings on cultural audit, gender equity tied to management compensation, retention rate of critical human capital, percentage gender initiatives fully implemented, average time for dispute resolution, employee referral rate by male and female employees, percentage gender based pay differentials and workplace flexibility index ratings.

Community perspective
For this organisation the community perspective is quite important as they partly exist to serve the communities need for energy. The organisation feels commitment to serve the community and therefore this perspective deserves special attention. For this reason the respondent also selected three indicators as being **very important**: *money given to the community, awards received from the community and company image (e.g. being an employer*

of choice for female potential employees). Percentage subcontracting euros to women-owned businesses was **not important** for the interviewee.

Leadership commitment perspective
Four indicators were selected as being very important under the leadership commitment perspective: *leadership participation in designing the vision and strategies for achieving gender mainstreaming / equality, the ability of the leader to overcome tension when it arises in the change process, money and other resources allocated by the leader to the gender mainstreaming initiative* and *leadership behaviour towards work–life balance issues (such as flexible working hours, glass-ceiling issues and family leave policies).* Of average importance were: the number of female employees in formal mentoring programmes with the leader, the representation mix on the organisation's board of directors, leadership representation on the gender steering committee and advisory boards, the degree of personal participation in creating an inclusive culture and the number of executives and managers that are competent due to training in dealing with gender mainstreaming issues. Not important were the number of female employees personally selected by the leader for special assignments and the percentage of gender objectives that are tied to key strategic business objectives connected to the bonus and compensation of the leader.

Workforce profile
Two indicators were selected as **most important**: *percentage female survival and loss rate* and *percentage absenteeism for male and female employees.* Of **average importance** were: percentage female new hires, percentage female managers and officials, percentage turnover by length of service for male and female employees, percentage voluntary turnover: exempt and non-exempt, percentage involuntary turnover: exempt and non-exempt, number of offers to female interviewees and number returning from leave for male and female employees. Not important was the cost per hire indicator according to the interviewee.

Case Study six
- **Type: Multinational**
- **Type of business: Telecommunications**
- **Country: Germany**
This is a **multinational** organisation with German roots. The organisation has been using the **traditional balanced scorecard**. The structure of the organisation is a **matrix** structure. The interviewee is head of a department and has been with this organisation for many years in different positions.

Part I: General background about the organisation

	World-wide	Germany
Industry	Telecom	
Turnover in 2004	> €30 billion	Not available
Number of employees; approx.	49.000	Not available
Number of female employees	Approx. 30%	Not available
Number of female employees working part-time	Not available	Not available
How many women are employed in middle and top management level (approx. percentage)?	Approx. 10%	Not available
How has the number of female employees changed in your organisation over the past three years? + /- ... %	Almost static/ little up	Not available

Part II: Gender measures
There are many measures and HR policies developed for personnel purposes. **Special guidelines** are available but no special agreements exist. Special **childcare measures** are offered according to the requirements of the government but also on specific demand of the individual employees. Also **work life / family life balance** support through flexible hours and home office possibilities are offered. **Coaching and mentoring** are measures that are available but it depends on the hierarchical level of the employee whether they apply and secondly the employee needs to ask for participation (participation is thus not automatically required). The **evaluation** of these gender measures is done via **satisfaction questionnaires** for the employees.

The following **advantages of gender mainstreaming** were **very important** for the organisation according to the interviewee: better use of the total workforce available, positive effect on company image, loyal & motivated employees – reduce absenteeism and loss of motivation of workforce & productivity.

The other **advantages of gender mainstreaming** were awarded **average importance** by the interviewee, these included: diverse work teams, more women in management positions, suitable organisational structures, "female customers prefer to buy from female employees", "female customers prefer to buy from women friendly organisations", avoid fines for discrimination and high retention costs.

According to the interviewee the **main problem with achieving gender equality** is **time pressure on managers**. Following this are the lack of family / work life balance support and culture of presentee-ism. 'Not a problem at all' is given as response to the following: ingrained attitudes, lack of child support and the organisational culture / climate.

Part III: Development of a gender balanced scorecard
The **traditional balanced scorecard** is used by the organisation. Also benchmarking is used extensively to develop new measures in HRM. The organisation aims to use total quality management in all processes and policies. The organisation has a special team of gender experts in the head office. These experts - among other activities - review specific gender statistics to review how female employees and male employees can be compared in certain aspects and issues. These statistics are probably similar to the indicators that would appear on a gender balanced scorecard. The group of experts also provides training to other personnel (in subsidiaries) in order that they are aware of the initiatives developed in the head office and increase there awareness towards achieving gender equality in the organisation. The initiatives toward gender equality are used by the organisation for marketing and PR purposes and awards of good practice have been given to this organisation.

According to the interviewee the **personnel department / HRM department** should carry the main responsibility for the design and implementation of a specific gender balanced scorecard. They should use the knowledge of the gender experts in the organisation.

To the question whether a gender balanced scorecard should be connected to bonus schemes for the top management the interviewee replied the following: *"The implementation and execution of a gender balanced scorecard may be connected to **bonus schemes of HR-top management** (not CEO-level), but with regard to the neutrality of career opportunities in* *respect of gender, religion, etc. Consequently, the existence of instruments serving as a frame should be assessed and related to bonus schemes, not the obligation itself to achieve certain quotas (to make sure that only qualification decides on staffing)."*

Implementation of principles helping to achieve gender equality in company guidelines could be another way (besides bonuses) to get the commitment from the top management for the implementation of a gender balanced scorecard.

The interviewee believes that **resistance** to a gender balanced scorecard would occur when certain committed quotas have to be achieved. If it would be designed as an instrument that only serves to achieve gender equality then the resistance should be limited.

The interviewee is not aware of any active attempts to **change the organisational culture** of the organisation.

To the question: **"Do you think that a gender balanced scorecard could be a tool that could help to change the organisational culture of your organisation in order that gender mainstreaming / gender equality becomes part of the culture?"** the interviewee answered as follows: *"A gender balanced scorecard could only be a good instrument if it was designed to monitor issues with regards to gender equality. However, if it would be used as an instrument to steer quotas for the sake of quotas then it would not be a very useful instrument and it would actually be received with high resistance around the organisation."* This organisation has already developed extensive measures and initiatives in the area of gender equality also by using statistical analysis. Some of these statistics could maybe be used on the official balanced scorecard to achieve a focus on them. However, a special gender balanced scorecard sounds too difficult to achieve and would also be very complex to implement in this organisation.

Part IV: The gender balanced scorecard perspectives and indicators
Question 1: Looking at the *four traditional perspectives* on a gender balanced scorecard: how important would the following **gender indicators** be for your organisation? (**A = really important, B = average, C = not important**)

Financial perspective
Under the financial perspective the following indicators were selected as being of **average** importance: *Amount of money saved as a result of gender initiatives, benefits costs as a percentage of payroll or revenue, return on investment for the gender initiatives, gender initiative expenses per employee, gender initiative budget as a percentage of sales* and *reduced litigation costs.* Turnover per employee, differentiating between men and women was seen as **not important** with the comment to it that this would again differentiate between men and women on the basis of quotas.

Customer perspective
For the customer perspective five indicators were selected as being **very important**, namely: *market share division between female and male customers and the representation in the workforce of male and female employees, percentage diverse customer satisfaction, number of new customers attracted by male and female employees, percentage customer retention by male and female employees* and *number of customer awards received.* The remaining four

indicators were given average importance and included: number of solutions offered per client by male and female employees, percentage on-time delivery rating by male and female employees, profitability by male and female customers and the number of customer complaints successfully dealt with by male and female employees.

Internal business processes perspective
Number of awards received for equality/diversity initiatives, employee satisfaction and female employee satisfaction (to be assessed with questionnaires) and *social audit results* were the three indicators under the internal business processes perspectives that were granted **high importance**. Throughput time per business action for male and female employees and new product introduction and design (male vs. female employees) were given **average importance** with the note from the interviewee that these indicators are very hard to measure because it is **teamwork** and cannot be granted to one employee.

Learning and growth perspective
The following four indicators were given high importance: *number of female employees, number and percentage of gender-competent employees, motivation index* and *ethic violations.* The other indicators were all given average importance: number of female managers / leaders, comparison of educational budget spend on women and men, productivity (male vs. female employees), cross functional assignments (male vs. female employees), personal goal achievement (male vs. female employees), percentage of employees with advanced degrees for male and female employees, number of innovations initiated by male vs. female employees and the empowerment index (i.e. the number of female employees vs. male employees that have received a certain level of power or authority to make higher level decisions).

Question 2: Which of the following (optional) **additional perspectives** would be relevant perspectives for your organisation to add on to the gender balanced scorecard?

Organisational culture is a very important additional perspective for the respondent. Reason for this is that all the different **existing orientations have to be represented** in the organisational culture. Also the outside **community** is important for this organisation and therefore this perspective would be included on the gender balanced scorecard. **Workforce profile** adds many statistical and interesting indicators and should be included. However, **leadership commitment** is not selected as a separate perspective.

Question 3: Which **gender indicators** would be important for your organisation for the additional perspectives you selected in question two? (**A = really important, B = average, C = not important**)

Organisational culture perspective
Under the organisational culture perspective four indicators were selected as being **really important**: *"employer of choice" ratings versus top 5 to 10 competitors, perception of consistent and equitable treatment of all employees, percentage favourable ratings on climate/culture surveys for male and female employees* and *percentage work-life balance benefits utilised.* Nine indicators were given **average importance**, these were: percentage favourable ratings on cultural audit, absence rate / percentage absenteeism, retention rate of critical human capital, percentage gender initiatives fully implemented, average time for

dispute resolution, employee referral rate by male and female employees, percentage gender based pay differentials, workplace flexibility index ratings and organisation's "openness" ratings. Only one indicator was seen as **not important** namely: gender equity tied to management compensation. Here again the same **note** from the respondent that compensation to management should not be connected to the obligation to achieve certain quotas.

Community perspective

The *company image* (e.g. being an employer of choice for female potential employees) indicator was selected as being **really important** under the community perspective. The following two indicators were given **average importance**: money given to the community and awards received from the community. The percentage subcontracting euros to women-owned businesses was seen as **not important** and also here again the business should go the best suitable supplier not specific women-owned businesses.

Workforce profile

Three indicators were selected as being really important, namely: percentage female survival and loss rate, percentage absenteeism for male and female employees and number returning from leave for male and female employees. The other indicators were seen as average important: percentage female new hires, percentage female managers and officials, percentage turnover by length of service for male and female employees, percentage voluntary turnover: exempt and non-exempt, percentage involuntary turnover: exempt and non-exempt, number of offers to female interviewees and cost per hire.

Appendix Two: In-Depth Interview Guideline

The Gender Balanced Scorecard explained:
A **traditional balanced scorecard** reviews **organisational performance** from the following four perspectives:

1) Financial perspective
2) Customer perspective
3) Internal business processes perspective
4) Learning and growth perspective

It is possible to take the traditional balanced scorecard a step further and develop a specific **Human Resources balanced scorecard** which reviews organisational performance from the Human Resources point of view. Then, this HR-Scorecard can be further developed into a specific **diversity scorecard** which measures the performance of the organisation with regards to diversity measures. Gender measures are part of the overall diversity strategy. The development of a **gender balanced scorecard** which shows the performance of the organisation with regards to gender initiatives and gender equality is the subject of this research.

A **Gender balanced scorecard** would be based on the outcome and comparison of a number of specifically designed **gender indicators** under several **business perspectives** (unique for each individual organisation). The traditional four perspectives of the general balanced scorecard can be expanded here with more specific perspectives for a gender balanced scorecard.

A gender balanced scorecard: *would serve as a strategic management tool to achieve gender mainstreaming in organisational culture. It is an instrument that would assist organisations with the review of organisational performance in the specific area of gender equality/mainstreaming.*

Structure of the interview:

Part I: General background information about the organisation

Part II: Gender measures *(four questions)*

Part III: Development of a gender balanced scorecard *(eight questions)*

Part IV: The gender balanced scorecard perspectives and indicators *(three ABC questions)*

Note: The complete interview was send to the respondents **before** the interview date in order that they could review all questions and with the request that they would fill out **part I and part IV** beforehand (or return it at a later stage after the interview). **Part II and part III** where the **actual discussion questions** during the in-depth interviews (approximately duration 60 to 90 minutes).

Part I: General background about the organisation

	World-wide	The Netherlands / Germany
Industry		
Turnover in 2004		
Number of employees		
Number of female employees		
Number of female employees working part-time		
How many women are employed in middle and top management level?		
How has the number of female employees changed in your organisation over the past three years? + /- ..... % (up / down/ static)		

Which **business structure** fits best to your organisation?

Organisational Structure:	
Bureaucratic / hierarchical structure	
Flat structure	
Network structure	
Matrix structure	

Part II: Gender measures

1) Which gender measures are included in the organisation's policy to improve the position of women in middle and top management:

Gender measures:	**Yes / No**
Special guidelines are available	
Special agreements exist	
Coaching	
Mentoring	
Special childcare measures	
Work life / family life balance support through flexible hours, home office, etc.	
Other measures, namely:	

2) How do you review and evaluate the effectiveness of these measures? (from intangible assets (i.e. gender measures) create tangible results)

3) How important are the following advantages of gender mainstreaming for your organisation? (A =very important, B= average importance, C= not important)

Advantage for organisation:	A, B, C	Reason when answer is *not important*:
Better use of the total workforce available		
Diverse work teams		
More women in management positions		
Suitable organisational structures		
Positive effect on company image		
Loyal & motivated employees – reduce absenteeism		
"Female customers prefer to buy from female employees"		
"Female customers prefer to buy from women friendly organisations"		
Avoid fines for discrimination		
Loss of motivation of workforce & productivity		
High retention costs		

4) In your opinion what are the main problems with achieving gender equality in your organisation? (A= is a huge problem / B = average problem / C = not a problem at all)

	A, B, C	*Notes:*
Culture of presentee-ism *(i.e. having to work late hours until the boss goes home)*		
Time pressures on managers		
Ingrained attitudes		
Lack of family/work-life balance support		
Lack of child support		
Organisational culture/climate		
Others, namely:		

Part III: Development of a gender balanced scorecard

1) Are you familiar with the traditional balanced scorecard and has your organisation implemented the **traditional** balanced scorecard *(why / why not)*?

2) In your opinion, who should be **responsible for the design and the implementation** of a specific gender balanced scorecard in your organisation?

3) Do you think that a gender balanced scorecard should be **connected to incentives / bonus schemes** for the top management?

4) Can you think of other ways to get the **commitment from the top management** for the implementation of a gender balanced scorecard?

5) If your organisation decided to implement a gender balanced scorecard do you believe that there would be **resistance** in the organisation? (*If so, from whom and why?*)

6) Would a specific **gender balanced scorecard** be a management tool that your organisation would **accept** as an instrument to achieve gender equality in the organisation? *If so*, would your organisation actually consider **implementing** this strategic instrument for gender equality? (*Why / Why not?*)

7) Do you think that a gender balanced scorecard could be a tool that could help to **change the organisational culture** of your organisation in order that gender mainstreaming / gender equality becomes part of the culture? (*Why?*)

8) Have there been any attempts to change the organisational culture? (*If yes, how was this process managed?*)

Part IV: The gender balanced scorecard perspectives and indicators

1) Looking at the *four traditional perspectives* on a gender balanced scorecard: how important would the following gender indicators be for your organisation?
A = really important, B = average importance, C = not important

1. Financial perspective	A, B, C
Turnover per employee, differentiating between men and women	
Amount of money saved as a result of gender initiatives	
Benefits costs as a percentage of payroll or revenue	
Return on investment for the gender initiatives	
Gender initiative expenses per employee	
Gender initiative budget as a percentage of sales	
Reduced litigation costs	

2. Customer perspective	A, B, C
Market share division between female and male customers and the representation in the workforce of male and female employees	
Percentage diverse customer satisfaction	
Number of new customers attracted by male and female employees	
Percentage customer retention by male and female employees	
Number of solutions offered per client by male and female employees	
Percentage on-time delivery rating by male and female employees	
Profitability by male and female customers	
Number of customer complaints successfully dealt with by male and female employees	
Number of customer awards received	

3. Internal Business processes perspective	A, B, C
Throughput time per business action for male and female employees	
New product introduction and design (male vs. female employees)	
Number of awards received for equality/diversity initiatives	
Employee satisfaction and female employee satisfaction (to be assessed with questionnaires)	
Social audit results	
Selection of critical core competencies / technologies (e.g. human capital as core competence)	

4. Learning and growth perspective	A, B, C
Number of female employees	
Number of female managers / leaders	
Number and percentage of gender-competent employees	
Comparison of educational budget spend on women and men	
Motivation index	
Productivity (male vs. female employees)	
Cross functional assignments (male vs. female employees)	
Personal goal achievement (male vs. female employees)	
Ethic violations	
Percentage of employees with advanced degrees for male and female employees	
Number of innovations initiated by male vs. female employees	
Employee suggestions (male vs. female employees)	
Empowerment index (i.e. the number of female employees vs. male employees that have received a certain level of power or authority to make higher level decisions)	

2) Which of the following (optional) additional perspectives would be relevant perspectives for your organisation to add on to the gender balanced scorecard?

Additional Perspectives:	Yes / No	Reason:
Organisational culture		
Community		
Leadership commitment		
Workforce profile		
Other, namely ...		

3) Which indicators would be important for your organisation for the additional perspectives you selected in question two?
(A = really important, B = average, C = not important)

Organisational culture	A, B, C
Percentage favourable ratings on cultural audit	
"Employer of choice" ratings versus top 5 to 10 competitors	
Perception of consistent and equitable treatment of all employees	
Gender equity tied to management compensation	
Absence rate / percentage absenteeism	
Retention rate of critical human capital	
Percentage gender initiatives fully implemented	
Percentage favourable ratings on climate/culture surveys for male and female employees	
Average time for dispute resolution	
Employee referral rate by male and female employees	
Percentage gender based pay differentials	
Percentage work-life balance benefits utilised	
Workplace flexibility index ratings	
Organisation's "openness" ratings	

Community	A, B, C
Percentage subcontracting euros to women-owned businesses	
Money given to the community	
Awards received from the community	
Company image (e.g. being an employer of choice for female potential employees)	

(A = really important, B = average, C = not important)

Leadership commitment	A, B, C
Leadership participation in designing the vision and strategies for achieving gender mainstreaming	
The number of female employees in formal mentoring programmes with the leader	
The number of female employees personally selected by the leader for special assignments	
The percentage of gender objectives that are tied to key strategic business objectives connected to the bonus and compensation of the leader	
The representation mix on the organisation's board of directors	
Leadership representation on the gender steering committee and advisory boards	
The degree of personal participation in creating an inclusive climate / culture	
The ability of the leader to overcome tension when it arises in the change process	
Money and other resources allocated by the leader to the gender mainstreaming initiative	
The number of executives and managers that are competent due to training in dealing with gender mainstreaming issues	
Leadership behaviour towards work–life balance issues (such as flexible working hours, glass-ceiling issues and family leave policies)	

Workforce profile	A, B, C
Percentage female new hires	
Percentage female managers and officials	
Percentage female survival and loss rate	
Percentage turnover by length of service	
Percentage absenteeism for male and female employees	
Percentage voluntary turnover: exempt and non-exempt	
Percentage involuntary turnover: exempt and non-exempt	
Number of offers to female interviewees	
Cost per hire	
Number returning from leave for male and female employees	

Forum Personalmanagement/Human Resource Management

Herausgegeben von Michel E. Domsch und Désirée H. Ladwig

Die Bedeutung des Personalmanagements für den Erfolg von Unternehmen ist in der Praxis wie in der Wissenschaft unbestritten. Allerdings zeigt sich national und international, daß nach wie vor zwischen Anspruch und Wirklichkeit große Unterschiede bestehen.

Diese Schriftenreihe will dazu beitragen, die Defizite zu reduzieren. So werden neue Entwicklungen im Bereich des Personalmanagements vorgestellt, erfolgreiche Praktiken präsentiert, interdisziplinäre Verknüpfungen verdeutlicht. Sowohl konzeptionelle Arbeiten wie empirische Studien werden in dieser Schriftenreihe aufgenommen. Im Einzelfall handelt es sich auch um Sammelbände und Konferenzberichte, wobei auch hier besonders internationale Aspekte des Personalmanagements diskutiert werden sollen. Die Autoren dieser Schriftenreihe sind entsprechend sowohl Vertreter verschiedener Bereiche der Praxis als auch der Wissenschaft.

Die Schriftenreihe spricht Fach- und Führungskräfte in der Privatwirtschaft wie im öffentlichen Bereich genauso an wie Wissenschaftler und Vertreter von Verbänden und der Politik.

Die Herausgeber vertreten die Institute für Personalwesen und Internationales Management der Universität der Bundeswehr Hamburg bzw. der OTA Hochschule Berlin. Sie leiten außerdem die F.G.H. Forschungsgruppe Hamburg.

Band 1 Andreas Geßner: Coaching – Modelle zur Diffusion einer sozialen Innovation in der Personalentwicklung. 2000.

Band 2 Katharina Köhler-Braun: Aufstiegsförderung weiblicher Führungs(nachwuchs)kräfte in den USA und in der Bundesrepublik Deutschland. Möglichkeiten der Einflußnahme und praktische Auswirkungen. 2000.

Band 3 Andreas Kammel: Strategischer Wandel und Management Development. Integriertes Konzept, theoretische Grundlagen und praktische Lösungsansätze. 2000.

Band 4 Michel E. Domsch / Désirée H. Ladwig (eds.): Reconciliation of Family and Work in Eastern European Countries. 2000.

Band 5 Ariane Ostermann: Dual-Career Couples unter personalwirtschaftlich-systemtheoretischem Blickwinkel. 2002.

Band 6 Michel E. Domsch / Désirée H. Ladwig / Eliane Tenten (eds.): Gender Equality in Central and Eastern European Countries. 2003.

Band 7 Maike Andresen: Corporate Universities als Instrument des Strategischen Managements von Person, Gruppe und Organisation. Eine Systematisierung aus strukturationstheoretischer und radikal konstruktivistischer Perspektive. 2003.

Band 8 Sonja W. Floeter-van Wijk: The Gender Balanced Scorecard. A Management Tool to Achieve Gender Mainstreaming in Organisational Culture. 2007.

www.peterlang.de